19

SECRET HEROES

ALSO BY PAUL MARTIN

Land of the Ascending Dragon:
Rediscovering Vietnam

FOR YOUNGER READERS

Messengers to the Brain: Our Fantastic
Five Senses

Science: It's Changing Your World

HarperCollins books may be purchased for educational, business, or sales promotional use. For information please write: Special Markets Department, HarperCollins Publishers, 10 East 53rd Street, New York, NY 10022.

FIRST EDITION

Designed by William Ruoto

Library of Congress Cataloging-in-Publication Data is available upon request.

ISBN 978-0-06-209604-3

12 13 14 15 16 ov/bvg 10 9 8 7 6 5 4 3 2 1

SECRET HEROES

★ ★ ★

EVERYDAY AMERICANS WHO SHAPED OUR WORLD

PAUL MARTIN

wm

WILLIAM MORROW
An Imprint of HarperCollins*Publishers*

FOR JANICE, EVAN, AND JUDY

CONTENTS

INTRODUCTION   xi

VOYAGERS

The Intrepid Leopard Wrestler
CARL AKELEY   3

On the Wings of an Angel
JIMMIE ANGEL   13

The Explorer with the Red Umbrella
GIACOMO BELTRAMI   21

The Genetics of Truth
KIRK BLOODSWORTH   31

The Slave Who Became a Union Spy
MARY BOWSER   39

The Black Swallow of Death
EUGENE BULLARD   47

Contents

The Last Stone Age Man in America
ISHI 57

General Washington's Genial Savior
HERCULES MULLIGAN 67

A Captive in Two Cultures
CYNTHIA ANN PARKER 75

An Act of Valor Denied
JAMES PARKER 87

The Yank Who United Canada
WILLIAM VAN HORNE 95

INNOVATORS

Why We Are What We Eat
WILBUR ATWATER 107

Mythmaker of the Old West
JOHN WALLACE CRAWFORD 117

The Inquisitive Benefactor
GEORGE FABYAN 129

Sealing the Victory at Gettysburg
HERMAN HAUPT 141

Contents

Keeping Eisenhower's Invasion Afloat

ANDREW JACKSON HIGGINS 153

The Lovely with the Lovely Brain

HEDWIG KIESLER 161

Choctaw Code Talker of World War I

SOLOMON LOUIS 169

A Thorn in the Side of Convention

ANNE ROYALL 179

The Man Behind the Checkout Counter

CLARENCE SAUNDERS 189

An Idea That Bloomed to Perfection

ELIZA SCIDMORE 197

Dispenser of Beauty and Truth

MADAM C. J. WALKER 207

HUMANITARIANS

Defender of the Defenseless

GRACE ABBOTT 221

The Man Who Fed Asia

HENRY BEACHELL 233

Contents

America's Joan of Arc
INEZ BOISSEVAIN 241

A Saint's Unassuming Assistant
JOSEPH DUTTON 249

A Life's Labor of Love
GERTRUDE ELION 257

The Mayor Who Just Wanted to Be Fair
GOLDEN RULE JONES 269

Healer of the Fallen
JONATHAN LETTERMAN 279

Warrior with a Conscience
HUGH THOMPSON 291

AFTERWORD 303

ACKNOWLEDGMENTS 305

SOURCES 307

Introduction

THIS BOOK IS about the accomplishments of a remarkable group of Americans—heroes all in different ways, although their names are largely unfamiliar. They represent a wide range of backgrounds—scientists, soldiers, spies, adventurers, inventors, businessmen, artists, activists. Among them are individuals from the earliest years of our country right up to modern times. What all these people have in common—other than an outsize measure of courage and determination—are their enduring legacies. Their achievements, though often overlooked, helped shape the world we know today.

A few of these secret heroes radically altered history, such as the Nebraska-born agronomist who saved millions in Asia from starvation through his plant-breeding experiments. Others had less dramatic though no less exceptional attainments, including the travel writer and Japanophile who struck upon the felicitous notion of gracing our nation's capital with flowering cherry trees. Despite their obscurity, such people are worth remembering.

To help me unearth these thirty uncommon characters, I solicited recommendations from every state historical society, along with more than a hundred history professors at colleges and universities around the country. Most of the discoveries, however, I made for myself, which provided half the fun of this undertaking. I love rummaging through history's back rooms in search of forgotten figures. For years, I've kept files on intriguing, little-known people I've come across in my reading—information that became the basis for this book.

Sometimes, a name alone has been enough to grab my attention. Poking through dusty tomes and faded documents in the Library of Congress and the National Archives, I encountered a parade of memorable monikers—Jimmie Angel, Anne Royall, Andrew Jackson Higgins, Golden Rule Jones. Once, while researching the first American to receive a military decoration, I made an unrelated find—an enigmatic colonial patriot named Hercules Mulligan. How could anyone not want to know more about someone with such a fantastic handle?

Delving into the backgrounds of these amazing Americans, I felt like I'd dropped in on an underground bash where every guest had a riveting yarn to spin—with each of their stories affording a new perspective on our country's heritage. So let me welcome you to the party. Now, if you'll come with me, I'd like you to meet someone interesting.

—Paul Martin

PART I

★

VOYAGERS

ONE

The Intrepid Leopard Wrestler

CARL AKELEY

THE PARCHED AIR pulsed with the feral melody of Africa at dusk—the guttural cough of a lion, the nervous shrieks of a restless troop of baboons, the insane cackles of a pack of hyenas. Gazelles and other small animals scurried through the brushy terrain. The interplay of sounds reflected a density of life found in few other places on Earth. Thirty-two-year-old Carl Akeley had quickly fallen in love with this untamed symphony. He was on the first of his five trips to Africa, an 1896 expedition to Somaliland to gather animal specimens for the Field Museum of Natural History in Chicago. Earlier this day, he'd shot a warthog, and now he was trying to locate the carcass to take it back to camp, where it would be prepared for shipment to the museum.

As Akeley searched in the fading light near a sandy riverbed, he spotted a hyena trotting through the tall grass. The hyena had the head of Akeley's trophy in its jaws. "That burned me up," he recalled, "because it was a fine specimen." Akeley turned toward camp in resignation. Trudging along, he glimpsed an indistinct shape slipping behind a bush. Another hyena, thought Akeley. Although he knew it was foolish, he raised his rifle and fired at the phantom hyena. The sound that answered startled him: a wounded leopard growled in anger.

Akeley knew he was in trouble. Leopards don't scare easily, and though smaller than lions, they're extremely dangerous when provoked. Deciding that retreat was the best option, Akeley picked up his pace. As he crossed the dry riverbed, he looked back and saw that the leopard was trailing him. Even though it was nearly dark, Akeley fired wildly—the last three bullets in his gun. He was sure he'd killed the animal with his final shot—until the leopard's snarls signaled it was about to charge. Terrified, Akeley started running, trying to load another cartridge in his rifle as he stumbled along. Just as he rammed home a cartridge and wheeled to face the leopard, the big cat pounced, knocking the rifle from his hands. The leopard went for Akeley's throat but missed and sank its teeth into his right arm near the shoulder.

Still standing, Akeley grabbed the leopard's throat with his left hand and squeezed its windpipe as hard as he could, causing it to loosen its grip. Akeley worked his right arm free and forced his fist deep into the animal's mouth to choke off its air. He threw the thrashing leopard to the ground, landing on top of it with his knees on its chest. His first shot had hit the leopard's right hind foot. "With one foot injured she couldn't get a purchase in the loose sand," he said afterward. "Otherwise I'd have been disemboweled in ten seconds by her hind claws." Akeley's weight on the leopard's chest broke at least two of its ribs, and the animal finally succumbed. Nearly done in from exhaustion and loss of blood, Akeley staggered back to camp, where his friends patched him up. He'd just survived the first of several tests that Africa would throw at him during thirty years of roaming the wilds to collect wildlife specimens, most of that time for New York's American Museum of Natural History.

The Intrepid Leopard Wrestler

During his adventure-filled decades from the 1890s to the 1920s, Akeley forged a reputation as the world's most talented creator of natural history dioramas. Experts said his exhibits raised the practice of taxidermy to the level of art. Perhaps that's because Akeley regarded his subjects as works of art themselves, whose beauty he tried to preserve forever. Most people who've seen Akeley's surging, trumpeting elephants in the American Museum of Natural History would agree that he succeeded. The majestic animals seem about to thunder off down the hallways just like they did in *Night at the Museum*. Although killing animals for display has thankfully been superseded by nature films and zoo exhibits featuring realistic habitats, Akeley made the wonders of far-off lands—both the animals and their settings— accessible to millions of people who would never get to Africa. He also had a surprising role in protecting Africa's wildlife.

Akeley spent his entire life around animals. Born in 1864, he grew up on a farm near Clarendon, New York. He became interested in taxidermy when he was thirteen. His first subject was his teacher's dead canary. Miss Glidden was thrilled when he gave her back her birdcage with her little friend inside, perched on a branch with its head cocked as if it were listening. Akeley took lessons in sculpture to help him accurately capture the shapes of animals, and he studied painting so he could depict realistic backgrounds for his mounted birds, something that had never been done before. When he was nineteen, he went to work for Henry Ward's Natural Science Establishment in Rochester, New York (at the lofty salary of $3.50 a week). The top taxidermy shop in the country, Ward's supplied mounted specimens to museums and universities and also trained museum curators. Akeley's first important assignment there was to help mount P. T. Barnum's beloved circus elephant, Jumbo, a huge

African specimen that had thrilled audiences in England and America for years until it died in a train accident.

At the time, taxidermy consisted chiefly of stuffing an animal's hide with straw or wood shavings and sewing it up—"upholstery," Akeley called it in derision. The slipshod method could result in such oddities as a mounted raccoon that looked more like a weasel. Akeley came up with a new technique. He built a wood-and-steel frame and covered it with thin, flexible strips of basswood to outline Jumbo's shape, then he fitted the elephant's hide over this life-size manikin. Akeley's realistic handiwork ultimately went on display in the Barnum Museum at Tufts University—after the circus had taken poor old Jumbo out on the road for two more years. (Jumbo suffered his final indignity in 1975, when he was lost in a fire that destroyed the Barnum Museum. The famous pachyderm lives on in memory as the mascot of Tufts University—and as the source of the adjective for something exceptionally large.)

After four years in Rochester, Akeley took a job at the Milwaukee Public Museum. It was there that he created the first of his lifelike dioramas. By arranging his specimens in realistic poses amid indigenous plant life and set against painted backgrounds, Akeley conveyed the appearance of animals in their habitats with astounding accuracy—innovations that would change the look of natural history museums around the world.

In 1895, Akeley went to work for Chicago's prestigious Field Museum, eventually heading its department of taxidermy. Always looking for ways to improve his exhibits, Akeley perfected the technique of sculpturing animals in clay over an armature of wood, wire, and bone. Working in clay allowed him to render tiny details such as muscles and veins. When the clay figure was complete, he used it to make a plaster mold, from which he cast a light, hollow manikin over which he fit the animal's skin. Soon, museums everywhere were using this method to create anatomically accurate displays.

Over the next fourteen years, Akeley made the first two of his expeditions to Africa. By the time he made his second expedition, Akeley had a new assistant—his wife, Delia. On that 1905 trip, Akeley brought back two enormous bull elephants from East Africa, which have been the centerpiece of the Field Museum's Stanley Field Hall for nearly a century. Akeley had been fascinated by elephants ever since his experience with Jumbo. He recounted that he was as excited as a kid to see the animals in their natural habitat. It was that experience of viewing wild creatures in their homes that he hoped to re-create for museumgoers, which was why he made sketches, photographs, and films of the animals and their surroundings. Such meticulous fieldwork helped him produce dioramas that were the next best thing to being there.

Akeley's work at the Field Museum launched a side career as an inventor—revealing his unusual combination of artistic and mechanical talents. To create his exhibits, Akeley developed a compressed air gun that enabled him to apply plaster as a spray; when the museum's deteriorating stucco walls needed repairing, Akeley adapted this device and made the repairs himself. He obtained patents for his new "cement gun," which was used in the construction of the Panama Canal and to make concrete ships and line battlefield trenches in World War I. Akeley received a gold medal for the invention from the Franklin Institute. (Pneumatically applied concrete, or "shotcrete," is still used for reinforcing reservoirs, mines, and tunnels.)

By 1908, Akeley was anxious to get back to Africa. That year he approached the American Museum of Natural History, the country's top natural history repository, with a novel plan: he proposed to work for the museum at no salary. All he asked for was a retainer; he would cover the costs of his expeditions by raising money on his own through his books and magazine articles and the popular lectures he gave all over the country. His lively talks were filled with anecdotes about his scrapes with lions and other wild creatures. The lectures were often attended by wealthy admirers who were thrilled to help fund his scientific endeavors. The museum went along, beginning a relationship that lasted the rest of Akeley's life.

On his first trip to Africa on behalf of the American Museum of Natural History, in 1909—his third expedition altogether—Akeley had another of his close encounters with wildlife. While tracking three bull elephants on the slopes of Mount Kenya, he was caught off guard when one of the bulls charged him. He was still fumbling with his rifle when the bull slammed him to the ground, pinning him between its tusks. The elephant's rough, heavy trunk broke Akeley's nose, ripped open his scalp and cheek, and smashed his chest, snapping several ribs. Akeley was convinced that the elephant's tusks hit a root or a rock, which kept him from being crushed to death. Fortunately, the elephant caught sight of Akeley's porters fleeing through the jungle and charged after them (they all escaped). A Scottish medical missionary was able to save Akeley's life, although his injuries forced him to cancel his plans to study gorillas on that trip.

Despite his accident, Akeley returned from his third expedition with an ambitious concept for the American Museum of Natural History: he would build a magnificent new hall filled with multiple groupings of African animals in their natural settings—a comprehensive permanent record of the panoply of wildlife that Akeley knew was quickly disappearing. The museum approved the idea and work commenced—only to be disrupted by World War I. Akeley had to wait until 1921 to resume his activities in Africa, this time in the Virunga Mountains near Lake Kivu, a wild volcanic region in the Belgian Congo. Akeley went there to collect specimens of the rare mountain gorilla—elusive creatures with an unwarranted reputation for aggressiveness.

Akeley gathered his specimens, and he also captured the animals on film, the first movies ever made of mountain gorillas in their natural habitat. He filmed the gorillas with another of his inventions, a movie camera that was far easier to operate than anything previously available. (The Akeley camera had been used to make newsreels during World War I, and, like his invention of the cement gun, it won Akeley an award from the Franklin Institute.) The gorillas that Akeley captured on film looked to him like a happy family at play. Akeley became so concerned about the preservation of the mountain gorilla that he persuaded King Albert of Belgium to create a wildlife sanctuary in the Kivu region. In 1925, Albert National Park became the first national park in Africa. (Now known as Virunga, it was declared a World Heritage Site in 1979; in 1994, the park was added to the list of sites in danger.)

As work on the African hall progressed, Akeley branched out artistically. He started casting bronzes from his original clay sculptures—an intentional attempt to link taxidermy and art. His first bronze, completed in 1924, was called *The Wounded Comrade*. It depicted two bull elephants holding up a third injured elephant between them—a scene someone had once described to him. The piece earned him membership in the American Sculpture Society. President Theodore Roosevelt praised it as "the finest tribute to a noble animal ever put in sculpture." (Akeley had met Roosevelt in Africa in 1909, and the two men became good friends; Akeley meant to name his African hall in Roosevelt's honor.) Akeley's other bronzes include the graphic *Lion and Cape Buffalo,* which shows a male lion bringing down its much larger prey by grabbing its nose. Akeley made bronzes of African tribesmen hunting lions with spears. He also executed a bronze figure called *The Chrysalis* as a symbol of evolution; the piece riled up creationists and was refused exhibition space by the National Academy of Design.

In the early 1920s, Akeley's personal life was in upheaval. He divorced his first wife, Delia, and married Mary L. Jobe, a writer, photographer, and explorer who'd made a name for herself through her expeditions to western Canada. Mary had set her sights on Akeley while he was still married, and she succeeded in supplanting Delia in Akeley's affections. Two years before Akeley divorced Delia, he rewrote his will and named Mary his sole beneficiary—not a very subtle message about his intentions. A photograph of the new couple shows Akeley to be a slight, leathery, gray-haired man with what appears to be a hand-rolled cigarette between his fingers. His left cheek bears the scars from his encounter with the bull elephant years before. Mary, a formidable-looking woman, stares off-camera with a look of impatience.

The second Mrs. Akeley accompanied her husband to Africa in 1926 on his fifth—and what turned out to be his final—expedition. Akeley spent eight hectic months gathering plant and animal specimens for his African hall. He also directed the work of the landscape artist who would paint the backgrounds for his dioramas. Sixty-two years old and already worn out from the strain of attempting to finish his grand project, Akeley fell ill with fever. He was hospitalized in Nairobi but insisted on returning to work before he was well. He wanted to get back to the Lake Kivu area of the Belgian Congo, where he'd first encountered the mountain gorillas. Perhaps he knew his time was running out. His team had to contend with intense heat and high humidity as it bushwhacked through the rugged Virunga Mountains. Akeley was so weak that he had to be carried at times. Shortly after his party reached the 11,000-foot saddle between Mount Mikeno and Mount Karisimbi, Akeley died. He was buried right there, a place he loved—"a country of marvellous beauty," he'd called it in his autobiography, *In Brightest Africa*. Four years earlier, when he'd stood on that same spot, he remarked to a companion, "I wish I could be buried here when I die."

For the next ten years, Mary Akeley and her husband's associates continued the project at the American Museum of Natural History. In 1929, New York City contributed $1,250,000 to build a new wing to house the exhibit. On May 19, 1936, Carl Akeley's dream became a reality. Regarded as one of the world's great museum displays, the twenty-eight dramatically lit dioramas of the Akeley Hall of African Mammals would be a fitting memorial to any man, although testimonials to Akeley's life also include the many impressive exhibits he created at Chicago's Field Museum.

Akeley's greatest commemoration is surely Virunga National Park—a living legacy rather than a static time capsule. A few hundred gorillas still cling to a precarious existence in the park, studied by groups such as the Dian Fossey Gorilla Fund International and protected by a brave corps of park rangers. (Nearly two hundred rangers have been killed by poachers and illegal loggers and miners in recent years, and continuing threats make the gorillas' long-term survival questionable.)

Akeley lived at a time when wildlife conservation was in its infancy, which makes it all the more remarkable that someone who killed and mounted animals for exhibition would also conceive of a sanctuary to safeguard the mountain gorilla. But then, Carl Akeley was an exceptional man. A lover of all wild things, he worked to protect America's bird life and the giant redwood trees, and he was an active member of the National Parks Association and many other conservation groups.

In his autobiography, Akeley offered this humble assessment of what he'd tried to accomplish through his work: "I hope that I have contributed something to the study of natural history and that I have stimulated a decent attitude toward wild life." He did both, of course. Virunga National Park reminds us that the fundamental purpose of natural history displays like those that Akeley created is to encourage us to honor all of our fellow passengers on this small spinning rock.

TWO

On the Wings of an Angel

JIMMIE ANGEL

PICTURE THIS: In the 1920s, a young American pilot named Jimmie Angel sits in a shabby cantina somewhere in Panama. He bears a faint resemblance to Humphrey Bogart. In walks a grizzled prospector named J. R. McCracken, who, if you squint your eyes just right, looks a little like actor Walter Huston. Overhead, a lethargic ceiling fan attempts to stir the cantina's syrupy air. The beer they serve here is cold. The senoritas smiling from the bar are not.

The two Yanquis strike up a conversation. McCracken starts telling young Angel about his prospecting days in Alaska. Then he confides in him about a mysterious mountain located in the wilds of southeastern Venezuela. There's gold there, McCracken says with a glint in his eye, gold just waiting to be picked up and made to glitter in coins and fancy jewelry. All McCracken needs is a pilot who can fly him there.

"I hear you can land on a dime," McCracken says.

"I'm your man," Angel replies. "It'll cost you $5,000."

It takes some time, but McCracken finally scrapes together the money and Angel buys a plane. They set off for Venezuela, landing in Ciudad Bolivar on the Orinoco River. From there they fly south. Using a miner's compass, McCracken guides Angel through the cloud-wreathed mountains. Finally McCracken spots the *tepui*—a flat-topped sandstone mountain—that he's been looking for. They land atop the tepui and hop out of the plane. They discover a riverbed glittering with gold. The men stuff their pockets with nuggets and hurriedly load the plane with as much as they can manage, but they have to get off the tepui before dark.

Back in civilization, McCracken falls ill and dies, taking the secret location of the mountain with him. Devastated, Angel vows to spend however long it takes to find the lost mountain and its river of gold once more.

That entire tale may sound like a variation of *The Treasure of the Sierra Madre*, but Jimmie Angel—an early barnstorming pilot, adventurer, and general defier of convention—swore it was true. His family, however, knew that he liked to embellish things now and then. Angel's niece, Karen Angel, who has made it her mission to document the truth about her uncle's exploits, admits that he "actively participated in the creation of the various legends about his colorful life." Be that as it may, this much is fact: Jimmie Angel would spend years searching for the river of gold in Venezuela. And in the process, he stumbled upon a different kind of treasure.

The entire life of James Crawford Angel reads like a movie script. Born in Springfield, Missouri, in 1899, Angel became fascinated with airplanes as a teenager. As he told the story, he ran away from home when he was fourteen and landed a job as an airplane mechanic. One day in 1914, he found himself working at an air show in Birmingham, Alabama. He was steering a plane being moved on the runway when he "accidentally" flipped a switch and the plane took off. Angel flew around the airfield until he ran out of gas, then he glided in for a landing. And that was how Jimmie Angel became a pilot.

Angel's early years as an aviator—again as he told it—had him heading to Canada during World War I, where he joined the Royal Flying Corps. He claimed to have flown a number of missions in Europe, shooting down three German aircraft and five observation balloons. Other adventures he described were even more fantastic: flying for Lawrence of Arabia, creating an air force for a Chinese warlord in the Gobi Desert, falling in love with a Russian countess. You have to wonder why he left out gunrunning and bootlegging.

None of those tales are documented, but what's indisputable is that somehow Angel became a crack pilot as a young man. After World War I, his accomplishments become more verifiable. His first job in Latin America involved flying payrolls to Mexican oil camps. Even here, though, Angel may have spun off into fantasy. He told people that he left the job following an attempted hijacking in which he shot and killed a man.

Back in the realm of the verifiable, Angel partnered with family members in the 1920s to form the Angel Brothers Flying Circus, a barnstorming troupe in which Jimmie flew and his brother Eddie specialized in a hair-raising act that entailed wing-walking and jumping from the plane dressed in a canvas "bat suit" that enabled him to spiral toward the ground like a falling leaf before popping open his parachute at the last moment.

Angel's aerial skills helped him win roles as a stunt pilot in Hollywood movies, including *Hell's Angels*, Howard Hughes's 1930 film about World War I. Other jobs included delivering airmail in Mexico and a short-lived promotional venture for one of the early airlines. What Angel never did was settle into a routine. Asked once why he refused to fly as a commercial airline pilot, he replied that it would be boring—"like driving a bus."

Adventure was Angel's addiction, which is why he never stopped thinking about that gold-strewn mountaintop in Venezuela. To get back to South America, he took a job with Santa Ana Mining, a Tulsa-based company searching for ore deposits in the untamed Gran Sabana region of southeastern Venezuela.

In the fall of 1933, Angel flew Santa Ana engineer D. H. Curry and mechanic José Cardona into the Gran Sabana. The most curious features of this region are its more than one hundred tepuis. The sheer-sided tabletop mountains poke up from the surrounding jungle like islands in a green sea, some of them over 4,000 feet high. Isolated from the rain forest below, the summits of these sandstone mesas are home to plant and animal species found nowhere else on Earth—a discovery that inspired Arthur Conan Doyle's 1912 novel The Lost World, a tale about dinosaurs surviving into the modern age atop a plateau in South America.

Angel became interested in one tepui in particular, a massive heart-shaped mountain called Auyantepui. The name means "Devil's House" in the language of the indigenous Pemon Indians, who consider tepuis to be the home of spirits. Auyantepui wasn't on any maps at the time. Angel became convinced that this was where he and J. R. McCracken had landed years before and found their river of gold.

On November 14, 1933, while making a solo reconnaissance, Angel flew into Devil's Canyon, part of the Auyantepui formation. As he reached the head of the canyon, a startling sight came into view—a waterfall like none he'd ever seen before plunged from the rocky brow of the tepui into the jungle below.

Based on altimeter readings, Angel estimated it to be a mile high. It was unbelievable, and when he told Curry and Cardona about it back in camp, that's just how they reacted—with disbelief. Angel never got to show them his discovery. Heavy rains soon forced the men to abandon their explorations.

In 1934, Angel signed on with a different mining company—Case Pomeroy—for another expedition into the Gran Sabana. On March 24, 1935, he flew Durand A. Hall and L. R. Dennison to the falls at the head of Devil's Canyon. The two men became the first to corroborate Angel's find. Later, Angel flew petroleum geologist F. I. Martin into the canyon. Martin made the first photographs of the falls. Angel had proof of his discovery, but he still hankered to find that elusive gold.

Over two years passed before Angel could put together an expedition with the goal of landing on Auyantepui. Its members included Angel's wife, Marie, and Venezuelans Gustavo Heny, Felix Cardona, and Miguel Delgado. After establishing a camp at the southern base of Auyantepui, Angel scouted out a landing spot at the top of the mesa. On October 9, 1937, the landing party boarded Angel's single-engine Flamingo aircraft and took off. Cardona stayed in camp to maintain radio contact with the group. Minutes later, the wheels of the plane touched down on Auyantepui.

The landing was fine, but as the aircraft taxied along it ran into a bog and pitched forward, its nose buried in the muck. The party couldn't free the plane. Even worse, after two days of searching they found no gold. They would have to hike out, empty-handed. Fortunately, they'd brought along plenty of supplies, although the climb down from the top of the tepui to their base camp proved to be difficult and dangerous. The group only made it through the harrowing two-week trek thanks to the exceptional mountaineering and jungle survival skills of Gustavo Heny.

Angel may have missed out on the golden bonanza that he'd been searching for, but he achieved something of even greater value: his tales about the wonders he'd seen in Venezuela helped spark the exploration and eventual protection of the unique Gran Sabana region.

Angel's enthusiastic descriptions of Auyantepui prompted scientific expeditions in 1937 and 1939. Scientists from the American Museum of Natural History took part in both trips. Ornithologist E. Thomas Gilliard described the initial expedition in the December 1940 issue of *Natural History* magazine. On the verge of starvation at times, the explorers discovered many rare species of plants and animals, including thirty-two kinds of subtropical birds. The article paid tribute to Jimmie Angel, calling him "the venturesome aviator and prospector whose fearless forays into one of the least known areas of the world led to the scientific exploration of the 'Lost World' of Auyan-tepui."

Although the public was learning about the singular nature of the Gran Sabana and its tepuis, several years would pass before that recognition spurred government action to protect the region. Then in 1962, Venezuela set aside part of the vast Gran Sabana as Canaima National Park, a reserve that was later expanded to more than 11,500 square miles (over three times the size of Yellowstone Park). In 1994, UNESCO declared Canaima a World Heritage Site because of its tepuis and their abundance of rare life-forms—proof that Jimmie Angel knew something special when he saw it.

The falls that Angel discovered were verified as the world's highest—over eighteen times higher than Niagara. It was Venezuelan Gustavo Heny who suggested naming them Angel Falls in Jimmie's honor. The government of Venezuela concurred. Of course, as Karen Angel points out, the decision was helped by the fact that Jimmie's last name wasn't Smith.

Besides naming the falls after the colorful American, the Venezuelan government made a national monument of his Flamingo aircraft abandoned atop Auyantepui. In 1970, the Venezuelan air force removed the plane in pieces and took it to the aviation museum in Maracay for restoration. Jimmie Angel wouldn't have been happy about this: he'd once commented to a friend that he wanted his plane to remain on Auyantepui. "As long as it stays up there, it will be a memory of me."

Angel was always protective of his legend. In November 1949, *National Geographic* published an article by American photojournalist Ruth Robertson, who'd led an overland expedition to Auyantepui. Robertson had established the official height of Angel Falls at 3,212 feet—over 2,000 feet shy of Angel's estimate of a mile high. Angel was incensed. He showed up on Robertson's doorstep and complained vociferously. "I've been tellin' folks for years that my waterfall was a mile high. Now you gotta go and spoil the whole thing. I tell ya it is a mile high."

That was Jimmie Angel—never one to let the facts get in the way of a good story.

Angel died in Panama in 1956 as a result of two strokes brought on by a minor flying accident. His widow, Marie, said of her husband, "He was the most interesting man I ever knew." In 1960, family members and friends flew to the top of Angel Falls, where they scattered Jimmie's ashes, as he'd requested.

In 2009, Jimmie Angel was in the news again. In December of that year, Venezuelan president Hugo Chavez declared that the falls should henceforth be called by their Pemon Indian name, Kerepakupai Merú. So far, though, Jimmie seems to be holding his own, since the new name Chavez is selling hasn't found many buyers. It would be a shame if Jimmie Angel were to be deprived of an honor he deserves, but at least no one can ever alter the fact that it was this daring, colorful pilot who introduced us to one of the world's great natural wonders.

THREE

The Explorer with the Red Umbrella

GIACOMO BELTRAMI

FORTY-FOUR-YEAR-OLD Giacomo Beltrami was about as far from home as he could possibly be. In August 1823, the Italian gadabout had the misfortune to find himself lost and alone in the wilderness of what is now northern Minnesota. Shortly after undertaking a dangerous personal quest to discover the source of the Mississippi River, Beltrami had been abandoned by his two Chippewa guides following an attack by a hostile band of Sioux. With the nearest settlement a hundred miles away, the tall, neatly dressed European aristocrat was left to fend for himself in a land of trackless swamps and serpentine waterways.

Beltrami's supplies were loaded in a single birch-bark canoe. He might have been able to continue on his way up the Red Lake River except for one minor detail: he'd never mastered the tricky technique of paddling the featherweight Indian craft. Each time he tried, the canoe tipped over, swamping his belongings and sweeping him back down the river away from his destination. Heavy rain added to his woes, and since the Chippewas had stolen his flint, he couldn't light a campfire to dry out. A normal person might have just sat back against a tree, had a good cry, and given up, but Beltrami wasn't about to admit defeat. You see, the irrepressible citizen of the world and honorary, if temporary, American was having far too much fun.

How Beltrami came to be alone in the wilds of North America—and what he accomplished on his search for the source of the Mississippi—constitute one of the most improbable records of exploration ever. It's a story filled with wackiness, coincidence, and dumb luck, as well as bravery and relentless determination. Beltrami's time in America had a bittersweet aftermath, since his enthusiastic claims to have found the Mississippi's headwaters were summarily rejected. Still, the book he wrote about his adventure conveys a joyous sense of wonder and accomplishment. And no one can deny the chutzpah of this peculiar dreamer who headed into the unknown beneath the jaunty banner of a red silk umbrella.

Beltrami was born in 1779 in northern Italy's Lombard region, in the town of Bergamo, then part of the Venetian Republic. Beltrami's father was a customs official when he could spare the time—he sired seventeen children. Giacomo, the sixteenth of the enormous brood, studied law and literature. Just as Beltrami reached adulthood, northern Italy came under the sway of Napoleon Bonaparte. A supporter of the liberal principles of the French Revolution, Beltrami joined the Little Corporal's puppet government, serving as an army inspector and judge. He grew wealthy through his positions, counting counts and countesses among his friends. In 1815, with Napoleon's empire imploding, Beltrami retired to the life of a gentleman farmer. Three years later, the new papal government labeled him a traitor for his ties to the French. Soon afterward, one of his closest friends, Countess Giulia Spada de Medici, died unexpectedly. Dejected over the countess's death and his own precarious situation, Beltrami went into exile at the age of forty-two. He made up his mind to see the world, making his own way and contending "with every sort of difficulty, privation and danger."

Setting out in October 1821, Beltrami began his peregrinations with an extended ramble across Europe. Like a medieval bard, he wrote florid accounts of his experiences in long letters home. After visiting several cities in Germany and France, he ended up in London in the summer of 1822. Around the beginning of November, he boarded a ship for America, relishing the chance to see the democratic principles he cherished being put into practice. His trip to the New World wasn't auspicious. Atlantic gales turned the ocean crossing into a roller coaster ride that completely disabled the Italian with seasickness. As the voyage stretched on, food supplies ran low, and passengers had to subsist on a meager daily ration of boiled rice. When Beltrami finally reached Philadelphia—two months after leaving Liverpool—he must have felt like getting down on his knees and kissing the ground.

From the City of Brotherly Love, Beltrami traveled to Baltimore, a city he described as "cheerful in all parts," with women who were "generally pretty." Then it was on to Washington, D.C., where he wandered into the White House unannounced and ran smack into President James Monroe. Next came Pittsburgh, an industrial center whose dense cloud of coal smoke, he observed, "enshrouds the sun by day and the stars by night." Beltrami traveled down the Ohio to Cincinnati and Louisville, then ventured on to the river's junction with the Mississippi. From there, he intended to board a boat bound for New Orleans. However, the first paddle wheeler to pull ashore was the *Calhoun*, which was headed north to St. Louis. On board were two men who would alter Beltrami's plans—Gen. William Clark, the superintendent for Indian affairs in St. Louis, and Maj. Lawrence Taliaferro, Indian agent at Fort St. Anthony, an army garrison near present-day Minneapolis. Intrigued by America's native peoples, Beltrami bombarded the two agents with questions about the tribes living in the country to the north. The more he learned, the more he wanted to see some Indians for himself. Postponing his visit to New Orleans, Beltrami joined the two army men aboard the *Calhoun*. The impetuous Italian was off to see the wilderness, an eager accidental explorer.

At St. Louis, Beltrami had his first glimpse of Native Americans, although their "grotesque appearance" didn't fit his image of the noble savage. Shaking off his disappointment, Beltrami transferred his gear from the *Calhoun* to the *Virginia*, the riverboat that would carry him and Major Taliaferro on the seven-hundred-mile voyage to Fort St. Anthony, which perched on a bluff above the confluence of the Mississippi and the St. Peter River (now known as the Minnesota). It was a historic and challenging trip. The *Virginia* was the first steamboat to travel the upper reaches of the Mississippi, where numerous sandbars and rapids made the passage difficult. The little paddle wheeler kept getting stuck, and the crew had to pull it free of the sand with ropes. Beltrami took advantage of any delays to poke around the countryside, crashing through the woods like a mad pirate, all decked out with a sword and pistols in his belt and toting a musket. On one occasion, he stayed ashore too long, and the *Virginia* left without him. Luckily, the boat soon got stuck on another sandbar, and Beltrami was able to catch up with it.

The vagabond Italian had another stroke of good fortune after the boat reached Fort St. Anthony. By coincidence, a military expedition led by Maj. Stephen H. Long arrived at the fort around the same time. Long and his men were assigned to journey up the St. Peter River and continue north along the Red River, ultimately delineating and mapping the U.S.-Canada border. Beltrami, who still had plans to return to St. Louis and then travel on to New Orleans, suddenly realized that if he could attach himself to Major Long's expedition, he'd be able to extend his trip into a region few white men had ever seen—a swath of Sioux and Chippewa territory that contained the source of the Mississippi. The explorer who discovered the river's headwaters would gain lasting fame, and Beltrami wanted to be that man.

Beltrami persuaded Major Taliaferro and the fort's commanding officer, Col. Josiah Snelling, to intercede on his behalf. Grudgingly, Major Long permitted Beltrami to join the expedition. It was clear from the outset, however, that the two men would never be chums. Long was a dour, no-nonsense soldier, totally opposite in temperament to the sunny, mercurial Italian. Long made it clear that he would grant no favors to the tagalong civilian. At the end of the first week of July, the band of thirty-three men left Fort St. Anthony. Beltrami immediately perceived that the major had it in for him. The two men argued constantly. A canoe carrying Beltrami's gear was wrecked. The talkative Italian was made to sleep on the exposed side of the tent he was assigned to, so that he got soaked whenever it rained. He was sure he was being cheated out of his share of the food. Even worse, Long's route meant that they were going to bypass the region where the Mississippi's headwaters lay.

In early August, the expedition straggled into the tumble-down frontier outpost of Pembina, along the U.S.-Canada border. Beltrami described the place as "the scene of every species of fraud, crime, and atrocities." There was some uncertainty about which side of the border the outpost was on, but Major Long proclaimed it was in U.S. territory and ran up the American flag. By this point in the trip, Beltrami was fed up with the army leader. The Italian left the expedition in a huff and joined two Chippewas and a mestizo who were headed for the Red Lake region to the southeast. Although Major Long had kept him guessing about the expedition's precise location, Beltrami was sure that the Red Lake River would lead him to the area where he expected to find the Mississippi's source.

The overland march to reach the Red Lake River was arduous. As the trip proceeded, things fell apart. The mestizo went his own way, leaving Beltrami alone with two Indians whose language he couldn't speak. Once the men were on the river, frequent rapids necessitated difficult portages. Then a band of Sioux started shooting at them, wounding one of the Chippewas. Before long, the Chippewas decided to quit the river and strike out for Red Lake on foot, leaving Beltrami alone in the middle of nowhere. The adventurer was in a dicey predicament, but he accepted it with surprising equanimity. (The man was either totally insane or literally afraid of nothing, although sometimes it was hard to say which. While staying at Fort St. Anthony, he'd attempted to bring down a bison by leaping onto the animal from his horse and stabbing it with a knife. He would have been killed if a companion hadn't shot the enraged bull.)

After the Indians decamped, Beltrami gamely hopped into his canoe, intending to continue upriver by himself. Unfortunately, he wrote later, "I was totally unacquainted with the almost magical art by which a single person guides a canoe, and particularly a canoe formed of bark, the lightness of which is overpowered by the current, and the conduct of which requires extreme dexterity." Almost immediately, the canoe flipped, pitching Beltrami and his supplies into the river. Again and again, he attempted to paddle the maddeningly difficult craft, but he was making no progress. Finally, he tied a leather thong to the canoe's bow and simply towed the boat upriver, trudging along in water up to his waist like Bogie in *The African Queen*. It was slow going, although at least he was headed in the right direction, and he kept himself amused by "holding conversation with the fishes beneath."

At night, Beltrami was unable to light a fire to dry out, thanks to the faithless Chippewas' having made off with his only flint. He huddled in a sodden ball, feasted upon by mosquitoes the size of swallows. The following day it rained, keeping him and his gear soggy. When the sun came out, he spread his possessions on the riverbank to dry. At the next threat of rain, Beltrami retrieved a large red silk umbrella he'd been carrying and propped it up in the canoe to protect his belongings. On the fourth day of his watery slog, two canoes appeared, paddled by Chippewas heading downstream. The Indians hung back when they beheld the apparition of a white man wading in the river and pulling a canoe covered by a shocking red canopy. Beltrami waved them over and convinced them—bribed them, really, with food and other goods—to take him to their village on Red Lake. There he shared a hovel with fourteen Indians, a roiling pack of dogs, and one wolf pup, which promptly ripped up his last decent pair of trousers. When Beltrami's Chippewa hosts weren't pilfering his supplies, they spent a good deal of time getting drunk.

After resting for a day or two, Beltrami hired a surly, possibly criminal, mestizo and an Indian to guide him to his destination. The men crossed Red Lake by canoe and commenced a weeklong journey to the south via numerous lakes, rivers, and streams. Eventually, they reached a boggy area where a gently sloping hill led to a small, heart-shaped lake. On the north side of the hill, Beltrami found a spring that flowed north. On the opposite side, another spring flowed to the south. Beltrami was ecstatic, certain that he'd found the sources of both the Red Lake River (which he called the Bloody River) and the Mississippi in a single location. Imagining himself surrounded by the ghosts of Marco Polo, Columbus, and other famous Italian explorers, Beltrami recorded his thoughts about "this most happy and brilliant moment of my life." He named the heart-shaped lake after Countess Giulia Spada de Medici, noting that the nearby south-flowing waters, "stealing cautiously through the rushes and briars," were "the actual sources of the Mississippi!" What joy, what a triumph. What a mistake.

Beltrami's heart-shaped lake was actually several miles north of the true source of the Mississippi, a lake identified nine years later by Henry Schoolcraft, to which he gave the faux Indian name Itasca. Beltrami wasn't alone in his error. Several other explorers—David Thompson, Zebulon Pike, Lewis Cass, and Schoolcraft himself—had previously misidentified the source of the Mississippi. It was easy to do, given the marshy terrain and maze of waterways in the region. Beltrami dismissed all of this, confident that he was the one to find the river's true source. Making his way back to Fort St. Anthony, he announced his triumphal return with a musket salute. The fort's inhabitants were startled to see him. No one had expected the eccentric Italian to survive after he'd left the Long expedition. His three-month sojourn in the wilderness was over, but his ties to the region were just beginning.

From Fort St. Anthony, Beltrami traveled down the Mississippi to New Orleans. There he spent several weeks shaping his notes into book form. The account of his journey was published in French in 1824 and in English four years later. The title of the two-volume work was as grandiose as its contents: A *Pilgrimage in Europe and America Leading to the Discovery of the Sources of the Mississippi and Bloody River; with a Description of the Whole Course of the Former, and of the Ohio.* Beltrami's writing was tinged with courtly floweriness, his words heaped up like sugar frosting slathered on marzipan. The lengthy, romantic account had relatively few readers, and Beltrami's claim of having discovered the source of the Mississippi was shot down by geographers and editorialists, one writer scoffing at the "exquisite dandy" traipsing through the wilderness. His old antagonist, Major Long, loftily dismissed the book's "fictions and misrepresentations."

Following an extended trip to Mexico, Beltrami returned to the United States to defend his reputation and promote the sale of his work. He visited Philadelphia to recover four hundred copies of his book that had been stashed in the cellar of a bar, a truly original publishing indignity. His memoir, however, was quickly forgotten in America. In the fall of 1826, Beltrami returned to Europe. He spent time in England, France, and Germany, becoming a respected member of several learned societies. Toward the end of his life, he moved back to Italy, living out his days in monklike simplicity. He died in Italy in January 1855 at the age of seventy-six.

By the time the peripatetic Italian passed away, few people in America would have recognized his name, other than historians and the citizens of Minnesota. Although he failed in his quest to discover the source of the Mississippi, Beltrami succeeded grandly in his larger mission of experiencing the world's marvels for himself. And he did it with high spirits, fortitude, and an eye for accurate detail (his writing may have been overwrought, but his descriptions of the Minnesota landscape and its inhabitants were dead-on).

In the journal Stephen Long kept during the 1823 expedition, the haughty major disparaged Beltrami as "an amateur traveller," a gross mischaracterization. Giacomo Beltrami may have been an amateur *explorer*, but he was, beyond all doubt, a consummate traveler—a "solitary pilgrim," as he described himself, whose only aim was "to see, to compare and to learn." Anyone driving across northwestern Minnesota today is still reminded of this Don Quixote of the wilderness. In 1866, the Minnesota legislature named one of the state's largest counties after the Italian adventurer. (Interestingly, Major Long received no such honors.) Considering the tribulations he endured in the American backcountry, Beltrami certainly earned his commemoration. His impact on the mapping of the country's geography may have been slight, but in the annals of outrageous individualism, he left an enduring mark.

FOUR

The Genetics of Truth

KIRK BLOODSWORTH

THIS WAS THE WORST day of Kirk Bloodsworth's life. As was the day before. And the day before that. Every long, pointless day for the past eight years had been a blur of fear and uncertainty, and tomorrow would be equally terrifying. The thirty-two-year-old Bloodsworth was suspended inside a gray void with no up, no down, no forward or back. Just three confining walls and those unyielding iron bars. Bloodsworth's cell in Baltimore's grim, medieval-looking Maryland Penitentiary measured three paces from end to end. If he stretched out his arms, he could touch both side walls at the same time.

For Bloodsworth, life inside this roach-infested pit consisted of one form of cruelty after another. Guards taunted him about his impending rendezvous with the gas chamber one floor above his cell. He'd seen acquaintances murdered by the barbaric thugs he was confined among. He'd survived two deadly prison riots—in one of them, he'd turned up the volume of his Sony Walkman in an attempt to drown out the screams of a fellow inmate being beaten and repeatedly raped. Just to survive, Bloodsworth passed himself off as an intimidating biker, growing his hair long and pumping weights. That didn't reflect who he was at heart. The worst thing about the physical and mental torture he endured every day was the fact that he had nothing to do with the crime he'd been convicted of—the rape and murder of a young girl. Kirk Bloodsworth was an innocent man.

Bloodsworth was accused of killing nine-year-old Dawn Hamilton on July 25, 1984. The pretty, sandy-haired girl lived in Essex, Maryland, just east of Baltimore. Bloodsworth had grown up in Cambridge, on Maryland's Eastern Shore, where he helped his father harvest oysters and crabs on the Chesapeake Bay. After a four-year stint in the Marines, Bloodsworth had married a hard-partying woman from Baltimore and gone to live with her in a row house in Essex—just three weeks before Dawn Hamilton was attacked.

Bloodsworth was picked up by the police based on an anonymous tip. Someone thought he looked like the man in the composite sketch of the suspect. Although prosecutors presented no hard evidence linking Bloodsworth to the crime, five eyewitnesses swore they'd spotted him at the scene. The most damning testimony came from two children, a seven-year-old and a ten-year-old. Despite the doubts raised by Bloodsworth's defense attorneys, prosecutors were certain that Bloodsworth was guilty, and they succeeded in convincing the jury of that.

Bloodsworth was originally sentenced to die in the gas chamber, but his appeals in higher courts resulted in his punishment being reduced to two consecutive life terms. It looked like Bloodsworth was doomed to spend the rest of his days in the Maryland Penitentiary. The only solace he had was that a Washington, D.C., attorney who specialized in defending death row inmates, Robert Morin, had agreed to look into his case in 1989. However, in three years Morin had made little progress.

To mentally free himself from his surroundings, Bloodsworth spent as much time as he could in the prison library, poring through newspapers, magazines, and books in hopes of finding some scrap of legal precedent that might help him prove his innocence. In 1992, he came across a book by Joseph Wambaugh called *The Blooding*. It described a criminal case in England in which two teenage girls from a village near the city of Leicester had been raped and strangled. Bloodsworth was startled to read about a new scientific technique that had been used to identify the girls' killer. The technique was based on profiling the composition of DNA—the molecular material in human cells that determines who we are.

Although 99.9 percent of the genetic information contained in DNA is the same in every person on Earth, a small amount is unique to each individual, which is why no two people are absolutely identical, including identical twins. Bloodsworth's excitement grew as he read about Alec Jeffreys, a professor at the University of Leicester who'd discovered how to capture a DNA "fingerprint" by recording the sequence of the four chemical bases within DNA that encode genetic information—the bar code of heredity stored in nearly every one of the body's trillions of cells. Dr. Jeffreys had developed a test that could positively identify individuals through a tiny sample of tissue or bodily fluid—a test that could pinpoint one person out of billions. Dr. Jeffreys made his discovery in 1984, the same year that Bloodsworth was arrested.

Police in England used Dr. Jeffreys's genetic fingerprinting technique to profile the DNA in blood samples taken from over 4,500 young men in the area where the two girls were raped and murdered. They hoped to find a match with the DNA in the semen found on the girls' clothing. The police had no success until they received a tip that a local man named Colin Pitchfork had asked a friend to submit a blood sample in his place. When the police tested Pitchfork's own blood, they found a perfect match. Pitchfork was convicted of the crimes in 1988, the first time that DNA profiling had been used to catch and convict a killer. Kirk Bloodsworth immediately realized that the new test could be used to prove his innocence. He contacted Bob Morin and told him about the book. The reply he received was discouraging.

Morin had looked into DNA testing when he originally agreed to represent Bloodsworth. The FBI had told him that no semen or foreign blood was found at the crime scene or on the victim's clothing. Some fluid samples had been taken from the victim and preserved on glass slides, but those samples were inadequate to ID the killer with the testing techniques available in 1989, and the test itself would have likely destroyed any existing DNA. Thankfully, Morin had the foresight to request that all the evidence be retained. Three years had passed since Morin's initial inquiries. At Bloodsworth's insistence, he agreed to pursue DNA testing once more. It was the only hope left for his client, whose innocence he believed in.

Morin contacted a California laboratory that was employing the most advanced DNA-testing techniques available. He sent them the glass slides and the clothes Dawn Hamilton had been wearing, along with scrapings from the dead girl's fingernails and the blood-speckled chunk of concrete used to crush her skull. He also sent a blood sample from his client. After three months, the lab finally got back to Morin: they had found semen stains on the girl's underwear. Another agonizing five months passed before Morin heard from the lab again. The test results were conclusive: DNA taken from the semen stains did not match his client's DNA—Kirk Bloodsworth had not raped and murdered Dawn Hamilton. When Morin broke the news to Bloodsworth, the tough, burly ex-Marine wept uncontrollably, then ran screaming down the hallways of the Maryland Penitentiary. "It's over! It's over! It's over!" he kept yelling.

It took two more months to obtain Bloodsworth's release from prison. The FBI insisted on completing its own DNA tests, which corroborated the earlier results. On June 28, 1993, Bloodsworth marched out of the Maryland Penitentiary and drew his first breath as a free man in nine years. As the cameras rolled, Bloodsworth thanked everyone who'd been kind to him, all those who'd helped him win his release. He also blasted the state for the unjust persecution he'd had to endure. He ended with these words: "Even though this is a small victory for me, to have proved my innocence, the real killer is still out there. And all of this won't be completed until the real one is behind bars."

Bloodsworth's life after his release began with a long stretch of partying. He couldn't endure being alone. Interviews by Oprah Winfrey and Larry King turned him into a temporary celebrity, and he spoke out against both the death penalty and wrongful imprisonment before the U.S. Congress. Bob Morin, meanwhile, won Bloodsworth a full pardon from the governor of Maryland and $350,000 in compensation for the nine years that had been stolen from him. Bloodsworth used the money to settle his debts along with those of his father, who'd spent all of his retirement savings trying to help his son. Bloodsworth kept on partying for over a year after his release, until the money ran out. That was when he knew he had to settle down and get a job. Divorced from his first wife, he married a woman in his hometown and took a job on an oyster boat. A short time later, he bought his own workboat, a lifelong dream. Things were going well, but something still nagged at him: Dawn Hamilton's killer hadn't been apprehended. It was possible he was committing additional crimes.

Ever since he'd been released from prison, Bloodsworth had been pushing the Baltimore County State's Attorney's Office, which had conducted his prosecution, to find Dawn Hamilton's real murderer. Why hadn't they looked for a match of the killer's DNA in the growing database maintained by the FBI? For ten years, he received nothing but evasion and excuses. After sparing no expense to prosecute Bloodsworth, the office now said it lacked the funding to search for a DNA match. In 2003, the *Washington Post* and the *Baltimore Sun* published articles that posed the same question Bloodsworth had been asking. Finally the state's attorney's office acted. The results of the DNA search were shocking: Dawn Hamilton's killer was already in the Maryland Penitentiary, serving a sentence for attempted rape and assault with intent to kill. His name was Kimberly Ruffner—a man who'd twice been arrested on child molestation charges. The first charge had been dropped. He was tried on the second charge but released just two weeks before Dawn Hamilton's death. Incredibly, Bloodsworth had served time with Ruffner. "I spotted weights for that man, brought him library books," Bloodsworth said when he learned of the search results.

Identifying Ruffner as the killer prompted a long overdue apology from the state's attorney's office, whose lawyers had remained skeptical of Bloodsworth's innocence even after he'd been released from prison. Their comments had tainted Bloodsworth's freedom, causing some people in his own hometown to shun him. Such continued persecution was unforgivable, but when one of the attorneys traveled to Cambridge to tell Bloodsworth in person how sorry she was for what the state had done to him, he forgave her. The state's attorney's office leaned toward seeking the death penalty for Ruffner. Bloodsworth opposed the decision, a remarkable stance given the pain Ruffner had caused him. Ruffner admitted his guilt and a life sentence was added to the term he was already serving.

Kirk Bloodsworth endured a terrible injustice. His release from prison after nine years came about through pure happenstance. He would never have been freed if attorney Bob Morin had not agreed to take on an apparently hopeless cause . . . if Morin hadn't had the foresight to insist that all the evidence in Bloodsworth's case be preserved . . . if DNA testing hadn't become available when it did . . . and if Bloodsworth himself hadn't read about the use of DNA in a criminal investigation and pressed Morin to pursue testing. It was a streak of good luck as improbable as the chain of coincidences that resulted in Bloodsworth's conviction.

In 2000, Bloodsworth became affiliated with the Justice Project, a nonprofit group working for criminal justice reform. Since then, he's told his story at universities and state legislatures all over the country. "I don't want the fact that I was the first person to be freed because of DNA testing to be my only legacy in life," he said. "I know there's more mistakes out there and none of us should ever sentence an innocent man to death or prison." Bloodsworth's testimony was key to the passage of the Innocence Protection Act, a law that instituted a postconviction DNA testing program named after him. Referring to his ordeal, he told members of Congress, "I don't ever want this to happen to anybody else."

In the years since Bloodsworth won his freedom, hundreds of wrongly convicted people have been similarly freed—all thanks to the DNA fingerprinting technology invented in 1984 by Alec Jeffreys. At a London ceremony honoring Dr. Jeffreys in March 2004, Bloodsworth had the opportunity to personally thank the man who'd played such an important role in his life and in the lives of other innocent victims. It was a moving experience for Bloodsworth—shaking the hand that had snatched him back from hell.

FIVE

The Slave Who Became a Union Spy

MARY BOWSER

SHE GAZES OUT from the photograph with disarming frankness, a young black woman wearing her neat and proper Sunday best. It's a formal portrait. She stands beside a chair, one hand resting on the handle of a parasol. A tightly cinched belt accents her narrow waist, and a jaunty straw hat perches atop her head. Her face seems to bear the faintest hint of a smile. (Could she have been smiling because she knew she'd pulled off one of the greatest deceptions of her time?)

Her name was Mary Elizabeth Bowser, and despite her demure appearance she was absolutely fearless. For much of the Civil War, she calmly walked a razor's edge of danger that would have incapacitated weaker souls. Throughout 1863 and 1864, Bowser spied on the South from inside the lion's den—in the Richmond, Virginia, household of Confederate president Jefferson Davis. During that period, she provided the Union with invaluable information about Southern military forces.

Aside from being brave, Mary Bowser was also undeniably lucky. Her pluck, her good fortune, and her association with another remarkable Virginia woman would shape a career that might have been conjured up by Ian Fleming.

Bowser began life as Mary Van Lew, born a slave around 1839 in the household of John Van Lew, a wealthy Richmond hardware merchant. Antebellum Richmond was a lively, colorful crossroads. A steady stream of cargo boats passed through town on the James River and Kanawha Canal, hauling goods from points east. Richmond's vibrant industrial center included iron works and flour mills that rivaled any in the country. Businessmen who made their fortunes here built fancy Greek revival or federal-style mansions in the Church Hill neighborhood, overlooking the Virginia state capitol building and the thrumming factories and chock-full warehouses of the Shockoe Bottom area. It was a city bursting with energy and enterprise.

Richmond also harbored one of humanity's most despicable creations—a slave auction. A major transshipping point for slaves bound for the Deep South, the city's slave market conducted its trade in a warren of cramped, haphazardly whitewashed rooms along Wall Street, near the riverfront. There, people were herded like cattle, pinched and poked to gauge their physical strength and size up their "breeding" potential. Friends and families were casually split apart, children torn from their mothers' arms without a thought. This most savage aspect of slavery was brought home to Mary Van Lew as a child, when John Van Lew sold off her own family members to other masters.

Mary's luck changed dramatically after John Van Lew died. Van Lew's daughter Elizabeth, a confirmed abolitionist, persuaded her mother to free all of their slaves. She even bought back Mary's family and gave them their freedom. Although Mary could have left the Van Lew home at that time, she stayed on as a paid servant.

Elizabeth Van Lew's kindness didn't end with the emancipation of the family slaves. Normally, slaves weren't taught to read or write. They were kept in mental fetters, their lack of knowledge holding them down as effectively as a ball and chain. Aware of Mary's intelligence and desire to learn, Elizabeth decided to pay for her education. She herself had been taught by Quakers, and in the late 1850s she sent Mary to a Quaker school for blacks in Philadelphia.

Mary returned to Richmond in the spring of 1861, just before the outbreak of the Civil War. She would have been in her early twenties. It was around this time that she married a free black man named Wilson Bowser. Though she now lived on the outskirts of Richmond, Mary Bowser continued her association with the Van Lew family.

When the war began, Elizabeth Van Lew committed herself to the Union cause. She delivered food and medicine to Northern soldiers held in the city's Libby Prison, and she hid escapees in a secret room in the family mansion. Her pro-Union sympathies earned her the enmity of most of Richmond, but she helped dampen resentment by appearing to be mentally unbalanced. In spite of her wealth and fine home on Church Hill, she adopted a slovenly appearance, going out in public in tatty dresses and bonnets. She walked the streets muttering to herself, her head cocked to one side. The locals began calling her "Crazy Bet."

As the capital of the Confederacy, Richmond was transformed by the war. It swelled with troops, government workers, Confederate wounded, and Union prisoners. Citizens often heard cannons booming in the distance, and peaceful outlying farms became bloody battlefields. In the midst of this chaos, Van Lew made her boldest move. She formed a spy ring of a dozen people, the so-called Richmond underground. She asked Mary Bowser to join her network. An educated black woman who could pass herself off as an ordinary slave would be an invaluable weapon against the South. Bowser readily agreed.

To plant her new spy, Van Lew arranged for Bowser to work part-time at several functions held by Varina Davis, the wife of Jefferson Davis. Calling on her acting skills, Bowser transformed herself into "Ellen Bond," a slow-witted but hardworking servant. Her dedication caught the eye of Mrs. Davis, and she landed a full-time job in the Davis home, the White House of the Confederacy, a gray-stuccoed neoclassical mansion two blocks from the Virginia state capitol.

Bowser's job included serving meals and looking after the Davis children. Her real assignment, though, was to collect as much intelligence as possible—information about the location of Confederate troops, Southern finances, and prisoners of war. She pulled this off with aplomb, aided by her ability to make herself inconspicuous. That effort was made easier thanks to Southern attitudes toward blacks, who were regarded as uncomprehending menials. To Southern aristocrats, slaves were virtually invisible. President Davis and his lieutenants would talk openly in front of Bowser as she served dinner or cleaned up afterward. And Davis felt safe leaving important papers on his desk in plain sight, assuming his servants were all illiterate.

Bowser soaked up this intelligence and passed it on. One of her contacts was Richmond baker Thomas McNiven. She would meet him at his bakery or on his frequent deliveries to the Davis mansion. McNiven later told his daughter that Bowser had "a photographic mind. Everything she saw on the Rebel President's desk she could repeat word for word."

Bowser and the other Richmond spies funneled all of the

information they gathered through Elizabeth Van Lew, who passed it on to Union forces in imaginative ways. She sometimes hid messages inside hollowed eggshells placed in a basket of fresh eggs. She hid letters under the false bottom of a food tray. She even secreted messages inside her servant's muddy shoes, which were unlikely to be searched by disdainful Southerners.

Of all the members of the Richmond underground, Bowser provided the best intelligence. Van Lew made sure this information went directly to Union generals Benjamin Butler or Ulysses S. Grant. Grant praised the work of Van Lew and her spies, telling her, "You have sent me the most valuable information received from Richmond during the war."

No one knows the specifics of the intelligence Mary Bowser obtained. When the fighting was over, War Department records on Union spies were destroyed to protect those who'd worked for the North from Southern retaliation. Still, it's easy to piece together the outlines of what Bowser picked up in the Davis home. President Davis was often confined to the White House by health problems, which meant that his military and political advisors routinely met with him there instead of at his office in the Treasury Building. Bowser would have found reasons to be close at hand whenever possible. She would have learned details about troop movements and the defenses around Richmond, information vital to Northern military strategy. In January 1864, the Van Lew spy ring discovered plans to relocate thousands of Union prisoners from Richmond to Georgia, which prompted Northern forces to attack the Confederate capital. Bowser would have had some part in that episode.

One thing is certain—the South felt the sting of Bowser's work. President Davis and his staff eventually began to wonder how the Union kept finding out about their plans. It's not known whether they suspected Bowser, but for some reason she abruptly fled Richmond in January 1865. Her last act on behalf of the Union was a failed attempt to set fire to the White House of the Confederacy.

Bowser disappeared after she left Richmond, and no further record of her exists, although she evidently left behind a diary. What that diary contained will forever remain a tantalizing mystery. In 1952, Mary's cousin McEva Bowser discovered the book while cleaning the room of her mother-in-law, who'd recently passed away. In reading the diary, McEva Bowser kept seeing references to a Mr. Davis, but "the only Davis I could think of was the contractor who had been doing some work at the house," she recalled. "The first time I came across it I threw it aside and said I would read it again." However, the next time McEva noticed the diary, she said she "just pitched it in the trash can."

The lack of written records about Mary Bowser doesn't detract from her accomplishments. The fact that she spent two years as a Union spy—smack under the noses of the highest officials of the Confederacy—is proof of her skill and audacity. At great personal risk, Bowser played a significant role in helping the North win the Civil War and preserve the Union. Her contributions were formally recognized in 1995 when she was inducted into the Military Intelligence Hall of Fame in Fort Huachuca, Arizona. During the ceremony, she was hailed for having "succeeded in a highly dangerous mission to the great benefit of the Union effort. She was one of the highest placed and most productive espionage agents of the Civil War."

It's natural to hope that Bowser lived a long and happy life after she disappeared from Richmond. Perhaps she returned to Philadelphia and settled down with her husband to raise a large, boisterous family, with all of her children attending school and going on to great success. That certainly would have been the life Mary Bowser deserved. And maybe, when she'd grown old, she sat in a rocking chair by the fire with a subtle smile on her face, thinking of the long-ago days when she'd fooled old Jeff Davis as simple little Ellen Bond.

SIX

The Black Swallow of Death

EUGENE BULLARD

THE AFTERNOON SUN glinted off the formation of trim little Nieuport 17s flying over the war-torn Verdun sector on Europe's Western Front. The wings of the silvery biplanes were painted with bright military roundels—concentric circles of red, white, and blue that identified them as French fighters. Developed for racing, Nieuports had been adapted for combat after the outbreak of World War I in July 1914. As the warplanes cruised along at 8,000 feet, the frigid air buffeted the fragile craft—gossamer constructions of wood, wire, and fabric.

Twenty-two-year-old American Eugene Bullard sat in the open cockpit of one of the planes. Bullard's ever-present companion and "copilot," a pet spider monkey named Jimmy, clung to the inside of his jacket. The engine of the single-prop Nieuport thrummed reassuringly as Bullard scanned the skies. He was on the alert for the distinctive tri-wing Fokker aircraft flown by the German army's air wing.

Looking down, Bullard spotted a group of enemy fighters. Their bold Iron Cross markings stood out against the irregular patterns of fields, roads, and trenches far below. Bullard signaled to the other pilots in his formation then dove toward the nearest German plane, his Vickers machine gun chattering wildly. Seconds later, a trail of black smoke marked the death spiral of Bullard's target. The young American had his first kill.

Bullard and his companions were part of the legendary band of pilots who made up the Lafayette Flying Corps, American volunteers serving under the French in the years before the United States entered the war against Germany. Only about two hundred men claimed membership in this exclusive group, and Eugene Bullard stood out from them all—simply because he was an African American, the first black combat pilot ever and the only one to serve in World War I. Twenty-five years before the Tuskegee airmen became the first African Americans to fly in the U.S. armed forces, during World War II, Bullard proved his mettle as a fighter pilot in an era of crushing prejudice. Bullard's trailblazing role as a pilot was just one highlight in an amazing string of adventures this son of a former slave experienced. Bullard saw the highs and lows of life as few people ever do, all because of his desire to be judged for his character, not his color.

Born in Columbus, Georgia, on October 9, 1895, Eugene James Bullard was the "lucky seventh" of William and Josephine Bullard's ten children. Eugene's father worked as a laborer and his mother took in washing and sewing. Although the family was poor, William Bullard instilled a sense of pride in his children. He told them there were places in the world where people of all races lived as equals. He also told his children that the best way to overcome discrimination was to maintain their self-respect and insist on fair treatment from others.

That was no easy feat in the Deep South. William Bullard barely escaped a lynch mob after he retaliated against a white bully at work. Eugene himself never experienced prejudice until after his mother's death in 1902. Josephine Bullard had not allowed her children to associate with whites, but after she died, her young son learned what racism was all about. Eugene knew that he had to escape Columbus and find one of those charmed places where he could live with dignity.

In 1906, Bullard set out on his own, an eleven-year-old boy with five years of schooling and $1.50 jingling in his pocket. Following the railroad tracks away from Columbus, the young runaway made it to Atlanta, where he took up with a band of English gypsies. The gypsies taught him their skills with horses, which he later put to use as a jockey and stable boy. They also fed Bullard's dreams of equality by telling him that black people were treated far better in Europe than in the United States, and they promised to take him with them when they went back.

Bullard traveled with the gypsies for over a year. He left them when he found out they had no intention of returning to Europe anytime soon. Bullard bummed around the South for the next few years, working on farms, in a barbershop, and in the households of white families. Sometimes he was treated with kindness and sometimes with contempt, but whenever any of his employers called him "nigger," he stopped what he was doing and refused to continue unless they agreed to address him as Gene.

Early in 1912, when he was sixteen years old, Bullard made a life-changing decision. He hopped a train for Norfolk, Virginia, where one night he stole aboard the *Marta Russ*, a German freighter bound for Europe. With a small supply of food and water, he hid inside a canvas-covered lifeboat—apropos for someone drowning in a sea of prejudice. As the *Marta Russ* steamed away from the dock at Norfolk, its master was unaware of the small cargo of hope and determination he had on board.

Bullard remained hidden in the lifeboat for three days. After his food and water ran out, he had to show himself. The captain jokingly threatened to toss him overboard but instead put him to work in the boiler room for the rest of the three-week voyage. When the ship reached Aberdeen, Scotland, the captain paid Bullard five English pounds and helped smuggle him ashore to avoid problems with the authorities. Bullard took a train to Glasgow, where he was startled by the absence of racial animosity. "Within twenty-four hours," he said, "I was born into a new world."

After a few months, Bullard moved on to Liverpool. He found a job in the cast of a minstrel troupe called Freedman's Pickaninnies. He also took up boxing, winning several professional bouts in Liverpool and London. In November 1913, Bullard traveled to Paris for a bout. He immediately fell in love with the French capital, intoxicated by the beauty of its boulevards, monuments, and parks and the friendliness of its people. He said that he "could never be happy for the rest of my life unless I could live in France." In the spring of 1914, Bullard accompanied Freedman's Pickaninnies on a tour of the Continent, performing in Moscow, Berlin, and, finally, Paris. When the troupe left Paris, Bullard stayed behind.

Bullard earned his living in Paris through prizefighting and working as a sparring partner. Adept at languages, he'd picked up enough French and German to act as a paid interpreter for other boxers. He delighted in the camaraderie of fellow expatriate African Americans and in the open acceptance he found among white Parisians. He felt like a burden had been lifted from him, since he no longer had to act according to someone else's expectations. Convinced that this was where he would spend the rest of his life, he adopted the Francophone version of his name, Eugène Jacques Bullard (his last name pronounced Bull-*ar*).

The summer of 1914 was magical. The lights of Paris blazed into the night, the music from the cabarets floating on the air. Events elsewhere in Europe, however, had turned threatening. Nations embroiled in a tangled web of alliances raced to stockpile armaments. At the end of June, Archduke Franz Ferdinand of Austria died from an assassin's bullet, and within weeks the major Continental powers were at war, dragging their colonial possessions into the conflict. France mobilized on August 1, following Germany's mobilization. The German army quickly rolled through Belgium and into northern France. The French government appealed to all able-bodied men to help defend the country. Among those answering the call was Eugene Bullard.

Just after turning nineteen in October, Bullard signed up with the French Foreign Legion. For the next year and a half, he endured the horrors of trench warfare on the Western Front, the contested strip of land separating territory controlled by Germany and that controlled by France and its allies. A machine gunner, Bullard saw action in some of the bloodiest conflicts of the war. He fought in the battle along the Somme River, where losses were so heavy among the three Foreign Legion regiments that they had to be consolidated into one. In gory mass charges, the opposing armies fought like animals, often hand to hand, driven into a killing frenzy with rations of 100-proof alcohol.

In the Champagne region, Bullard suffered a head wound. His Foreign Legion regiment had been so depleted that its soldiers were transferred to regular French units. Bullard ended up in the 170th Infantry, a regiment whose ferocious fighters were nicknamed the "Swallows of Death." In early 1916, the unit took part in the savage fighting at Verdun. The opposing armies lobbed millions of artillery shells onto each other, many filled with poison gas. Bullard began to imagine the incoming shells were screaming his name. The battlefield was a nightmare scene, a cratered, denuded landscape with body parts hanging from skeletal trees.

Some three hundred thousand men died in the months-long battle at Verdun. Bullard survived, although an exploding shell knocked out all but four of his teeth. Shortly after that injury, he suffered a severe thigh wound while carrying a message under fire. Bullard's gallantry earned him the Croix de Guerre. It also ended his time as a foot soldier. Evacuated to Lyon, he spent three months in the hospital and another three months in a convalescent center. As he hobbled about the streets of town, he was greeted as a hero.

Unfit to return to the trenches, Bullard began thinking about transferring to the aviation service as a gunner. While on leave in Paris, he upped his aspirations considerably after accepting a $2,000 bet with a friend over whether he could qualify as a combat pilot, which no black person had ever done. Bullard applied to flight school and was accepted. Seven months later, in May 1917, he received his wings. His accomplishment was noted in an article in the Paris edition of the *New York Herald Tribune*, although not a word appeared in newspapers back in the United States.

Bullard would fly more than twenty missions, downing two enemy planes (only one was corroborated as an official kill). His career as a pilot lasted just over two months. The United States had joined the fight against Germany in April 1917, and when its forces arrived in Europe later in the year, Americans flying under French command were transferred to the U.S. Army Air Service—except for Bullard. U.S. authorities told him he wasn't qualified—not even to serve as a member of an aviation ground crew. It didn't matter that he'd proven his abilities to the French—his countrymen still regarded him as an incompetent. Bullard had escaped American racism by moving abroad, only to see it follow him to Europe. He was sent back to his old French regiment, where he served until he was discharged in October 1919.

At twenty-four, Bullard returned to civilian life in Paris. Following the horror of the war years, the city provided a welcome dose of gaiety. In the cabarets of Montmartre, African American performers such as Josephine Baker fueled the hedonistic frenzy of the Jazz Age. Bullard learned to play the drums and found work at Zelli's, a club that opened at midnight just as other cabarets were closing. Selling only bottles of champagne and offering pretty young dancing partners, the club was the "in" spot of Montmartre. In his elegant tuxedo, Bullard became a fixture at Zelli's—Ernest Hemingway based a character on him in *The Sun Also Rises*. Bullard later managed another popular club, Le Grand Duc, and eventually he owned his own bar, L'Escadrille, as well as a health club.

During the war, Bullard had met a young woman named Marcelle Straumann, a member of a well-to-do Parisian family. Bullard often took her dancing, and although he had many other lady friends, he realized he'd fallen in love with Marcelle. In July 1923, they were married. After honeymooning in Biarritz, they moved into a luxury apartment with a view of the Eiffel Tower—quite a contrast to the shabby three-room house where Bullard grew up. The couple had two daughters (a son died in infancy). The marriage lasted until 1935, ending,

Bullard said, because his wealthy wife insisted that he give up his businesses and live a life of ease, something the hardworking Yankee refused to do.

Throughout the 1920s, Bullard hobnobbed with renowned musicians, actors, and writers. He was friends with Dooley Wilson, who later played Bogie's piano man in *Casablanca*. At Le Grand Duc, Bullard met Louis Armstrong, Cole Porter, Sophie Tucker, Charlie Chaplin, and the Prince of Wales—and at Zelli's, he hired fledgling poet Langston Hughes as a dishwasher. Although he had violent run-ins with racist Americans, Bullard enjoyed a life filled with friendship and financial success. But this halcyon period was drawing to a close. After the New York stock market crash in 1929, the free-spending patrons who'd kept the Paris night scene bubbling began to disappear. By the late 1930s, Adolph Hitler loomed over Europe like a vulture on a barren snag.

As the menace of Nazi Germany grew, Bullard again stepped forward to aid his adopted country. In late 1939, he joined French counterintelligence, spying on Nazi supporters who frequented his bar and gym. In May 1940, the Germans attacked France, and by June they'd captured Paris. Bullard fled the city before it fell. He joined French forces defending Orléans, but the Germans drove them from the city. On June 18, Bullard suffered a spinal injury when the concussion of an exploding shell threw him against a wall in the village of Le Blanc.

Knowing that the racist Nazis would execute a black combatant, Bullard's commander—an officer he'd served with at Verdun—ordered him to escape from France. Walking in constant pain, and later riding a bicycle that a French soldier gave him, Bullard made the long journey to Biarritz. From there, he slipped into Spain, then traveled on to Lisbon, where he boarded the American steamship *Manhattan*. A week later, he was looking up at the Statue of Liberty, back home for the first time in twenty-eight years.

Life in America was a tremendous comedown. Bullard made a nostalgic trip to Columbus, Georgia, although he failed to locate any immediate family members. Holding down a variety of jobs—longshoreman, security guard, perfume salesman—he lived alone in an apartment in New York's Harlem, surrounded by photos and paintings of his friends from the old days. He found companionship among New York's French community and World War I veterans. His biggest shock was once again having to deal with discrimination, the worst instance coming in 1949, when he was clubbed by police at a civil rights benefit concert in Peekskill, New York. This cosmopolitan, entrepreneurial, multilingual war hero was just a "boy" in America, someone who didn't know his "place." In France, he had soared; here at home, his feet were still nailed to the ground.

In 1950, Bullard returned to Paris, hoping to win a settlement for the property he'd lost in the war and resume his career as a club owner. Unsuccessful in his litigation—and disappointed by the changes in Montmartre—Bullard went back to New York, realizing that the Paris he'd known was gone forever. The following year, he toured Europe with Louis Armstrong, serving as Satchmo's interpreter. In 1954, the French government brought Bullard to Paris to participate in the relighting of the eternal flame at the Tomb of the Unknown Soldier below the Arc de Triomphe. It was his last trip to the city he loved. In October 1959, France bestowed its highest award on Bullard, making him a knight of the Legion of Honor, his fifteenth military decoration. Two months later, Bullard enjoyed a moment of recognition in his homeland when he appeared on the *Today*

Show. Host Dave Garroway displayed his medals as Bullard related his incredible story.

Bullard died of stomach cancer in October 1961. Dressed in his Legionnaire's uniform, he was buried in Flushing, New York. It was many years after his death before Americans finally began to honor Bullard's accomplishments. In 1989, he was inducted into the Georgia Aviation Hall of Fame. In 1990, he was depicted in a mural honoring pioneer aviators at the St. Louis International Airport, and a year later the Smithsonian Institution unveiled a bust of Bullard at the National Air and Space Museum. In a long overdue gesture, Bullard was posthumously commissioned a second lieutenant in the U.S. Air Force in September 1994—seventy-seven years after he'd been rejected as a pilot by American forces in World War I, simply for the color of his skin. Today he serves as inspiration for Americans of all races and backgrounds—anyone aspiring to accomplish more than is expected of them.

In his last job before his death, Bullard worked as an elevator operator in New York City's Rockefeller Center. Very likely, few of his passengers were aware that they were rubbing elbows with a genuine war hero. The homely image of Eugene Bullard confined in a tiny elevator car is depressing. He was a man who lived a daring, passionate life. Far better to remember him in his younger days, soaring over the patchwork French countryside in his jaunty little Nieuport 17, his pet monkey Jimmy perched on his shoulder and the sun sinking low as he heads for home after a mission. Look up toward the clouds and you might see him now, waggling his wings in salute and diving headlong for glory.

SEVEN

The Last Stone Age Man in America

ISHI

THE LATE AUGUST heat and humidity had settled like a soggy blanket over Oroville, California, a former gold rush town squatting at the foot of the Sierra Nevada northeast of San Francisco. Out on Quincy Road, sunlight glistened on the wet concrete floor inside the Ward slaughterhouse as workers went about cleaning up at the end of the day. Before they'd finished, the men heard dogs barking outside, and one of them stepped into the corral to investigate. What he saw gave him a start. Cowering nearby was the sorriest-looking human being the worker had ever come across—a scrawny, sun-scorched Indian dressed in a tattered canvas tunic. The Indian's eyes reflected the desperation of a wild creature caught in a trap, which is exactly what he was—a once unfettered soul now held fast in a web of time and circumstance. The slaughterhouse worker had no clue about the significance of this pathetic figure, but what he was looking at on this steaming afternoon in 1911 was the last Stone Age man in America.

The worker telephoned the Butte County sheriff, telling him they'd captured "something," but they didn't know what it was. When the sheriff arrived, the Indian submitted to being handcuffed and obeyed willingly when the sheriff motioned for him to follow. At the sheriff's office, the Indian wolfed down a hot meal. Officials tried to communicate with him by gesturing, since he didn't seem to understand English, Spanish, or any native dialect the locals were familiar with. Before long, people were crowding into the jail to gaze at the "Wild Man of Oroville." A reporter from the *Oroville Register* concluded that he was "probably the surviving member of the little group of uncivilized Deer Creek Indians who were driven from their hiding place two years ago." The newspaper stated that "these Indians were originally proud and warlike, and their frequent depredations upon the white settlers led to an organized war against them."

It was a very effective war. The day after the Indian was discovered, he was taken back to the slaughterhouse in hopes that he might explain how he'd gotten there. The Indian eventually understood what he was being asked. Using pantomime, he indicated that he'd once had three companions, all of whom were dead. The Indian then held up one finger and pointed at himself, meaning that he was the last member of his tribe. As a sign of mourning, he'd singed off his hair, traditionally worn long. The citizens of Oroville might have been surprised at the man's state of mind: he later revealed that he'd resigned himself to being put to death after his capture, since white men had always killed his people.

When word of the Indian's discovery reached San Francisco, two anthropologists at the University of California at Berkeley—Alfred Kroeber and Thomas Waterman—urgently discussed the importance of this rare cross-cultural encounter. The opportunity to study a member of a vanishing society was an anthropologist's dream. The two men had investigated California's indigenous populations extensively, and they guessed that the Indian might belong to the Yana tribe, whose people had once lived in a sixty-mile-long territory stretching from the Sierra foothills around Oroville northward to Mount Lassen in the southern Cascades. The anthropologists telegraphed the sheriff, stating that one of them would be coming to take custody of the Indian and accept responsibility for him. "Matter important account aboriginal history," the telegram explained.

An excited Professor Waterman left for Oroville immediately. Arriving at the sheriff's office, Waterman sat down beside the Indian in his cell and began reading from a list of Yana words. The Indian understood none of them. Then Waterman read the word *siwini*, which means "yellow pine." When he pointed to the pine frame of the bed they were sitting on, the Indian beamed. After all the strangers barking incoherent words in his face, here was someone who had uttered a word he knew. For several minutes, the two men kept slapping the bed frame and repeating the word *siwini*. The Indian began pouring out a torrent of thoughts, thrilled to be freed from his prison of mutual incomprehension. Waterman had no idea what the ecstatic Indian was saying, although gradually the two men discovered enough words they both understood to conduct a rudimentary conversation. In the process, Waterman learned that the Indian belonged to the Yahi tribe, the southernmost Yana subgroup, thought to be extinct.

Waterman sought and received permission to take charge of the Indian and escort him back to San Francisco, where he would be housed and studied at the University of California's Hearst Museum of Anthropology. It was the beginning of one of the strangest personal odysseys of the twentieth century, a cultural adventure of heroic proportions. Here was a man who had emerged from a hunter-gatherer society into the age of the railroad, airplane, automobile, and radio. He was like a Rip Van Winkle who'd slept for twenty centuries, not twenty years. For a modern-day American, an equivalent shock would be having to adapt to time travel or interplanetary vacations.

Decked out in a donated suit (though he refused to wear shoes), the Indian docilely followed Waterman to the Oroville train station. Their eight-hour journey ended light-years away from everything the Indian had previously known, at the four-story museum next door to the University of California's medical school in Parnassus Heights, a neighborhood at the eastern end of Golden Gate Park in the busy heart of San Francisco. There, the Indian met Professor Alfred Kroeber, who was to become his closest friend and principal guardian in this strange new world. A doctor from the medical school next door, Saxton Pope, estimated the Indian's age to be around fifty. Kroeber realized that they needed a name for their guest, but he knew that California Indians rarely revealed their tribal names, which were considered sacred. Kroeber resolved the issue by christening the Indian "Ishi," which means "man" in the Yana language.

Except for a few months when he lived with Thomas Waterman, Ishi would spend the next four and a half years at the Hearst Museum, shielded from vaudeville promoters, carnival impresarios, and other schemers wanting to make a buck off his unusual circumstances. Kroeber and Waterman did their best to pick up the Indian's language, and Ishi learned enough pidgin English that the men could communicate (one of Ishi's favorite phrases was "Sure, Mike," a reply that must have mystified the poor female visitor who earnestly asked him if he believed in God). Shy with strangers, Ishi proved outgoing around his small circle of friends, which included curators, guards, and janitors as well as other Indians who visited the museum to share their tribal lore. Accompanied by chaperones, Ishi loved to roam the city—riding streetcars and ferries, shopping, attending the theater. He easily took to eating with a knife and fork, and his manners were impeccable. He was so tidy that the museum hired him as a caretaker. Dr. Pope invited him to observe surgical procedures at the medical school. Afterward, Ishi visited the hospital regularly, making his rounds to cheer up the patients.

Despite his remarkable adaptation to his new life, Ishi never shook off the mournful awareness of his cultural solitude. In photographs, he often wore a distant, pensive look, as if he were meditating on his vanished people. "I am here," his expression seems to say, "but my spirit is not." That solemn demeanor is understandable. The man was a real-life E.T., a Neolithic denizen of nature marooned in a materialistic, industrialized society. But instead of gazing at the stars like E.T. and longing to return home, Ishi recalled the Sierra foothills, with their streams, forests, and meadows of tawny grass—the benign setting of his people's lives for thousands of years, lives that he alone remembered.

Fortunately for Kroeber and Waterman, Ishi was happy to share the details of that former existence. He patiently demonstrated his many outdoor survival skills, from building a shelter with tree branches and boughs to starting a fire with a wooden drill. He showed how to make arrowheads by knapping, a Stone Age technique that involves chipping away flakes from materials such as flint or obsidian to produce a razor edge. Ishi even knapped arrowheads from pieces of glass bottles. Crafting his own bow and arrows, he taught archery to his friends. Saxton Pope became so adept that he later hunted African lions with a bow and arrows. On several occasions, university staff members accompanied Ishi to his former hunting grounds, where the Indian revealed his prowess with his handmade weapons by hunting deer and rabbits and spearing salmon. Kroeber also arranged annual trips to gather acorns, a staple of Ishi's people.

Besides re-creating his old way of life for documentation, Ishi helped the anthropologists with their linguistic studies by allowing them to record his voice onto wax cylinders. Decades later, the recordings were painstakingly transferred to tape. A company also made a movie of Ishi, showing him working at his crafts and doing chores around the museum. Unfortunately, the old celluloid film stock deteriorated, and no viewable copies are known to exist today. Without a doubt, the most poignant information Ishi shared—with great reluctance and only in bits and pieces—was the story of the extermination of his people, including his immediate family.

Before the California gold rush, an estimated four hundred Yahi Indians lived in the Sierra foothills along Mill Creek and Deer Creek, with a few thousand other Yanas living to the north. The influx of miners and ranchers that began in 1849 inevitably led to clashes. Like all the native cultures that settlers encountered as they spread across the continent, the Yanas were inexorably overwhelmed. The newcomers followed the usual pattern of dehumanization, writing off the indigenous people as filthy savages, little more than animals. The settlers saw no reason not to shoot them down, burn their villages, capture them as slaves. So-called Indian fighters—"riffraff from the mining camps and saloons," as Trappist monk Thomas Merton described them in his book *Ishi Means Man*—scalped the Yanas they murdered for the five-dollar bounty. It was easy to justify such brutality when the Yanas fought back with equal cruelty or stole cattle to replace the diminished herds of deer they'd once depended on. By 1865, the Yanas had been reduced to a remnant group of Yahis.

The remaining Yahis fled to areas that cattle or horses couldn't reach. They sustained themselves by raiding livestock and isolated homesteads. It was a dangerous, unsettled life that bore little resemblance to their former existence. The bad blood between the white settlers and the Indians led to the Three Knolls massacre, an attack that decimated Ishi's tribe. It's possible that Ishi's father was killed at Three Knolls, with Ishi and his mother among the survivors. Subsequent attacks whittled the band's numbers down even further. Afterward, the remaining Yahis went into an extended period of hiding, retreating deeper into the Sierra hills. Ishi would have been about ten years old at the time.

From the early 1870s to the mid-1880s, the Yahis vanished from sight. They ceased their raids on white property and lived completely off the land. They camouflaged their houses and storage shelters and left no trace of their movements, walking on rocks or in streams and obliterating every footprint. They built small fires to minimize smoke and avoided creating trails that might give away their presence. It was the lifestyle of a ghost clan. Unfortunately for the group, most of the able-bodied men had died by the mid-1880s, forcing the Yahis to resume their raids on cattle herds and lonely cabins. Also by that time, the white settlement had reached their latest stronghold, making contact inevitable. By the 1890s, only Ishi and two or three other males were left to forage for the group. Then in the mid-nineties, the raids once again ceased. Only five Yahis remained. Their final retreat was a march to oblivion.

Leaving their hideout along the upper reaches of Mill Creek, the Yahis relocated to Deer Creek Canyon, building a tiny encampment in a remote thicket no whites ever entered. Their refusal to give themselves up is a testament to their will to survive as a culture, although their numbers had long since been too few to sustain a viable population. An observer had once commented on the Yahis' determination to resist white incursions "to the last man, and the last squaw, and the last papoose"—which turned out to be the literal truth. The once thriving tribe had been diminished to just Ishi, his aged mother, a sister, an elderly uncle, and a younger man who soon died.

The end of the group came in 1908, after two surveyors working for the Oro Light and Power Company surprised Ishi as he stood fishing in Deer Creek. The next morning, a search party discovered the nearby Indian camp. Only Ishi's mother remained in camp, covered by blankets and hides in an attempt to conceal her. She was too ill and feeble to be moved. The search party stole most of the Indians' belongings as souvenirs but left the old woman where she lay. The next day, one member of the search party returned to the camp, but the old woman was gone. Anthropologist Thomas Waterman later spent a month looking for the Yahis, although none of them were seen again until the morning Ishi gave himself up in 1911.

After the raid on their camp, Ishi had returned and carried his mother to safety. It's believed she died within days. From that moment until he appeared at the slaughterhouse in Oroville, Ishi was alone. He never saw his sister or uncle again. He assumed they'd drowned or been killed by wild animals. In the end—driven by hunger, grief, and loneliness—Ishi sought out the company of his enemy. What powerful emotions he must have wrestled with to reach the decision that any form of human contact was preferable to the life he was leading, even if it meant surrendering himself to being killed. It was a situation few human beings have ever had to face—like a lone shipwreck survivor walking willingly into the camp of cannibals.

Given the decades of sorrow he experienced, it's good to know that Ishi was relatively happy for his last few years. Surrounded by his friends at the Hearst Museum and safeguarded from exploitation, he lived a life of simple joys, practicing his own folkways as a living cultural treasure. He seemed to think that the best thing the white man had invented was the ice-cream soda. Ishi died in March 1916 after developing a cough that led to tuberculosis. He faced death with courage and stoicism. Cared for by his friend Saxton Pope, he remained cheerful until the end, uttering the consoling farewell "you stay, I go" as he lay dying.

Kroeber and Waterman were devastated by Ishi's death. Waterman declared, "I loved the old Indian." Kroeber, who was in New York at the time, showed his affection and respect by demanding that Ishi's body not be subjected to an autopsy. "If there is any talk about the interests of science, say for me that science can go to hell," he wrote. Nevertheless, an autopsy was performed and Ishi's brain preserved (the disposition of the brain became a subject of controversy, documented in a 2004 book by anthropologist Orin Starn). Ishi's body was cremated according to Yana custom, his ashes placed in a black clay Pueblo Indian pot and interred at Mount Olivet Cemetery south of San Francisco.

Ishi's death brought the historical cycle of the Yana to a close. Not a lot can be added to the many public acknowledgments of our inhuman treatment of Native Americans. It's a collective guilt our country will always bear, along with the shameful stain of slavery. We'd like to think, in these enlightened times, that such behavior is a relic of a different age, although Thomas Merton feared that "we learned little or nothing about ourselves from the Indian wars." Aside from the lives that were snuffed out in the extermination of the Yanas, we lost the richness of another human culture. In the introduction to the 2002 edition of the 1961 biography *Ishi in Two Worlds*, written by Alfred Kroeber's second wife, Theodora, their son Karl lamented "how little we know of Ishi's life. This deepens the sorrow of his story, because we feel in the death of the man the disappearance of thousands of years of Yahi family life, the loss of the Yahi impoverishing by that much the diverse antiquity of all California Indians."

That Ishi emerged from a half century of oppression without bitterness or hatred for white people is perhaps the greatest marvel of his exceptional life. His friends described him as a gentle, civilized man, although his civility went far deeper than simple good manners. There was a Zen-like quality to his acceptance of and adaptation to white society. He was a visitor from another age who lived among us briefly and then was gone, leaving countless lives enriched. Theodora Kroeber called Ishi "a stone skipped randomly across the surface of a quiet pond," one whose "riffles of contact and influence formed round him in widening circles."

It's unfortunate that we only came to appreciate the worth of the Yana people after we realized that Ishi was the last of his kind. By demonstrating his native crafts while interacting with museum guests, Ishi altered the perception of a so-called barbarian culture, and he taught anthropologists a significant amount about the language and traditions of his vanished tribe. Ishi's ghostly voice still speaks to researchers on the recordings he made a century ago, a farewell message from the last living native speaker of the Yana language.

EIGHT

General Washington's Genial Savior

HERCULES MULLIGAN

IT WAS A DAUNTING prospect for Hugh and Sarah Mulligan to pack up and leave their home in County Antrim, Ireland, in 1746, but they were determined to trade the oppression of the British-imposed Penal Laws for the freedom of the American colonies. Across the sea, their children would be able to own property when they grew up, attend the college of their choice, even marry a Protestant if they wished. In Ireland, those simple rights, along with countless others, were forbidden to Catholics.

The Mulligans settled in New York City. In short order, Hugh Mulligan opened a wig-making business, and the family prospered. Later, Hugh started a successful accounting firm. The Mulligans' sons received good educations and practical business training. The eldest, Hugh Jr., went to work for a prestigious import-export company. After attending Kings College, the forerunner of Columbia University, his younger brother Hercules gave the import-export business a try as well, but he didn't take to it. In his early twenties, Hercules decided to become a tailor. It was a career choice that would reward him handsomely—and place him in a position to become an important Revolutionary War spy, one who had an unparalleled impact on the lives of two prominent American leaders.

In person, Hercules Mulligan was every bit as colorful as his name, a large, round-faced man who could sling the blarney as well as anyone. His shop on Water Street, located near lower Manhattan's busy East River wharves, attracted a parade of wealthy colonists and British businessmen and military officers, men who strode the city's avenues with a proprietary air. In his early thirties, Mulligan married Elizabeth Sanders, the niece of an admiral in the Royal Navy. As he moved up in the world, Mulligan relocated his shop to a tonier area, still close to the East River waterfront. A sign with a golden thimble and shears hung in front of his new establishment at 23 Queen Street (today's Pearl Street). The simple wooden plaque over the door announced: H. MULLIGAN, CLOTHIER.

Inside his shop, Mulligan hobnobbed with the clientele, advising them on the latest fashions and measuring them for new garments made by his staff of tailors. His newspaper ads touted his swank merchandise: "superfine cloths," "gold and silver spangled buttons," "epaulets for gentlemen of the army and militia," "silk breeches and silks of all colours." Mulligan's shop must have been quite a sight, filled with preening dandies hoping to make a sartorial splash. What all those fine gentlemen weren't aware of, though, was that their genial Irish host was one of the most ardent patriots in the colonies, a man who hated the British yoke as much as his parents had back in Ireland.

Mulligan took up the patriot cause at least a decade before the start of the Revolutionary War. In 1765, he joined the Sons of Liberty, an underground group that engaged in anti-British agitation. In January 1770, he fought in the Battle of Golden Hill, a skirmish with British soldiers that was one of the first violent incidents leading up to the American Revolution. In the summer of 1775, he helped the Sons of Liberty steal a cache of muskets from the city armory. Mulligan was also a member of the New York Committee of Correspondence, a group that rallied opposition to the British through written communications.

Mulligan continued to fight for liberty following the Declaration of Independence. On July 9, 1776, he led a group of patriots to New York's Bowling Green, a park at the lower end of Broadway. In the center of the oval greensward stood a hated symbol, a huge gilded statue of King George III, perched regally astride a horse. Mulligan and his fellow Sons of Liberty broke through the iron fence surrounding the park and toppled the gleaming British monarch. As cheers rang out, the men hacked the statue apart and paraded the pieces through the streets. Beneath its gilt, the statue was made of lead, which colonists melted down and cast into bullets to be used against the British.

Mulligan's career as a spy came about through sheer coincidence. In 1773, he and his new bride took in a young boarder named Alexander Hamilton. Born on the island of Nevis in the West Indies, Hamilton had later moved to St. Croix, where he became an apprentice clerk in a branch office of Hugh Mulligan's import-export firm. In his midteens, Hamilton left the islands to complete his education in the American colonies. He brought with him a letter of recommendation addressed to Hugh. Hugh introduced Hamilton to his brother Hercules, and the two hit it off. When Hamilton enrolled in Kings College, Hercules invited the slender, reddish-haired young man to board in his home.

Hamilton often shared his evenings with the Mulligans, sometimes dashing off doggerel to amuse his hosts. Hamilton also took part in serious political discussions with the Mulligans and their friends. Despite her upper-crust British connections, Elizabeth Mulligan sided with her husband on the question of independence. Up until this time, Hamilton had supported British rule over the colonies, but as he listened to his impassioned hosts make the case for liberty, he gradually came to share their views. Hamilton joined the Sons of Liberty, and in February 1775—at the age of eighteen—he wrote a lengthy essay that persuasively laid out the case for independence. Published as a pamphlet entitled *The Farmer Refuted; or, a more comprehensive and impartial View of the Disputes between Great Britain and the Colonies*, Hamilton's essay caused a sensation and helped hasten the revolution.

While still in college, Hamilton prepared himself for war by taking gunnery training. In the summer of 1775, he and Mulligan helped steal twenty-one cannons from the seawall along the Battery, coming under fire from a nearby British ship. In July 1776, Hamilton assumed command of an artillery company and fought in several early battles around New York. However, Hamilton was known more for his writing than his military prowess. In March 1777, General Washington made him his aide, with the rank of lieutenant colonel.

For the next four years, Hamilton handled all of Washington's correspondence, becoming intimately involved in every facet of the war effort, including intelligence operations. General Washington depended on good military intelligence, and he employed a wide network of "confidential correspondents" to supply it. At the end of the revolution, the head of British intelligence in the colonies would comment, "Washington did not really outfight the British, he simply outspied us."

When Washington spoke of his need for reliable information from within New York City—which the British had held since the Continental Army was driven out in September 1776—Hamilton recommended his friend Hercules Mulligan. Washington already had a handful of spies in New York, but as a tailor to British bigwigs, Mulligan was ideally placed. With his jocular demeanor and affable banter, he could surely pry valuable information from his patrons, some of whom held important positions in the British Army or Royal Navy. Any useful intelligence Mulligan picked up would go straight to General Washington.

Mulligan agreed to the arrangement and soon proved his worth. In the winter of 1779, he picked up a piece of information that literally saved the commander-in-chief's life. Late one evening, a British officer called at Mulligan's shop to purchase a watch coat. Curious about the late hour, Mulligan asked why the officer needed the coat so quickly. The man explained that he was leaving immediately on a mission, boasting that "before another day, we'll have the rebel general in our hands." As soon as the officer left, Mulligan dispatched his servant to advise General Washington. Washington had been planning to rendezvous with some of his officers, and apparently the British had learned the location of the meeting and intended to set a trap. Thanks to Mulligan's alert, Washington changed his plans and avoided capture.

Two years later, Mulligan warned Washington about a second attempt to waylay him. This time, Mulligan's brother Hugh played a crucial role. Hugh's firm did considerable trade with the British military. In February 1781, the British placed a rush order for provisions to be loaded onto a transport ship. Hugh casually asked the British commissary officer in charge what the supplies were for. The officer revealed that three hundred cavalrymen were being dispatched to New London, Connecticut, to intercept General Washington as he traveled to Newport to confer with the French general Rochambeau. Hugh Mulligan passed the information to his brother, who relayed it to Washington's camp. Washington altered his route to Rhode Island and arranged a surprise welcome for the British forces.

An amazing aspect of Mulligan's life was his ability to take part in so many rebellious activities yet maintain his position as a respectable merchant. Most likely, it was his marriage to a British admiral's niece, along with his many contacts among British officials, that helped him avoid being strung up as a traitor. In addition to meeting people at his shop and through his brother Hugh's business, he made friends with several officers who were billeted in his home during the seven years the British occupied New York. Even with all his connections, Mulligan was hard-pressed to worm his way out of trouble on two occasions. The first came in September 1776, when the Continental Army evacuated the city. Mulligan decided to leave as well, but he was stopped by the British and held prisoner for a month. Somehow, he talked his way out of jail and went back to his tailoring. His second scrape came four years later. This one was more serious.

In September 1780, Gen. Benedict Arnold's treachery to the American cause was discovered. Arnold fled to New York, where he was made a brigadier general in the British Army. Having served with Washington, Arnold knew about his network of spies in the city, and he rounded up over fifty suspects, including Hercules Mulligan. The British tossed Mulligan into prison and tried him on charges of espionage, but even though Arnold himself testified against him, Mulligan again talked his way out of a conviction. Some of his fellow prisoners weren't so lucky, especially those sent to the British prison ship *Jersey*. More than a thousand prisoners were stuffed into the fetid holds of the rotting ship, a spectral hulk coated with green slime. Few survived there for more than six months.

When the war finally ended in 1783, anyone who'd supported the British was in potential danger. Many Loyalist homes and businesses were destroyed. A few New Yorkers may have felt that Hercules Mulligan had been a bit too friendly with the British. No one but Washington and his staff knew of the valiant efforts of his spies. Worried about his confidential correspondents, Washington made a point of personally visiting each of them and very publicly thanking them for their contributions. The morning he arrived back in New York, General Washington called on Hercules Mulligan. The men shared breakfast, and afterward General Washington ordered a complete civilian wardrobe from the Irish tailor. Mulligan promptly installed a new sign outside his shop: CLOTHIER TO GENL. WASHINGTON.

Mulligan prospered after the revolution. His business grew and so did his family (he and Elizabeth had three sons and five daughters). Mulligan retired from business at the age of eighty and died five years later. He is buried in the churchyard of the same house of worship in which he was married, New York's venerable Trinity Church (he'd become an Episcopalian as a young man). The grave of his friend Alexander Hamilton lies just a few yards away.

Trinity Church stands at the intersection of Wall Street and Broadway, its neo-Gothic spire and gold cross a familiar sight to the thousands of people who pass by the Manhattan landmark every day. Odds are that few of those people have ever heard of Hercules Mulligan. Even those who step inside the churchyard and chance upon Mulligan's small, weathered gray tombstone are probably unaware that beneath it lies a true hero of the American Revolution. One of the few honors ever accorded this colorful patriot came in 1970, when several historical groups placed a plaque at the site of Mulligan's home, now occupied by the 160 Water Street skyscraper.

Hercules Mulligan is a name every schoolchild should know—and not just because it's fun to say. The man didn't utter a memorable last line like his famous fellow spy Nathan Hale, but what he did was infinitely more important. Probably no other individual had such a dramatic impact on the lives of two of the leaders who charted the course for our country. Certainly no one else can make the claim of having inculcated the desire for freedom in one of the founding fathers—in addition to twice saving the life of the father of our country. Those were feats that required the might of Hercules.

NINE

A Captive in Two Cultures

CYNTHIA ANN PARKER

THE RESIDENTS OF Fort Parker felt their prayers were being answered. It had been a challenging four years since they'd left their Illinois homes in 1832 and made the trek to eastern Texas. Settling at the headwaters of the Navasota River, in present-day Limestone County, the small band of devout Baptists had found a new life here in the fertile, grassy region along the southeastern edge of the Great Plains. The members of the settlement—eight or nine families led by the Parkers, a prolific clan that included four generations—had built cabins and cleared the rolling hills of brush and scattered oaks for farming. Being prudent, they'd constructed a sturdy stockade to protect themselves from hostile Indians, especially the Comanche, the nomadic warriors whose fighting skills and horsemanship had helped them rebuff Spanish and French explorers on the prairies of North America—and who were making life hazardous for American pioneers.

Two recent milestones had cheered the people of Fort Parker: Texas had been freed from Mexican rule, and a company of Texas Rangers, under the command of their own Silas Parker, had been formed to protect the settlers from Indian attacks. Only a month before, in April 1836, Mexican forces had been defeated at the Battle of San Jacinto following the declaration of independence by the new Republic of Texas. Since Mexico had forbidden Protestant churches in Texas, the residents of Fort Parker could now practice their religion without fear. And the local company of Texas Rangers was taking its job seriously. The men attacked every Indian they encountered. That ruthless policy, however, was about to backfire.

On the morning of May 19, 1836, most of the men of Fort Parker were working in the fields when an alarm went up inside the stockade. A war party of Comanche and allied tribes had been spotted nearby. Benjamin Parker, Silas's brother, attempted to parlay with the Indians, offering them food and other supplies, but the warriors weren't in a peaceful mood. The men and women inside the fort looked on in horror as the Indians speared and scalped the envoy. Incredibly, the gate to the fort had been left open, and some of the warriors stormed inside. Only a few men were on hand to protect the women and children. When the workers from the fields made it back to the fort they found a scene of chaos. Silas Parker and four other men were dead. Silas Parker's wife, Lucy, had attempted to escape with their children, but the Indians had taken the two oldest, nine-year-old Cynthia Ann and her six-year-old brother John. The Indians also abducted two women, Elizabeth Kellogg and Rachel Plummer, along with Plummer's two-year-old son James.

Still harassed by the Indians, the survivors—twenty-six of the community's three dozen or so members—made their way to the safety of Fort Houston, some sixty miles distant. The Indians, meanwhile, stole or destroyed everything at Fort Parker. It was an ignoble end to the settlement. For young Cynthia Ann

Parker, though, it was a beginning. For the next twenty-four and a half years, she would dwell among the Comanche, becoming so fully integrated into their culture that she all but forgot her former life, her native language, even her family. In essence, she became a Comanche.

Cynthia Ann's transition to her new life was filled with hardship. Initially, her captors abused her and the other prisoners. In the best of times, the Comanche weren't a love-thy-neighbor tribe. They didn't sit around weaving baskets and wishing for peace. Theirs was a militant culture, dedicated to hunting buffalo and making war. In battle, they fought to the death. Riding their ponies with the mastery of Mongol warriors, they dominated other Plains Indians, so why would they open their arms to white settlers? Following the attack on Fort Parker, Cynthia Ann and the four other captives were beaten, taunted, and starved (their treatment was described in the autobiography Rachel Plummer later wrote).

After several days, the war party divided the captives among the various bands. As a result, each prisoner faced a different fate. Elizabeth Kellogg was ransomed in just a few months. Rachel Plummer toiled as a slave for a year and a half before being ransomed. James Plummer lived with the Comanche for six years until he was ransomed in 1842. Some accounts say that John Parker was ransomed at the same time as James Plummer, while others claim he rode with the Comanche until he was a young man. Regardless of what her brother's fate may have been, long after all the other prisoners from Fort Parker were released, Cynthia Ann Parker was still with the Comanche. It's likely she was taken in by a family and indoctrinated into tribal customs, a common practice with young female captives. (Basically, Comanche men hunted and fought; the women did just about everything else.)

No one knew of Cynthia Ann's whereabouts during her early years of captivity. Then in the spring of 1840, a white trader named Leonard Williams noticed the blue-eyed girl in a Comanche camp where he was conducting business. The Indians refused Williams's offer to buy the girl's freedom. They did allow him to talk with her, although she refused to answer his questions. Williams thought she was either afraid of her captors or had forgotten how to speak English.

When he returned from his trading expedition, Williams sent word of his encounter to the Parkers. Despite the family's ongoing search for Cynthia Ann, another five years passed before two federal agents thought they spotted her at a Comanche camp in Oklahoma. The agents tried to ransom her, but again the Indians were unwilling to let her go. By that time, the eighteen-year-old captive was thoroughly acculturated as a Comanche. The would-be rescuers reported that the girl had hidden herself to avoid being ransomed. An 1847 article in a Houston newspaper reported on Cynthia Ann's refusal to return to white society: "Even if she should be restored to her kindred here, she would probably take advantage of the first opportunity, and flee away to the wilds of northern Texas." One or two other attempts were made to ransom the girl, but she remained unwilling to leave her Indian family.

Cynthia Ann had a compelling reason to stay with the Comanche. Sometime in the mid-1840s, she married a Comanche chief named Peta Nocona, one of the leaders of the raid on Fort Parker. Evidently it was a happy marriage. War chiefs often claimed multiple brides, but Cynthia Ann was Peta Nocona's only wife. She eventually bore her Comanche husband three children—two sons, Quanah and Pecos, and a daughter, Topsannah ("Prairie Flower"). From then on, the tug of war for

Cynthia Ann's loyalties involved blood relatives on both sides, although it's understandable that she would have felt a stronger kinship to her own children than to family members she hadn't seen since she herself was a child.

As the years became decades, Cynthia Ann continued to follow the nomadic life of her adopted people. Then, once again, her fate was taken out of her hands. Friction had been increasing between the Plains Indians and the Texas settlers throughout the mid-1800s. War parties raided settlements that encroached on tribal hunting grounds. The U.S. Army and Texas Rangers retaliated with attacks on Indian camps. The frontier bristled with forts, and although attempts were made to reach an accord with the Indians, the general attitude among settlers was that all of them should be driven from Texas.

In December 1860, following a series of Comanche raids on farms and ranches in north-central Texas, a force of 150 Texas Rangers, army troops, and volunteers overtook a band of Comanche camped near the Pease River. The Indians were led by Cynthia Ann Parker's husband, Peta Nocona. Catching the Indians unawares, the avenging white men swept down on the encampment and slaughtered everyone they could find. Tales about the number of Comanche killed spun off into fantasy, with estimates varying from a dozen to several hundred. The claim that Peta Nocona had been killed was later disputed. There were, however, two unusual survivors: a woman with blue eyes and her infant daughter—Cynthia Ann and Topsannah.

The mother and daughter were taken back to the nearest army post, Camp Cooper, where authorities questioned Cynthia Ann in order to establish her identity. At first she refused to talk, but then, through an interpreter, she asked about her two sons. The soldiers told her that no young boys were among the dead, so Quanah and Pecos had escaped. Cynthia Ann revealed that most of the men in her band had been away trading stolen goods for provisions, and the remaining warriors had left camp shortly before the attack. Only women, children, and a few male helpers were present, she said, left behind to prepare meat for the oncoming winter. Although the "battle" of Pease River went down as a fabulous victory in Texas lore, more than one account paints the raid as a one-sided affair, an inglorious turkey shoot whose true nature was underscored by the fact that none of the white attackers were killed or even wounded.

Everyone at Camp Cooper was certain the blue-eyed "squaw" was Cynthia Ann Parker, since the story of her capture and refusal to return to white society was widely known. Officials contacted one of Cynthia Ann's uncles, Isaac Parker. When he arrived at Camp Cooper in late January, Parker did all he could to jog Cynthia Ann's memory about her childhood and family. She didn't respond when he spoke English, but through an interpreter he managed to get her to recall her home at Fort Parker. Speaking to his interpreter, Parker said, "If this is my niece, her name is Cynthia Ann." The woman touched her breast and muttered, "Me Cincee Ann." The lost girl of Fort Parker, now a thirty-four-year-old woman, was finally—reluctantly—back with her white kinfolk, after having spent three-quarters of her life among the Comanche.

With assurances that her sons would be brought to her if they were captured, Cynthia Ann agreed to accompany her uncle back to his farm. When they passed through Fort Worth, a photographer took a picture of the woman as she nursed Topsannah. Her expression is vacant, forlorn. She'd cut her hair short as a sign of mourning for her lost family members. Cynthia Ann's remarkable situation caused quite a stir. Texas newspapers carried stories about the rescue of the white captive and her return to civilization, with editors opining about how fortunate Cynthia Ann had been to be saved from the clutches of savages. What none of those spinmeisters realized was that the woman was miserable. For the second time in her life, she'd been torn from her loved ones. She feared for the safety of Peta Nocona, Quanah, and Pecos, longing to return to them as soon as possible.

At Isaac Parker's farm, relatives and friends descended on Cynthia Ann and her daughter with well-intentioned zeal, intending to rid them of their Indian ways. They quickly outfitted the pair with new clothes. (Another photograph made at the time shows Cynthia Ann in a new dress and shawl, a white lace collar at her throat. She sits with her hands clutched tightly in front of her, a grim look on her face. She reflects the wary, cheerless attitude of a convict. She might as well have been dressed in prison stripes.) To remedy the effects of being born among heathens, little Topsannah—who was only two years old and spoke no English—was bombarded with scripture readings.

In spite of the Parker family's loving attention, Cynthia Ann tried to escape several times. It's said that the Parkers had to lock her and Topsannah in their room every night. By day, Cynthia Ann spent hours sitting on the front porch of the Parker cabin, weeping and staring wistfully into the distance. Isaac Parker finally told her that he'd take her to visit the Comanche if she'd try to adapt, but no such visits ever took place.

In April 1861, the Texas legislature granted Cynthia Ann a pension of $100 a year for five years to help her get by and to pay for Topsannah's education. She was also granted a plot of land. Both acts were compassionate, but they probably meant little to the befuddled creature. What would she buy with the white man's money? And what did a speck of land mean to someone who considered the entire prairie her home? She certainly gave no positive response. Her uncle eventually grew weary of dealing with her and asked Cynthia Ann's younger brother, Silas Jr., if he would take on his brooding sister and her child. Toward the end of 1861, the pair moved to Silas's farm. Her brother also promised to allow Cynthia Ann to visit her Comanche friends and to help search for her sons, although the Civil War disrupted those plans.

Silas's wife, Mary, disliked having the two newcomers in her home, even though Cynthia Ann helped with the chores. Mary was always quick to punish Topsannah if she addressed her mother by her Comanche name, Naduah (some accounts give her Indian name as Preloch). Mary referred to her niece as the "little barbarian." Before long, the two guests were fobbed off on another family member, Cynthia Ann's sister Orlena, who gave her two relatives a friendlier reception. Topsannah quickly picked up English. She was described as a "pretty and sprightly" youngster. Then in the fall of 1863, the five-year-old girl caught the flu, which led to pneumonia. She died in December 1863 (her brother Pecos died earlier that same year of smallpox). Topsannah's death took away Cynthia Ann's last reason for living. Alone, alienated, and uncertain about the fate of her husband and surviving child, Quanah, she withdrew into a self-imposed prison of silent grief. In 1870, she came down with the flu. Weak from refusing to eat, she passed away at the age of forty-four.

That wasn't the end of her story, however.

Quanah Parker, who was still a boy at the time of his mother's "rescue," grew into a prominent war chief. He became a leader of the Quahadis, fiercest of all the dozen or so Comanche bands. Even other Comanche treated them with respect.

The Quahadis shunned all exchanges with whites. Their only contact was when they attacked homesteads, settlements, and wagon trains, which they did with regularity. After the Civil War, growing numbers of U.S. Army troops chased the Quahadis and other Comanche bands all over the prairies, but what finally brought down the defiant Indians was the destruction of the immense herds of buffalo they depended on for food, clothing, and hides for their tepees. Throughout the 1870s, tens of millions of buffalo were slaughtered by white hunters, nearly pushing the species to extinction. The old way of life for the Plains Indians was ending. In May 1875, the Quahadis surrendered—the last band of Comanche to submit to the indignity of reservation life.

Quanah Parker soon became the most influential leader on the Comanche-Kiowa-Apache reservation, one of over two dozen Indian reserves in Oklahoma. Politically and financially astute, he grew rich in the cattle business, built a large house, had multiple wives, and fathered a substantial brood. Although he still wore his hair in braids, he adapted remarkably well to white society, traveling often to Washington, D.C., to negotiate on behalf of his people. He even became friends with Teddy Roosevelt and marched in Roosevelt's 1905 inaugural parade.

Throughout his life, Quanah never forgot the white mother who'd been taken from him. After his surrender, he tried to find her so they could be reunited, only to learn that she'd died five years earlier. In 1910, he had his mother's remains moved to Post Oak Mission in Oklahoma. Quanah died the next year and was buried next to his mother. More than a thousand people—Indians and whites alike—attended the funeral of the last principal chief of the Comanche. (The graves of Cynthia Ann, Quanah, and Topsannah Parker were later moved to Fort Sill, in Lawton, Oklahoma.)

At Cynthia Ann's reburial in 1910, Quanah remarked that whites and Indians were "all same people." That wasn't a widely shared opinion. Cynthia Ann was a casualty of one of humanity's oldest hang-ups: the belief in cultural superiority. The material existence of the Comanche may have been primitive by European standards, but Cynthia Ann seems to have experienced years of happiness among them. Her life could well have been more meaningful and fulfilling than any number of alternatives. Four walls and a roof have certainly never guaranteed contentment. She was the wife of a chief, a mother, an accepted member of her community. She probably lived more intensely than most people, acutely aware of the intertwining of nature and human existence. The moon and stars were her artwork, prairie thunder and howling coyotes her music. Her white relatives simply couldn't accept the fact that for Cynthia Ann to be wrenched from that life of freedom—cut off from her husband and sons and locked up in stuffy, silent rooms—was the worst torture imaginable. From a life of respect, she became an object of pity. The least charitable even called her an ingrate.

What Cynthia Ann Parker endured was heartrending. This unfortunate woman was doubly victimized—twice ripped from her family and thrust into an alien society. That she survived and flourished in her first period of change, the nearly quarter of a century she spent with the Comanche, confirms her tenacity and adaptability. That she withered and died during her second period of upheaval, surrounded by well-intentioned but sometimes thoughtless relatives, is a testament to the strength of a woman's love for her children and mate, among the most tenacious bonds in nature.

Cynthia Ann's life was a classic illustration of the mutability of personality and identity. She changed so radically during her years with the Comanche that she became, in every way, another person, dooming efforts to reintegrate her into white society. The Cynthia Ann her relatives remembered had ceased to exist years before. It was as if they had kidnapped a stranger off the street. Though the Parker family thought they were doing what was best for her, they robbed Cynthia Ann of her freedom of choice. In the end, this captive in two cultures was, quite literally, loved to death. An irony of Cynthia Ann's life is that her son Quanah readily succeeded in bridging the two worlds that she herself could not. Quanah's ability to lead his people in both war and peace may have been his mother's greatest gift.

The memory of Cynthia Ann Parker is kept alive in northern Texas by the town of Crowell, which holds an annual festival to celebrate the region's Native Americans and white settlers. Groesbeck, Texas, holds a Christmas festival each year on the grounds of the old Parker family settlement, which has been re-created. And in Abilene, Hardin-Simmons University has established the Cynthia Ann Parker College of Liberal Arts. Oklahoma's Fort Sill Cemetery holds Cynthia Ann's gravesite along with a memorial to her famous son. In literature, Cynthia Ann's experiences are believed to have inspired the Alan Le May novel *The Searchers*, which was adapted into the classic John Ford Western of the same name. Such continuing interest in this remarkable woman shows that her fate touches something deep inside us. That's not surprising, since it's all too easy to find ourselves wondering how well we could endure the hardships Cynthia Ann Parker faced.

TEN

An Act of Valor Denied

JAMES PARKER

THE HOTTEST TICKET around in the summer of 1901 was the Pan-American Exposition in Buffalo, New York. Since the fair's May 1 opening, several million visitors had plunked down the fifty-cent admission fee to gawk at the latest technological wonders. Billed as a celebration of the ties among Western Hemisphere nations, the exposition gave perennially unglamorous Buffalo a chance to show off its industrial and commercial might. To house the exhibits, the "Queen City of the Lakes" created a 350-acre fantasyland of brightly painted Spanish Renaissance–style buildings, gussied up with a profusion of flower beds, sculptures, tree-lined walkways, lagoons, and canals.

The fair's main attraction was electrical power, which was just emerging as an alternative to gas. At night, visitors thrilled to the sight of tens of thousands of light bulbs outlining the exposition's buildings. "The lights do not go on at once," wrote one enthusiast. "There is at first a slight rosy glow, which becomes brighter and brighter until the whole place is ablaze, and when the lights are turned off at eleven o'clock they do not go out suddenly, but fade gradually like a dream." The light show came courtesy of Nikola Tesla, the Serbian genius who'd invented a way of transmitting alternating current electricity over long distances, enabling generators at Niagara Falls, twenty-five miles away, to power the exposition's colored bulbs and floodlights.

By day, gents in bowler hats and ladies with Gibson Girl hairdos could amuse themselves at the nearly three hundred concessions along the midway. They could sample the goods at dueling chocolate companies Baker's and Lowney's, or marvel at the infant incubator, where actual premature babies were on display. They could stop by the Acetylene Building and learn about the supposed virtues of the impractical and potentially dangerous acetylene gas lamp, which thankfully never caught on as a home lighting source. For lunch, visitors could pop into the Nebraska Sod House for the thirty-cent fricasseed-chicken special (a fairly dicey proposition, given that the kitchen was shut down in August for gross violations of health standards).

In the heat of summer, parasol concessions dotted the grounds, and the *Buffalo Courier* joked that crowds ran the risk of getting an "Exposition tan." When it got too hot, visitors could cool off beside one of several elaborate fountains or stop in for a beer at the Pabst Pavilion, which, according to the company's advertisement, wasn't meant to make money but was instead "a colossal courtesy extended by the Pabst Brewing Company to its cosmopolitan clientele."

By the first week of September the weather had moderated, with daytime highs averaging in the low 70s. It was the perfect time to visit the exposition. Those lucky enough to be there on September 6 would even have the chance to shake the hand of President William McKinley, who was scheduled to greet fairgoers that day in the Temple of Music, a garishly painted performance hall encrusted with music-themed sculptures.

The Temple of Music was where Big Jim Parker meant to be. He'd been holding down a $5-a-week job at the exposition's Plaza Restaurant, and he couldn't pass up the opportunity to stand face to face with the president of the United States. As a black man, how many chances would he have to do that?

Ruggedly handsome and a natty dresser, forty-four-year-old James Benjamin Parker had come to Buffalo by a circuitous path. Born and educated in Atlanta, Parker had traveled throughout much of the eastern half of the country. He'd been a constable for a magistrate in Savannah, Georgia, where it was said he never failed to serve a warrant. At six feet, six inches tall and 250 pounds, Big Jim had no trouble getting offenders to submit peacefully. In Chicago, Parker signed on as a waiter with the Pullman Palace Car Company. He'd been a newspaperman at one time, working for the *Southern Recorder* in Milledgeville, Georgia. It was journalism that brought him to Buffalo, where he hoped to land a sales job with the *Gazetteer and Guide* magazine. He'd taken the temporary job at the Pan-American Exposition while waiting for a position to open up.

When the day of McKinley's visit arrived, Parker was more than willing to brave the jostling crowd of several thousand people waiting to meet the president. Big Jim had shown up outside the Temple of Music at midmorning, even though McKinley wasn't scheduled to greet visitors until 4:00 p.m., following a tour of Niagara Falls.

Once the reception began, the line moved quickly. Inside the building, an organist softly played selections by Bach. At one point, Parker was shouldered aside by a mother with a young girl, allowing a boyish-looking, twenty-eight-year-old man named Leon Czolgosz to step in front of him. Czolgosz's right hand, apparently injured, was wrapped in a handkerchief. Parker grinned as the president addressed the woman and her daughter. In just a moment, it would be his turn to meet the man he admired so much. McKinley looked every inch a president, a distinguished, silver-haired gentleman in a black frock coat.

The president acknowledged Leon Czolgosz. As he reached to shake his hand, two shots rang out, striking McKinley in the midsection. Czolgosz's handkerchief had concealed a pistol. In a fury, Jim Parker grabbed the president's assailant by the shoulder and spun him around, punching him hard and knocking him to the floor. Czolgosz tried to raise his revolver to fire a third shot, but Parker batted the gun away. The president's guards fell on the writhing assailant and began beating him.

President McKinley watched the struggle in shock, his face ashen. As guards dragged Czolgosz away, McKinley's assistants led the president to a chair. Within minutes, an ambulance arrived, and McKinley was taken to the exposition's emergency hospital, where doctors found that one of Czolgosz's bullets had only grazed the president's ribs. The other had passed through his stomach and lodged near his back. Though doctors weren't able to retrieve the bullet, there was hope that the president would survive.

Jim Parker, meanwhile, wandered outside the Temple of Music, where he described what had happened to some of the people milling around. Several witnesses to the shooting talked to newspaper reporters, confirming the heroism of the tall black man. Secret Service agent Samuel R. Ireland, who'd been standing near McKinley, told reporters, "The big Negro standing just in back of him [Czolgosz], and who would have been next to take the President's hand, struck the young man in the neck with one hand and with the other reached for the revolver. . . . While on the floor Czolgosz again tried to discharge the revolver, but before he could get it pointed at the President it was knocked from his hand by the Negro." Agent Ireland admitted to the Associated Press that "the colored man was quicker than we. He nearly killed the man."

As word of his heroism spread during the next few days, Parker received financial offers to tell his story on the exposition midway, but Big Jim was reluctant. He told a reporter for the *Buffalo Commercial*, "I happened to be in a position where I could aid in the capture of the man. I do not think that the American people would like me to make capital out of the unfortunate circumstances. I am no freak anyway. I do not want to be exhibited in all kinds of shows. I am glad that I was able to be of service to the country."

Parker's modesty didn't stop others from honoring him. The *New Haven Leader* wrote, "Secret Service men, soldiers, detectives were standing all around, but it was Jim Parker whose timely blow saved the President's life. It was Jim Parker who thrust his burly form right in the teeth of danger, thinking of nothing, caring for nothing except to preserve the President's life." *Colored American Magazine* proclaimed Parker "Our Uncrowned Hero." The *New York Journal* said, "A Negro is a National hero today. He is James Parker, the giant who hurled himself on the would-be assassin at Buffalo and kept him from firing a third shot that might have proved fatal."

Newspapers called for public contributions to a fund for Parker, and several testimonials and benefits were held in his honor. The country was thrilled and grateful that the president had survived. Big Jim was naturally pleased as well, proclaiming, "It's the very best day's work I ever did. . . . Just think, old Father Abe freed me, and now I saved his successor from death." Indeed, President McKinley appeared to be doing remarkably well. On September 10, one of McKinley's attending physicians, Dr. Herman Mynter, announced that if the president "continues to improve as he has in the last 24 hours we will have him out of doors inside of three weeks." Vice President Theodore Roosevelt was so certain of McKinley's recovery that he left Buffalo that same day for a vacation in the Adirondacks.

Unfortunately, the optimism about the president's condition was unfounded. On September 12, McKinley took a turn for the worse, complaining of a headache and nausea. Despite his doctor's best efforts, McKinley rapidly declined. On September 14, eight days after he'd been shot, the president was dead at the age of fifty-eight.

A fateful chain of circumstances had contributed to McKinley's death. The hospital where the president was operated on was little more than a first-aid station, with poor lighting and insufficient equipment. The top surgeon in Buffalo, Dr. Roswell Park, was out of town, leaving Dr. Matthew Mann, an obstetrician and gynecologist, to probe for the bullet still inside the president. Mann opted not to drain the wound, and he was unable to adequately disinfect it. As a result, gangrene set in, dooming the president.

Suddenly, Leon Czolgosz went from presidential assailant to assassin. The trial of the unrepentant, self-proclaimed anarchist took two days, the outcome preordained. The jury returned a verdict of guilty in less than thirty minutes. On October 29, McKinley's murderer was executed by electrocution at Auburn State Prison. At his burial, jailers poured acid over Czolgosz's body in an attempt to erase all traces of the man.

The most surprising aspect of Czolgoz's trial was that James Parker wasn't called on to testify. No one identified Parker as the man who had knocked down the president's attacker and prevented him from firing a third shot. Whether from overt racism or out of embarrassment that Parker had acted faster than the president's own bodyguards, all of those who testified at the trial simply invented a new narrative surrounding the events of September 6. One witness, Secret Service agent George Foster, had written a report to Washington just after the attack in which he stated that Parker had hit Czolgosz's arm, causing him to miss his third shot, yet at the trial Foster testified, "I never saw no colored man in the whole fracas."

Suddenly newspapers that had been celebrating Jim Parker as a hero began to question his participation, even his motives. The *Buffalo Express* quoted attorney James Quackenbush, who said he'd been standing six feet from the president when the shots were fired. Quackenbush said Czolgosz had been subdued solely by Secret Service men and military guards. *Buffalo Morning Review* reporter John D. Wells made the same claim. The *Buffalo Courier* and the *Buffalo Commercial* piled on, reporting that Parker had nothing to do with the assassin's capture. The two papers added that Parker deserved none of the money he'd received from lecturing or public donations.

Parker himself was mystified by the turn of events. Asked why he thought he wasn't called on to testify at Czolgosz's trial, he responded, "I don't know why I wasn't summoned. . . . I don't say this was done with any intent to defraud me, but it looks mighty funny, that's all." Naturally, African Americans were incensed that their hero was being robbed of his due and accused of undeserved profits. Was this the old familiar pattern they were seeing—the establishment doing all it could to render a black man invisible?

Jim Parker, however, didn't dwell on the controversy. He simply got on with his life. He managed to land the sales job he'd been after on the *Gazetteer and Guide* magazine. And he continued to have his supporters. The black community of Savannah, where Parker's mother and many of his relatives still lived, announced plans for a "substantial testimonial" in his honor.

In December 1901, Parker received a belated gesture of official recognition. At the behest of several government dignitaries, including two U.S. senators and presidential assistant George B. Cortelyou, who'd been with McKinley in Buffalo, he was given a job as a Senate messenger. These distinguished men, at least, were convinced that Parker had acted heroically in defense of the president.

It's a travesty that a shadow was cast over James Parker's valor. Without hesitation, he threw himself in harm's way to protect his president—a split-second reaction that revealed his true character. In contrast, those who begrudged him his recognition only succeeded in showing themselves as small, mean-spirited men.

In Buffalo, Big Jim Parker was instantly lifted from obscurity and just as quickly returned, but his selfless act of courage remains a lasting testament to a man who was as large in spirit as he was in stature. Though he is only a single thread in the fabric of our nation's history, that thread is strong. Parker's own words provide a fitting coda to his brief moment of fame: "I would have tried to save any man's life, but I would have given my life for that of the president," he said in a newspaper interview. "I tried to do my duty. That's all any man can do."

ELEVEN

The Yank Who United Canada

WILLIAM VAN HORNE

TALL, BEARDED, AND barrel-chested, American railroad executive William Cornelius Van Horne was an outsize man with equally large appetites. According to one acquaintance, "Van Horne liked big things: the largest and best locomotives . . . big Cuban cigars . . . the grandeur of the Rocky Mountains." With his easy grin and booming laugh, Van Horne took every one of his pleasures with gusto. When a friend marveled at an immense midnight snack he was washing down with copious amounts of champagne, Van Horne blithely told him, "Oh, I eat all I can; I drink all I can; I smoke all I can; and I don't care a damn for anything."

Van Horne was a man of big ambitions, too, and he wasn't afraid to take a chance to achieve them. An avid poker player, he knew when it was time to shove all of his chips to the center of the table, which is precisely what he did in late 1881 when he agreed to take on a job that had already overwhelmed two other men—building a railroad across the untamed Canadian interior. To link eastern Canada with the Pacific, thousands of miles of track and scores of bridges and tunnels needed to be built—through the rocky, boggy country above the Great Lakes, across vast prairies, and over the looming Rockies and bear-toothed mountain ranges of British Columbia. Van Horne didn't ask for the job—the directors of the new Canadian Pacific Railway Company came looking for him. One of them, James J. Hill, told his associates, "You need a man of great mental and physical power to carry this line through. Van Horne can do it."

Hill knew what he was talking about. It was said that the thirty-eight-year-old Van Horne could personally perform every job related to railroading, be it driving a locomotive, operating a telegraph, managing a rowdy track crew, or running a company. He needed every one of those skills to pull off the feat he was taking on up north. It was, as an observer of the time described it, "the greatest railway project ever undertaken in any part of the world." Van Horne had spent his whole life preparing for it.

Born on a farm near Chelsea, Illinois, in 1843, Van Horne moved to Joliet with his family when he was eight. His father, Joliet's first mayor, died when Van Horne was eleven, leaving the family financially strapped. In school, Van Horne was a bright but lazy student. He spent more time wrestling and fighting than on his studies. At fourteen, he dropped out of school to help support his family, although he had another motivation as well. A practical joker and quick sketch artist, Van Horne had drawn some caricatures of his principal and shown them to his classmates. He got into so much trouble that he decided never to return to school. Instead, he began his lifelong association with the railroad business, initially as a telegraph operator. He became so proficient that he could understand complete messages just by listening to the rapidly clicking stream of dots and dashes, without having to write down the individual letters as they came over the wire. (He also lost one job because of his practical jokes: while working at a freight yard, he wired a metal plate so that anyone stepping on it got a mild shock; unfortunately, the shop foreman—who apparently lacked a sense of humor—fell victim to the prank.)

Over the next few years, Van Horne rose steadily through the ranks on a succession of midwestern railroads—from ticket agent with the Chicago & Alton to general superintendent of the St. Louis, Kansas City & Northern to president of the Southern Minnesota. Along the way, he married Lucy Hurd of Joliet, the daughter of a railroad civil engineer. In 1879, Van Horne became general superintendent of the giant Chicago, Milwaukee & St. Paul Railway, his last job before being hired away as general manager of the Canadian Pacific, with what was reported to be a very generous salary. He would earn every penny of his pay.

The engineering challenges facing the Canadian Pacific ranged from having to lay track over unstable muskeg—where rails would sink out of sight if not properly ballasted—to dealing with steep mountain grades where railroads were never meant to go. Toss in hostile Indians, arguments over the route the rail line should follow, and repeated political and financial flare-ups, and you had a chin-deep swamp of difficulties. That was the situation Van Horne stepped into on January 2, 1882, his first day on the job. He immediately announced that he would lay five hundred miles of track across the prairies in his first year, more mileage than had ever been completed in that length of time.

Despite spring floods that delayed the start of construction, Van Horne's crews put down 418 miles of main line and 110 miles of branch line track. They also strung 897 miles of telegraph wire. It was an unprecedented achievement, one that Van Horne accomplished by driving his assistants, his workers—and himself—relentlessly. Whether riding in his personal railcar or bumping across the prairie in a buggy, Van Horne kept close watch over the progress his men were making—and he let them know when they needed to step it up. Observing the general manager exhort his men, a reporter for the *Winnipeg Daily Sun* wrote: "Van Horne is calm and harmless-looking. So is a she-mule, and so is a buzz-saw."

Van Horne mixed easily with his workers, chatting with a lowly laborer as readily as with a bank president. Somehow, he managed to keep his men going even when funds ran low, which was often. When one contractor fretted over not getting paid, Van Horne told him to go sell his boots and buy Canadian Pacific stock. The comment would prove prophetic, although it seemed like shaky advice at the time. More than once, the company's directors were ready to cancel the ambitious project, but Van Horne always rallied them with assurances that he'd finish the job.

Van Horne's race across the prairies had its lighter moments. When the Blackfoot tribe objected to the railway's plan to cross its territory, the Indians had to be pacified with assurances of government compensation. To seal the arrangement, Van Horne ceremoniously presented their elderly chief, Crowfoot, with a fancy pass granting him free transportation on the Canadian Pacific for life—as if the old Indian was itching to hop a train and set off to see the world! Inexplicably, Crowfoot seemed pleased with the gift, and while he didn't use it to rack up frequent-traveler miles, he wore the pass on a chain around his neck for the rest of his days.

Aside from the tremendous distances Van Horne had to cross in Ontario and the prairie provinces, the other major obstacle he faced was the mountainous terrain between Calgary and the Pacific coast. The Rockies and the Selkirks presented

an intimidating barrier—a giant's battleground strewn with for-
tresses of stone. A railroad here had to snake around precipitous
peaks, thread deep valleys, and bridge numerous mountain tor-
rents. One hundred and sixty-nine miles of track needed to be
laid from Kicking Horse Pass, on the Continental Divide near
Lake Louise, to just west of Eagle Pass, on the western slope of
the Gold Range not far from Revelstoke. There the line would
link up with tracks extending eastward from the Pacific. On the
prairies, a mere 169 miles of track took just three months to lay,
but here in the mountains, with a short construction season, it
would take Van Horne's crews two years to do the work.

As Van Horne's men labored down the western slope of the
Rockies below Kicking Horse Pass, they were forced to lay track
on the Big Hill, a treacherous slope with a gradient of 4.5 percent—a pitch over twice as steep as the maximum allowed in the
construction contract and one of the steepest sections of railroad
track in the world. In the Selkirks, Van Horne decided to build
the rail line over Rogers Pass, the shortest route to the coast. It
was a dangerous region that even the local Indians avoided. The
crews had to contend with avalanches, forest fires, and mud-
churning rainstorms, but the tracks finally crossed Rogers Pass
in August 1885. (In 1909, the Spiral Tunnels eliminated the Big
Hill section of the railway, and in 1916, the Connaught Tunnel
eliminated the hazardous route over Rogers Pass.)

On November 7, 1885, the rails from the east met the line extending from the Pacific at a spot Van Horne named Craigellachie, in honor of the railway's president, George Stephen, whose
ancestors hailed from Craigellachie, Scotland. Van Horne and
other company officials looked on in their derbies and top hats
as financier Donald Smith, one of the godfathers of the Canadian Pacific, drove the final spike in the rail line that united

British Columbia with the rest of Canada—a transcontinental link from the Pacific to Montreal, where the St. Lawrence River gave access to the Atlantic. (The line was later extended to the all-weather port of Saint John, New Brunswick.)

More than ten thousand men had a hand in building the railway, and many gave their lives, including at least six hundred Chinese laborers, but no one played a greater role in the grand enterprise than William Van Horne. Through force of will, the American completed a project many believed couldn't be done, and he finished it in four years—more than five years ahead of schedule. His work, however, wasn't over.

Van Horne had been promoted to vice president of the Canadian Pacific shortly before the transcontinental line was completed. In 1888, he was named president of the company. By then, he was already busy tackling the new railway's biggest problem: for the most part, the line ran through wilderness. To become profitable, it needed paying customers—western lumbermen, importers of goods from the Orient, farmers wanting to ship their grain to eastern markets, vacationers eager to see the wonders of the mountain west. Van Horne set about creating those customers. He assembled a fleet of ships to carry passengers and freight between the Orient and Vancouver (a town he'd chosen the site for and named). He launched a fleet of Great Lakes ships and acquired two existing Atlantic shipping lines—making it possible to travel from London to Hong Kong exclusively on Canadian Pacific ships and trains, a major new link uniting the British Empire. (In 1894, Queen Victoria knighted the railroad magnate for his achievements.)

As part of its contract with the government, the Canadian Pacific had been granted 25 million acres of land, mostly in the prairies, making the company one of the world's largest private landholders. To populate the prairies, Van Horne promoted land sales by advertising in Europe. Thousands of immigrants poured into Canada, transported, naturally, by the Canadian Pacific. They bought land for as little as $2.50 an acre, financed with loans from the railway. Immigrants from Germany, Hungary, Sweden, and Ukraine turned the "idle" prairies into fields of wheat—their crops transported on Canadian Pacific trains, stored in Canadian Pacific grain elevators, and processed in Canadian Pacific mills.

To entice eastern tourists out west, Van Horne employed artists and photographers to portray the grandeur of the mountains. He directed the construction of the Banff Springs Hotel and Chateau Lake Louise in the Rockies of Alberta, personally choosing the Banff Springs site and helping design the hotel. (Van Horne also helped design Quebec City's stately Château Frontenac.) The Canadian Pacific's two Rocky Mountain hotels popularized newly established Banff National Park and sparked the creation of other parks in the region.

Van Horne continued to expand the company's rail operations throughout his eleven-year tenure as president. He vowed to retire when the railway reached ten thousand miles of track and its stock hit par. Both of those things happened in 1899, and Van Horne kept his promise, stepping down as the active head of the company to become chairman of the board.

During the previous seventeen years, Van Horne's efforts had created enormous wealth for the Canadian Pacific—and he'd shared handsomely in that prosperity. He owned a palatial home in Montreal, filled with an impressive collection of Japanese pottery, along with one of the country's finest art collections, containing works by old masters, Asian artists, and French impressionists. He summered on Ministers Island off

St. Andrews, New Brunswick, in a forty-room mansion he named Covenhoven in honor of his family's Dutch heritage. He owned a 4,000-acre farm in Manitoba, and winters often found him at his estate in Camagüey, Cuba. (Just to keep his hand in the game, he built a railroad in Cuba after his "retirement.")

Besides overseeing his many business interests—he was a director of dozens of companies—Van Horne made time to pursue his personal passions. He was an accomplished classical violinist and enthusiastic orchid collector. He turned out hundreds of landscape paintings, often completing a piece in a single night. He enjoyed fine dining, good whiskey, and card games. He liked to entertain guests with parlor tricks, including a bit of mind reading. (At one dinner party, he reproduced a sketch done by a friend sight unseen.)

Though never a major philanthropist, Van Horne had his soft spots. He contributed to hospitals and schools, and he donated much of his ceramics collection to the Royal Ontario Museum. For nearly twenty years, he served as a trustee of Montreal's McGill University. Van Horne was also a steadfast friend. Aboard his private railcar, his personal porter—and fellow jokester—was a black man from Chicago named Jimmy French. Like Jack Benny's sidekick Rochester, French was an inveterate wisecracker, tossing off droll remarks about Van Horne's guests. When Van Horne played host to a pair of European royals—the Marquis of Lorne and Princess Louise—French innocently addressed the young lady as "Your Succulency." In 1901, French died unexpectedly from heatstroke. Van Horne paid for an elaborate funeral and marched at the head of the mourners.

Van Horne himself passed away in September 1915. His zest for life had driven him like a charging locomotive throughout his seventy-two years. Though he'd become a naturalized

Canadian citizen a quarter of a century before he died, Van Horne chose his hometown of Joliet, Illinois, as his final resting place. A special Canadian Pacific train transported his remains to Joliet following his funeral in Montreal. He was buried in the family plot, a wandering Yank who'd finally come home to stay.

Few other Americans have had the impact on a foreign country that Van Horne had on Canada. The railroad he built became the engine for Canada's settlement and economic growth. His hotels lured thousands of travelers to Canadian cities and resort areas. Today, Banff Springs Hotel, Chateau Lake Louise, and Château Frontenac remain the crown jewels of Canadian lodgings, and the Canadian Pacific Railway still knits the nation, a mainstay of the Canadian economy. William Van Horne may have taken a career risk when he moved north to oversee the construction of a struggling railway, but his gamble paid off. He did much more than complete a monumental engineering project. He helped to build a nation.

PART II

★

INNOVATORS

TWELVE

Why We Are What We Eat

WILBUR ATWATER

A FIRST-GRADER IN a small town in Tennessee—call him Jimmy—files by the school lunch counter. The other kids in line are jostling and joking, but Jimmy hungrily eyes the array of food laid out on the steam table. The ladies behind the counter pile Jimmy's tray with his choice of chicken tenders and rice, tossed salad, chunks of pineapple, a slice of whole wheat bread, and a carton of milk. This will be the boy's main meal of the day, its cost subsidized by the federal government. In order to receive the subsidy, the school's lunch program must meet nutrition guidelines that ensure students receive one-third of the recommended daily allowances of protein, vitamins A and C, iron, and calcium, as well as sufficient calories—with no more than 30 percent of the calories coming from fat, and less than 10 percent from saturated fat.

At the Olympic Training Center in Colorado, swimmer Michael Phelps sits down to his typical training breakfast: three fried-egg sandwiches garnished with mayo, cheese, lettuce, tomato, and onion; an omelet; a bowl of grits; three slices of French toast topped with powdered sugar; and three chocolate chip pancakes just to fill in the empty corners. Phelps consumes a staggering 6,000 to 8,000 calories a day when he's swimming those endless laps that have made him a champion. As monstrous as that breakfast menu appears, it's a good foundation for a competitive athlete—high in protein and loaded with the fat and carbohydrates needed to propel Phelps's lanky, muscular body through the water during his grueling training regimen.

In chichi Santa Barbara, California, a young attorney named Bronwyn shops at her local Whole Foods grocery store. As she strolls down the aisle, she picks up a container of hummus and reads the label to make sure the product isn't a diet-buster (she'd give up her new Lexus before she'd part with her size 2 dresses). She's shocked to see that a 2-tablespoon, 100-calorie serving contains 70 calories from fat. "Isn't hummus made from vegetables?" she says to herself. Checking the ingredients, Bronwyn sees that the hummus contains chickpeas, sesame seed paste, soybean oil, and feta cheese—all relatively high in fat. With a sigh, she puts the container back on the shelf.

What Jimmy the schoolboy, Michael Phelps, and Bronwyn the svelte barrister all have in common is that their daily lives are regulated by nutritional information—school-lunch program guidelines, training table menus, self-imposed diets. Like all of us, they are what they eat—but today they can know exactly why. Since the second half of the nineteenth century, scientists have known how the major components of food—fat, carbohydrates, and protein—are used by the body. In the twentieth century, the vitamins and minerals vital to human nutrition were identified. Today—if we choose to look at the federally mandated nutrition facts label appearing on most prepackaged food—we can tell fairly accurately what the impact on our bodies will be from everything we stick in our mouths. How did this surfeit of waistline-saving (or guilt-inducing) information come to be? In the United States, we can trace its origins to one man, Wilbur Olin Atwater, a nineteenth-century agricultural chemist whose research laid the groundwork for the science of nutrition in this country.

The son of a Methodist minister, Atwater was born in Johnsburg, New York, in 1844, although he grew up in Vermont. After attending the University of Vermont for two years, he completed his undergraduate degree in 1865 at Wesleyan University, a small liberal arts college founded by Methodists in Middletown, Connecticut. Atwater taught high school for a short time before deciding to seek an advanced degree. He enrolled as a graduate student in agricultural chemistry at Yale's Sheffield Scientific School, earning a PhD in 1869. His doctoral thesis on maize represented the first modern chemical analysis of a food conducted in the United States. He spent two more years studying in Germany, where he visited several agricultural experiment stations. There he met scientists who were investigating every aspect of food production. No comparable research centers existed in the United States, and Atwater came away determined to do something about it.

After returning home, Atwater resumed teaching, first at East Tennessee University, then briefly at the Maine State Agricultural College. In 1873, he landed a position as a chemistry instructor at Wesleyan University. About that same time, Atwater discovered another type of chemistry at work in his life. In August 1873, he met a young lady in Bangor named Marcia Woodard. The two had much in common. Like Atwater, Marcia had studied in Germany—music and art, in her case—and, also like Atwater, she spoke French and German. (They quoted the poetry of Goethe and Heine to each other.) In August, a week after they'd met, Atwater wrote Marcia a letter, referring to her as "My dear Miss Woodard." He requested that he be considered a friend; she responded positively, asking for a photograph of him. In October, they met a second time, and the sparks must have flown. From then on, Atwater's letters began with "My Dearie," "My Darling," "My love." In June of the following year, the two were married. He was thirty, she was twenty-three. It turned out to be a good match. The couple spent the rest of their lives together in Middletown, raising two children, Helen and Charles.

The year after his marriage, Atwater made history by establishing America's first state agricultural experiment station. With the support of a wealthy patron of Wesleyan University, he persuaded the Connecticut legislature to fund a temporary facility at the school. He started working with local farmers on fertilizer trials and conducting experiments on field crops. However, his efforts were undermined two years later when the legislature moved the experiment station to the larger, more prestigious Yale University. Following that setback, Atwater began to shift direction, focusing his research on the composition of foods and human nutrition. (Nutrition is defined as the process by which the body takes in and utilizes food substances, that is, chemicals. As the eighteenth-century French scientist Antoine Lavoisier observed, "Life is a chemical process.") Atwater's first research paper, published when he was thirty-four, dealt with the measurement of the fat content of foods.

Atwater's work gradually won recognition for himself and for the emerging field of nutrition. From 1879 to 1882, he analyzed the nutritive value of fish and invertebrates for the U.S. Fish Commission, and he did similar studies on meat for the Smithsonian Institution. In the winter of 1882–1883, he traveled to Germany to study new methods of food analysis. In 1885 and

1886, he evaluated workers' diets in Massachusetts by analyzing data collected on the foods they ate. Atwater found that the workers seemed well fed, but that they spent half or more of their income on food, often on expensive items such as steaks and butter. To cut costs, Atwater recommended cheaper sources of fat and protein, including cheese, beans, and margarine.

In 1887, Atwater began a series of articles for *Century Magazine* promoting nutrition science. The series was called "The Chemistry of Foods and Nutrition." Atwater wrote that providing an adequate diet to workers was a Christian act. He quoted Bishop R. S. Foster: "If we will care for men's souls most effectively, we must care for their bodies also." Atwater's articles gave him a national reputation, one that he used to help persuade the U.S. Congress to fund agricultural experiment stations in every state. Atwater became the first director of the new Office of Experiment Stations in the Department of Agriculture. During his three years in that role, he launched two publications to document the findings of the state experiment stations, and he traveled to Europe to convince researchers there to contribute articles.

By 1891, Atwater had concluded that nutrition science should focus on four areas: the chemical composition of foods; the effects of cooking and processing on nutritional value; the amounts and kinds of food eaten by different groups of Americans; and the amount of food energy that people require each day. Atwater had a good idea about how to tackle that last point. During his previous visits to Germany, he'd observed scientists using a machine called a respiration calorimeter, a device that measured the relationship between food intake and energy output in humans at various levels of physical activity. The machine was expensive to build and operate, but it provided vital information about nutrition, and Atwater knew he had to have one. He drummed up financial support from business groups, wealthy donors, and government officials. In 1893, he publicized nutrition science by staging an exhibition at the Chicago World's Fair. Four years later, Atwater flipped the switch on the country's first respiration calorimeter, constructed at Wesleyan University. It took sixteen people to run the machine and cost $10,000 a year to operate, but it enabled Atwater to conduct landmark studies on diet and human energy production.

Essentially, the respiration calorimeter measured the heat energy produced by the body's burning of fat and carbohydrates. The unit of measurement was the calorie (one food calorie represents the amount of energy needed to raise the temperature of one kilogram of water by one degree Celsius). Atwater's research with the respiration calorimeter demonstrated that different kinds of food produce different amounts of energy. It showed that cheaper sources of fat, carbohydrates, and protein can be just as useful to the body as more expensive ones. (One of his findings was that alcohol provides usable calories, a fact that the liquor industry immediately promoted—subjecting Atwater to criticism from the temperance movement.) Atwater's studies helped plant the term "calorie" firmly in our collective consciousness, and they underscored a fact that still reverberates in this country: on the whole, we consume too much fat and sugar and don't get enough exercise.

Even as he conducted his own research, Atwater continued to work with the U.S. Department of Agriculture to expand our knowledge of nutrition. He coordinated the studies being done at sixteen of the state agricultural experiment stations on the composition of different foods and the diets of various groups of Americans—including students, teachers, athletes, laborers, farmers, and immigrants. Always concerned about the disadvantaged, Atwater supervised studies on the diets of black sharecroppers, poor whites, Mexican families, and mental patients. He looked abroad for information about eating habits, investigating the diets of people in Europe and India.

In 1896, Atwater published the definitive collection of data on the foods we eat. It appeared in the USDA's *Office of Experiment Stations Bulletin*, one of the publications that Atwater started. The sober title was "The Chemical Composition of American Food Materials." It was a lengthy piece filled with dense tables listing the nutritive values of every type of food that had been analyzed to that point—every meat, fish, vegetable, dairy product, fruit, grain, and nut you could think of. The tables spelled out the fat, carbohydrate, and protein content of each food, along with its "fuel value" (in calories). The tables were expanded in 1899 and reprinted with minor changes in 1906. The findings stood until 1940 and served as the model for today's USDA *Agriculture Handbook No. 8*, a catalog of the nutritive value of American foods relied on by dieticians and nutritionists.

Despite his unceasing commitment to science, Atwater knew how to have fun. He was dedicated to his family and had a wide circle of friends. He loved canoeing and fishing as well as art, literature, and travel. He wrote accounts of his frequent trips to Europe for his hometown newspaper. In September 1897, he visited Leo Tolstoy at his Russian estate. Atwater had tea and stayed for supper, chatting with Tolstoy and his family in French, English, and German. The famous author showed the American scientist his private study, and the two men discussed ethics and sociology. Tolstoy encouraged Atwater in his work, stating that science hadn't paid enough attention to human nutrition. Atwater was so impressed that he wrote a twenty-five-page letter about his visit to his daughter, which included drawings of the grounds of Tolstoy's estate.

Atwater's vigorous, productive professional life came to an end in November 1904 when he was disabled by a stroke. He lingered for three years, cared for at home by his wife and daughter after doctors had done all they could for him. He died on September 22, 1907, leaving a legacy that still influences the health of Americans. His careful studies of nutrition and those that followed helped spur federal policies that have done much to alleviate childhood hunger. We see reflections of his influence on the labels of products in our grocery stores, and we're beginning to see nutritional information on the menus of restaurants. (In the Great Depression and during World War II, the government relied on nutrition guidelines to ensure that Americans and liberated populations received adequate nourishment.)

Today's familiar food pyramid, a quick and easy visual guide to the recommended daily intake of food, is a tribute to Atwater and his successors. (Recently, the USDA introduced a new nutrition graphic called MyPlate.) The research Atwater began over a century ago continues at the Beltsville Human Nutrition Research Center in Maryland and at similar facilities around the country, with national nutrition surveys now conducted by the USDA's Human Nutrition Information Service and the Department of Health and Human Services' National Center for Health Statistics.

Not surprisingly, some of Atwater's findings have become outmoded: the amount of protein he recommended in the diet has been revised downward, and—because the discovery of vitamins and many trace nutrients didn't occur in his lifetime—he failed to appreciate the importance of fruits and vegetables to good health. Still, Wilbur Atwater achieved great things, though he was never boastful about his abilities. In a letter to his future wife, he wrote, "I have a strong faith in what may be accomplished by energy and devotion to any cause even when one's abilities are not great. I am not gifted with any remarkable talent in any direction. Years ago I made up my mind that whatever I accomplished must be the result of plodding and not of genius and so I work along in my moderate way."

It's clear that Atwater sold himself far short in that self-assessment. The man was certainly persistent, but he also possessed the genius of knowing how to devote his talents to the betterment of people's daily lives.

THIRTEEN

Mythmaker of the Old West

JOHN WALLACE CRAWFORD

THE MURKY AUGUST night enveloped the buckskin-clad rider as he slipped through the silent, chaparral-covered hills just west of the Laramie Mountains. The only sounds were the creak of the man's saddle and the soft, steady thud of hooves. The rider had removed his horse's iron shoes to prevent any hostile Sioux who might come across his trail from identifying him as a white man. To encounter a Sioux war party in the Wyoming Territory in the summer of 1876 would mean certain death, and John Wallace Crawford—known to his friends as Captain Jack—intended to keep his scalp. He'd already spotted the tracks of a band of at least fifty warriors and peered from hiding as an Indian patrol passed by—praying that his horse wouldn't whinny and give him away.

Recently appointed as a scout for Col. Wesley Merritt's Fifth Cavalry, the tall, slender, twenty-nine-year-old Crawford had ridden north from Medicine Bow, Wyoming, several days earlier. He'd hoped to catch up with his regiment at nearby Fort Fetterman, but Merritt's forces had already departed for the Montana border region, where they were to join the command of Gen.

George Crook, the renowned Indian fighter assigned to drive
the Sioux back onto their reservations. The Indians had gone
on the warpath over the flood of prospectors invading their sacred Black Hills homeland following the discovery of gold in the
Dakota Territory. Just a month back, a large force led by Lakota
chief Sitting Bull had slain Lt. Col. George Armstrong Custer
and his 216 men near the Little Bighorn River, and Crook was
bent on revenge.

Jack Crawford finally caught up with the Fifth Cavalry near
Rosebud Creek, in the south of the Montana Territory. By that
time, he had ridden for twelve days and covered nearly four hundred miles, dodging hostile Sioux the entire journey. He'd only
made it through by traveling at night and lying low during the
day. It was a feat not many men could have pulled off, or would
even have attempted, but Captain Jack accomplished it with pa-
nache. One of the first things he did after linking up with his
regiment was to deliver a fifth of sour-mash whiskey to his friend
Bill Cody, a gift from a mutual acquaintance. Buffalo Bill, the
Fifth Cavalry's head scout, later wrote that "Jack Crawford is the
only man I have ever known that could have brought that bottle
of whiskey through without *accident* befalling it, for he is one of
the very few teetotal scouts I ever met."

John Wallace Crawford was more than a daring and re-
sourceful guide (he would succeed Buffalo Bill as the Fifth Cavalry's chief of scouts). He embodied an image we associate with
the essential American character—the indomitable pioneer who
helped conquer the West. No one today celebrates the exploits
of Detroit factory workers or Boston accountants. Our enduring
heroes are frontiersmen—men who represent grit, self-reliance,
honesty, and a dedication to justice, traits we think of as inher-
ently American. Since the late nineteenth century, Westerners

have dominated our folklore. Captain Jack Crawford became a frontier legend himself, one who used his dramatic experiences to create a romanticized cast of western characters in his writing. In that regard, he was in excellent company.

The settlement of the frontier took roughly half a century, from the 1840s until the 1890s. No doubt most of the men and women who ventured beyond the Mississippi had plenty of courage. The West was no place for the faint of heart. A fair number of pioneers may have even been heroic on occasion, but few of them could have reached the lofty heights of strength and goodness ascribed to storybook heroes. Rather than wait for those rare creatures to mosey along, the mass media in the East manufactured them, with the enthusiastic complicity of Westerners themselves.

Following the invention of the steam-powered rotary printing press in 1845, the public was inundated with heroic accounts of western trappers, scouts, prospectors, Indian fighters, and lawmen—firmly planting their larger-than-life images in America's collective imagination. Outlandish portraits of these characters emerged through the exaggerations and fabrications of newspaper and pulp magazine articles, dime novels, and sensationalist biographies. Stage plays and Wild West shows helped establish the perception of rootin' tootin' Westerners battling bloodthirsty savages and making the frontier safe for civilization. As in war, truth was the first casualty. Real-life scout and Indian fighter Kit Carson didn't recognize himself after the dime novelists got through with him. "That thar might be true," he commented after seeing himself depicted heroically on the cover of one book, "but I hain't got no reckerlection of it."

A sizable posse of purple-prose-slingers and entertainers had a hand in creating the myth of the Old West, but a single name stands out: William F. Cody—Pony Express rider, buffalo hunter, Indian fighter, army scout, and showman extraordinaire. For more than forty years, Cody made a living peddling an over-wrought version of western life, first in dime novels and stage melodramas and later through his famous Wild West show. De-buting in 1883, his extravaganza featured elaborate mock battles between real cowboys and Indians, along with trick-shooting ex-hibitions and demonstrations of western skills such as roping, riding, and bronco-busting. Though based on actual western characters and events, the show hyped everything for dramatic impact. The spectacle was one of the most influential forces in shaping the image of frontier figures as valiant men of action, whose chief means of expression was armed violence. As far as Buffalo Bill was concerned, the more the bullets flew, the bet-ter the show. Cody loved "noisy, rattling, gunpowder entertain-ment," and so did his audiences.

Captain Jack Crawford had the distinction of being one of Buffalo Bill's chief allies in creating the exaggerated image of the Wild West. Crawford wove fanciful tales of bold, upstand-ing Westerners in newspaper and magazine stories, poetry, and plays, and he embellished those heroic images on the stage and in the lecture hall. Out on the prairie, Crawford kept his note-book and pencil right next to his gun. Between 1877 and 1908, he turned out a half-dozen books of verse, a one-act temperance play, and three full-length melodramas filled with adventurous scouts, settlers, and prospectors. The star of most of Crawford's literary works was himself. He had a bounty of material to draw on, since his life was filled with blood and thunder.

Crawford was born in Donegal, Ireland, in 1847, the son of a struggling tailor. Crawford's father left his wife and children in 1854 to travel to America, where he went to work in the coal mines of Pennsylvania. Not long after the family was reunited in 1860, Crawford's father joined the Union Army, leaving young Jack to find work in the mines. In 1864, just after he turned seventeen, Jack Crawford enlisted in the army as well. He was wounded in two Civil War battles, at Spotsylvania and Petersburg, Virginia. His life took a fateful turn while he was recuperating in a Philadelphia hospital. A Sister of Charity taught the young soldier, who'd never had the luxury of attending school, how to read and write. He immediately made his first venture into poetry, finding he had a natural talent for rhyming.

Crawford returned home after the war to help support his family. His mother, a descendant of Scottish hero Sir William Wallace, died a short time later, quickly followed by his alcoholic father. Before his mother passed away, Crawford promised her he would abstain from strong drink, a vow he reportedly never broke. Although Crawford married and fathered several children, he left his wife and kids behind in Pennsylvania sometime in the early 1870s to seek his fortune on the frontier. Like so many other Easterners, Crawford fell under the spell of the West by reading lurid newspaper accounts and dime novels. He became convinced that adventure and maybe a bit of glory awaited him out west.

In Nebraska, Crawford found work as a newspaper reporter. At the outset of the Black Hills gold rush, he traveled on assignment to the Dakota Territory. He did some prospecting there himself, and he began to piece together the persona he would cultivate the rest of his life—Captain Jack, the Poet Scout. Appointed a captain in a local militia, Crawford donned the prairie scout's buckskin uniform and soon became widely known for his versifying around the campfire. He grew his light brown hair to his shoulders and sported a flowing mustache and a goatee, a rakish broad-brimmed hat, and a bowie knife and pistol at his waist—the very picture of the insouciant Westerner. "He was a jolly fellow, and very popular with the ladies," noted his long-suffering wife, Maria, years later.

The role of a Black Hills scout threw Crawford into some precarious situations. While camped at a mining claim outside Custer City in the early part of 1876, he and some fellow prospectors came under attack from a Sioux raiding party, which made off with most of the men's horses. Bands of Sioux repeatedly attacked Custer City that spring, stealing horses and other livestock. Crawford led several posses to try to recover the animals, although the Sioux always eluded their pursuers.

A short time later, Captain Jack took up his army scouting duties in the campaign that followed Sitting Bull's massacre of Colonel Custer and his men. After his daring four hundred-mile ride to join Merritt's Fifth Cavalry in Montana, Crawford faced near starvation as the weary troops trailed the Sioux around the countryside. The cavalrymen were reduced to eating their horses in order to survive. Crawford showed his courage on several occasions. In one dawn raid on a Sioux village, he rode among the Indians like a madman, his pistol blazing. While under fire, he searched some of the tepees, finding saddles and other gear that the Sioux had taken from the soldiers they'd killed at the Little Bighorn.

From those real-life Indian dustups, Crawford turned to pretend encounters. Near the end of 1876, he agreed to appear in Bill Cody's stage productions. Crawford was a natural actor, but despite his familiarity with weapons, he accidentally shot himself in the groin during one raucous performance. While recuperating in Virginia City, Nevada—where he met Mark Twain—he wrote his first melodrama, *Fonda; or, The Trapper's Dream.*

Crawford toured California with the play, which received favorable reviews. He later wrote *The Mighty Truth; or, In Clouds or Sunshine*, followed by *Colonel Bob: A Western Pastoral* and *The Dregs*, his one-act temperance play. In 1879, the first of Captain Jack's poetry collections appeared, titled, not surprisingly, *The Poet Scout*. Crawford never made much money from his acting or his writing—he called his own poetry "the crude, unpolished offspring of my idle hours"—but both endeavors reinforced his public reputation as an authentic western "character," a role he played to the hilt.

Crawford ended up spending half his life out West. In addition to chasing Indians and gold all over the Black Hills, he went prospecting in the Yukon and worked for many years as a scout, rancher, and government agent in New Mexico, where he was finally reunited with his family. The names of his frontier "pards" (partners) conjure up lonely prairie bivouacs, Indian skirmishes, and mining camp shoot-outs: Pawnee Bill, Buckskin Johnny, Antelope Smith, Colorado Charley, California Joe, Texas Jack, Ranger Pierce. He crossed paths with a remarkable number of future western icons—from Colonel Custer, Buffalo Bill, and Sitting Bull to Jim Bridger, Billy the Kid, and Wild Bill Hickok.

Crawford's meeting with Billy the Kid typified his incredible western adventures. One night while Crawford was sitting around a campfire in New Mexico, a stranger appeared and asked if he could join him. As the two men talked, Crawford discovered that he was sharing his fire with the notorious killer William Bonney. Since Bonney and Crawford hit it off, Crawford felt safe in asking his dangerous companion why he'd taken up his violent ways. Crawford later wrote that Bonney said he'd been led astray by the dime novels he'd read as a child.

Captain Jack hung out with Wild Bill Hickok—the former

marshal of Abilene, Kansas—in the lawless Dakota mining town of Deadwood (which Crawford had helped settle, along with Custer City, Gayville, and Spearfish). Wild Bill got all weepy whenever Crawford recited his saccharine poem about how he'd promised his "angel mother" that he wouldn't drink:

> And I made her one dear promise—
> Thank the Lord, I've kept it, too;
> Yes, I promised God and mother
> To the pledge I would be true.

After Wild Bill was shot and killed in a Deadwood saloon, Crawford memorialized his friend in verse:

> Sleep on, brave heart, in peaceful slumber,
> Bravest scout in all the West;
> Lightning eyes and voice of thunder,
> Closed and hushed in quiet rest.

Captain Jack knew that Wild Bill had his shortcomings, but he chose to portray him as uncommonly noble, a tendency that colored Crawford's fictional characters as well. The protagonists of his plays were invariably brave, wise, and supremely competent, and the Westerners he wrote about in his poetry, while often rough in appearance and speech, had the dignity of kings. That was the sort of man the West attracted, Crawford believed—a debatable contention, but one that made for uplifting copy. Crawford liked to think he was revealing the real West in his writing, which was loosely autobiographical (the lead characters in his three melodramas were named Jack Crawford, Jack Wallace, and Colonel Bob). However, since Crawford romanticized his characters so extensively, he only succeeded in reinforcing the stereotype of the dashing, fearless, sentimental, impossibly virtuous yet eternally modest western cavalier.

The exaggerated images Crawford and his contemporaries created had an unexpected effect. Life began to imitate art as the over-the-top figures depicted in dime novels, melodramas, and Wild West shows were accepted as real not only by gaping Easterners but also by Westerners, who identified with the values attributed to frontier characters. By the final years of the nineteenth century, the many permutations of the western hero—army scout, Indian fighter, gunslinger—coalesced around the most popular figure of all: the cowboy. No other western character has had a more lasting cultural impact than the six-shooter-packing rowdy in chaps and spurs—the purported embodiment of individual freedom and derring-do.

That rustic image became fixed in American folklore even though the actual heyday of the trail-riding cowboy lasted barely twenty years, from just after the Civil War to the mid-1880s, when railroads reached the western rangelands, ending the need to drive cattle over long distances. Ironically, three privileged eastern dudes helped immortalize the cowboy. Following a yearlong sojourn in the Dakota Territory, Teddy Roosevelt published several books on the West in which he pronounced that cowboys displayed all the best attributes of the American character. Artist Frederic Remington created dramatic, if often imaginary, scenes of the Old West in paintings of soldiers, cowhands, and Native Americans. And in his best-selling novel *The Virginian*, writer Owen Wister first evoked the cowboy as a lone knight-errant living by a code of honor. (It was Wister who invented the ritualized six-gun showdown in the street—"Slap leather, pilgrim"—a virtually nonexistent occurrence in the real

West, where gunfights were usually spontaneous, liquor-fueled free-for-alls.)

The landmark 1903 film *The Great Train Robbery* reinforced the colorful depiction of the cowboy, an image burnished by the hundreds of Wild West movies and TV shows that followed. When we picture a cowpoke today, we see John Wayne or Clint Eastwood, Paladin or Marshal Dillon—taciturn hombres with a soft spot for women, kids, and horses, but who will blow a hole the size of a grapefruit in anyone who crosses them. As popularly conceived, "cowboys" no longer needed a connection to the cattle industry. If they rode a horse, carried a gun, and wore a big hat, they belonged to the dusty fraternity.

Americans still cling to the romantic conception of the cowboy with cultlike tenacity. President Ronald Reagan, who played a few cowboys during his Hollywood days, certainly believed in the virtues of the storied figures of the Old West. Reagan called Wild Bill Hickok, Calamity Jane, and Annie Oakley "courageous and self-reliant heroes." Historian David H. Murdoch poured a ten-gallon hatful of cold water on Reagan's fond assessment in his book *The American West: The Invention of a Myth*. Murdoch wrote that "James Butler Hickok was a cold-blooded killer who spent most of his time gambling and chasing prostitutes. Martha 'Calamity Jane' Canary was a sad transvestite alcoholic, an inveterate liar who was reduced to exhibiting herself as a sideshow freak. Phoebe Anne Oakley Mozee was entirely the creation of showbusiness; the tiny trick-shot star was born in Ohio and had never been in the West when she joined Buffalo Bill Cody's Wild West show."

America's idealization of the cowboy was peculiar, Murdoch went on, if not downright absurd: "To make an itinerant agricultural worker an epic hero was to create a cultural curiosity.

Then to insist that this hero have the maturity of a [backward] teenager, the moral outlook of a Sunday School teacher and the skills of an assassin was bizarre." In truth, cowboys were widely regarded as dangerous, drunken riffraff prior to their literary deification. Decent people hid the kids—and themselves— whenever these mostly young, seasonally employed laborers galloped into town.

For over four decades, Captain Jack Crawford played a leading role in stoking the public's fascination with the characters of the Old West. In the end, though, an unadorned account of his own life is more dramatic—more believably heroic—than the fanciful tales he spun. Crawford took part in all the archetypal experiences our western folklore is based on, from tangling with Indian war parties to prospecting, cattle ranching, and settling frontier towns. He may not have attained the fame of his cohort Buffalo Bill, but, as a writer and a performer, he earned celebrity status in his day, even appearing in a movie in 1915, *The Battle Cry of Peace*. When Crawford died in Brooklyn in February 1917, his passing was noted in the *New York Times* and newspapers across the country. The *Literary Digest* mourned Crawford as the last of "the great scouts who led Custer and the Seventh Cavalry into the sage-lands or 'took the dust' of the wily Apache chief Geronimo."

In a more personal tribute, Crawford's close friend and fellow adventurer James Barton Adams described how he'd watched Captain Jack write poetry every night in the West, even when the men couldn't light a campfire for fear of being attacked by Indians. "With saddle for seat and buckskin-covered knee for table he would sit in the bright light of the Southwestern moon and write, and write, and write. . . . He saw poetry in everything from the awe-inspiring grandeur of the mountains to the sneaking coyotes which sang us to sleep at night from their perch on a distant sandhill." Crawford clearly loved the sweeping western landscape, the crucible in which his fictional homespun princes were forged.

It would be easy to laugh at the ersatz Paladins and phony Virginians of the never-was Old West, all those glorious made-up knights of the open range, riding tall in the saddle and living by their imaginary code of honor. But it would be wrong to do so. Our western heroes may have been exaggerations, but, just like the characters of Greek mythology, they serve their purpose. By creating an idealized figure that embodies the virtues Americans hold dear, John Wallace Crawford and his compadres bequeathed us more than a sizable community of latter-day Shanes. They gave us an enduring cultural touchstone. And isn't that what heroes are for?

FOURTEEN

The Inquisitive Benefactor

GEORGE FABYAN

THE BIG GENT with the Vandyke beard sauntered across the parklike grounds of his estate at the close of a mellow summer afternoon. He was dressed in riding breeches, his long legs encased in tall leather boots. Clutching an ever-present cigarette, the man seemed supremely confident and at ease. He looked over his property—several hundred acres of prime farmland—with an air of satisfaction. In one lush field, prize Jersey cattle tugged at the grass contentedly, tawny smudges against the vivid emerald backdrop. Nearby, a Dutch-style windmill pinwheeled slowly in the evening breeze. The Fox River lazily eddied and swirled through the heart of the estate. The scene was reminiscent of a Constable landscape, with its dreamy timelessness.

There were hints of the military reflected in the man's upright carriage, or perhaps it was the patrician courtliness of a European count. The gentleman's farm, however, was far from Europe. Millionaire businessman George Fabyan's Riverbank estate lay just south of Geneva, Illinois, a country hamlet forty miles west of Chicago. If the squire of Riverbank seemed satisfied on this summer eve in 1916, it was because his staff of several dozen workers had put in another fruitful day in their curiously varied pursuits, all conducted under the close supervision of this wealthy semiretired textile merchant.

The duties of the Riverbank staff went far beyond typical farm chores. Oh, there were crops to be harvested and barns to be mucked out. But the estate also claimed a group of men and women who had loftier tasks. With Fabyan's financial backing, some of the nation's top scientists had been gathered here, brought together to investigate a range of subjects that held their patron's interest—from plant genetics, animal husbandry, and health and fitness to architectural acoustics, military technology, and ciphers and codes. This eclectic team of privately funded researchers constituted one of the world's first think tanks.

"Some rich men go in for art collections, gay times on the Riviera, or extravagant living," Fabyan declared. "But they all get satiated. That's why I stick to scientific experiments, spending money to discover valuable things that universities can't afford. You never get sick of too much knowledge."

Fabyan's unquenchable inquisitiveness, coupled with his private fortune, made him a rustic Renaissance man of the early twentieth century. His life offered proof that amateur dabblers can have as great an impact on scientific progress as government or academia. It was also a reminder of the good that can come from wealth coupled with generosity. By following his private passions, George Fabyan became a public benefactor. It was a role he was born for.

The eldest son of a wealthy Boston businessman and philanthropist, Fabyan enjoyed all the perks of growing up rich— frolicking with his four brothers and sisters at tony retreats such as the Eastern Yacht Club of Marblehead and the Jekyll Island Club of Georgia. In a fit of youthful rebelliousness, he ran away from home at sixteen, becoming a purchasing agent for the Union Pacific Railroad—and getting disinherited in the process. His job took him throughout the Pacific Northwest and upper Midwest, where he met his future wife, Nelle Wright. The two were married in Minneapolis in 1890.

For a short time, Fabyan worked as a cotton broker in Memphis. Later, he took a job in Chicago with the family firm, Bliss Fabyan Company, one of the largest textile businesses in the world. Fabyan kept his identity a secret until his sales record earned him an introduction to the head of the company—his father—who welcomed him back into the family. When his father died, Fabyan inherited $3 million (equivalent to $70 million today) and control of the firm's Chicago operation. His inheritance enabled him to ease back on office work and pursue his outside interests. In 1905, at the age of thirty-eight, Fabyan purchased the first ten acres of his Geneva estate, which would eventually grow to six hundred acres.

Fabyan cut quite a figure around bucolic Geneva. An energetic man with a booming voice, he was known for his sense of humor. He often gave out copies of a book he'd "written" entitled *What I Know About the Future of Cotton and Domestic Goods*. All one hundred pages were blank. An unapologetic autocrat, Fabyan enjoyed barking orders to members of his staff, be they respected scientists or humble farmhands. He also exhibited a quiet generosity. Whenever he bumped into any new parents around town, he would shake hands and surreptitiously pass them a ten-dollar gold piece. During the Depression, he handed out food baskets to hard-pressed families. The baskets contained five silver dollars, along with a note asking the recipients to never mention his gift to anyone.

In 1901, Fabyan was granted the rank of colonel for his

service on the National Guard detail assigned to the governor of Illinois. He went by that honorific for the rest of his life. It's a title that's sometimes handed out like party favors—slapped on everyone from Colonel Sanders to Colonel Mustard—but in Fabyan's case, it was a perfect fit. Swaggering around his estate in his jodhpurs and riding boots, he looked exactly like a British colonial just back from India.

Once the colonel and his wife were ensconced at Riverbank, Fabyan threw himself into his scientific pursuits. His interest in acoustics grew out of his experiments with a sound-activated antigravity machine, an improbable contraption that comprised a rotating wooden cylinder and sets of vibrating piano strings. Though the levitation device never got off the ground, it led to Fabyan's introduction to Wallace Clement Sabine, a Harvard physicist and the country's leading expert on architectural acoustics. At the time, Sabine was attempting to measure the reverberation and absorption of sounds, but he was frustrated by the loud ambient noises in the city of Cambridge, Massachusetts. (The unit now used to measure sound absorption is called the "sabin" in honor of the professor, who is regarded as the father of architectural acoustics.) Fabyan offered to build a laboratory at Riverbank, where Sabine could work amid the quiet of the Illinois countryside. "Hell, what do you want?" Fabyan snorted. "I'll build it."

The result was the Riverbank Acoustical Laboratory. Finished in 1918, it was the first independent research facility dedicated to architectural acoustics. Wallace Sabine died soon after the lab was completed, but his cousin Paul Sabine, a Harvard-trained scientist, took over. During his years at Riverbank, Paul Sabine created a sound-absorbing plaster for walls, led the design of the first Hollywood soundstage, and provided guidance on acoustics to the architects of Radio City Music Hall, the Chicago Civic Opera House, and other major public venues. While investigating noise abatement, Sabine conceived the idea of restricting airplanes to precise flight paths as they passed above cities. Sabine's research was key to the development of the electronic hearing aid. When he retired in 1947, the Illinois Institute of Technology assumed control of the lab. Today, Alion Science and Technology continues to run the updated facility, still a leading research center.

Colonel Fabyan kept his own office at the rear of the acoustics lab. To reach his private lair, visitors had to negotiate a funhouse maze that began in the entryway, where a bell hung above a sign reading RING BELL FOR SERVICE. When a visitor tugged on the pull-wire, the bell came loose and clattered against the wall—the colonel's little joke. An attendant would then appear and direct the guest to an adjacent room, which was empty. The room had three additional doors, one leading to a staircase and the other two opening onto closets. At the back of one of the closets was another door, which, if the visitor hadn't yet lost his sanity, would admit him into an office where the colonel sat grinning behind a huge desk. Guests running that gauntlet for the first time must have thought they'd stumbled onto the set of a Marx Brothers movie.

Another of Colonel Fabyan's academic interests was cryptology—the science of ciphers and codes. (At their simplest, ciphers use a letter-substitution system to create hidden messages, while codes rely on a list of arbitrary numbers or letters that correspond to actual words or phrases.) Fabyan's fascination with the mysteries of secret writing was fueled by an offbeat literary theory he subscribed to. He believed that Sir Francis Bacon had written the works attributed to William Shakespeare, and that Bacon had hidden secret messages in the plays and son-nets to confirm his authorship. (Never mind the question of why Sir Francis would bother with such an elaborate ruse.)

The conceit that someone other than Shakespeare had penned the Bard of Avon's masterpieces has consumed a small army of fanatics over the centuries. Once bitten by that peculiar bug, Fabyan became determined to build a convincing case for Bacon. With money to lavish on the project, he hired investiga-tors to find and decipher the supposedly hidden messages. His quest included an expensive wild-goose chase in London that entailed digging through twelve feet of river muck in search of lost manuscripts.

Fabyan's lead researcher on the Bacon project was Elizabeth Wells Gallup, a matronly English teacher who'd been immersed in the subject for years. The dour, gray-haired Gallup looked downright mean in her photographs. One resident of Riverbank said she resembled Whistler's Mother, with her austere black outfits. The lady cast a spell over Fabyan. He put her and her sister up in a cottage on the estate and assembled an extensive collection of Elizabethan and Jacobean literature for their use.

Gallup was always wildly imaginative. One of her pet theo-ries was that Bacon was the illegitimate son of Queen Elizabeth I and thus should have inherited the British throne. Gallup's method of proving that Bacon was the author of Shakespeare's literary creations consisted of interpreting the "biliteral cipher" that Bacon invented. Bacon's cipher used the letters *a* and *b* in different combinations to represent the entire alphabet—much as computer binary code combines the digits 0 and 1 to rep-resent letters, numbers, and other symbols. Gallup was certain she could detect Bacon's cipher in Shakespeare's work through minute differences in the typefaces used to print the original editions of the plays. Fabyan had such faith in Gallup's theories that he published half a dozen slim volumes about her work, with detailed illustrations. Perusing these books is a surefire way to get a headache. The colonel's introductions are marvelous examples of pretzel logic, and the illustrations of old-time type-faces that are supposed to prove Bacon's hidden meaning look like nothing more than penmanship exercises.

Mrs. Gallup had a helper in her arcane endeavors, a petite, dark-haired young scholar named Elizebeth Smith. Smith arrived at Riverbank in 1916 with a new English degree from Hillsdale College and absolutely no background in cryptology. However, she took to the subject and found it interesting. Even more interesting was another newcomer at Riverbank—William Friedman, a slender, Adolphe Menjou look-alike hired by Fabyan the previous year to research plant genetics. (When Friedman asked his prospective employer what he raised at Riverbank, the colonel replied, "I raise hell.")

The instant that Friedman and Smith caught sight of each other, a message was transmitted—and it didn't need decoding. Friedman soon began helping out on the Bacon project by taking close-up photographs of the typefaces used in Shakespeare's plays. Before long, he'd assigned his work on plant genetics to an assistant and was devoting himself to cryptology . . . and Miss Smith. In May 1917, Friedman and Smith were married—just as the United States was preparing to join Britain and France in the war against Germany.

Suddenly, cryptology had a new importance. Deciphering enemy communications was vital, but the government had no agency to do the work. Colonel Fabyan offered the services of his staff at no charge (he also funded training on his farm in trench warfare). For several months, the scholars at Riverbank were the country's only cryptanalysts, relied on for making and breaking secret messages for the government and its wartime allies. William and Elizebeth Friedman went from the frivolous academic exercise of trying to unmask Shakespeare to the life-or-death matter of providing the American military with battlefield intelligence.

Both proved adept at the task. Besides decoding German transmissions, they revealed a group of plotters in the United States who were hoping to stir up trouble in India. Asked to vet a new cipher the British had devised, the Friedmans cracked it in less than three hours. (The hidden message read: "This cipher is absolutely undecipherable.") After the army set up its own Cipher Bureau, the Friedmans trained its officers in cryptology, and William later joined the army himself, serving the final months of the war on Gen. John J. Pershing's staff in France.

During and after the war, William produced a flurry of writing on creating and solving ciphers and codes—the first major effort to document the science. His monograph *The Index of Coincidence and Its Applications in Cryptography*, published by Riverbank Laboratories in 1920, has been called "the most important single publication in cryptology." William revolutionized cryptology by applying mathematics and statistical analysis to the discipline for the first time. The army was so impressed that it hired both of the Friedmans as civilian experts. The couple left Riverbank for good at the end of 1920, spending the rest of their lives in government service.

During World War II, William led the team that cracked Japan's supposedly unbreakable Purple cipher, revealing key communications between Japan and Nazi Germany—a triumph equal to the solving of Germany's vaunted Enigma cipher. William held leadership roles with the Signal Intelligence

Service, the Armed Forces Security Agency, the National Security Agency, and the Department of Defense. His books became classics and remain required reading for cryptanalysts. Elizebeth worked for the War Department, the OSS, the Treasury Department, the U.S. Navy, and the coast guard. She aided law enforcement agencies by breaking codes used by rumrunners and a Chinese opium-smuggling gang. She cracked a code that revealed the identity of a spy for the Japanese in New York. Near the end of her career, she established a secure communications system for the International Monetary Fund. The Friedmans are still hailed as the most brilliant cryptanalysts the country has ever produced—a reputation forever linked to George Fabyan's obsession with Francis Bacon.

Colonel Fabyan hated to lose the services of the Friedmans. He tried to retain them with salary increases and the promise that they didn't have to support the Bacon theory if their investigations refuted it. Despite the absence of the talented couple, a full slate of research continued at Riverbank Laboratories. Riverbank scientists developed a highly accurate bimetallic, temperature-compensated tuning fork widely used in hearing tests. Other advances included new electromechanical frequency control devices. Fabyan's researchers paved the way for the country's first cross-country wire photo services, and they continued to set new standards for testing the acoustical properties of architectural components.

Of course, life at Riverbank wasn't all work. The Fabyans hosted a parade of distinguished guests, among them Teddy Roosevelt (as president, Roosevelt had tapped Fabyan to help negotiate the 1905 Treaty of Portsmouth, which ended the Russo-Japanese War). Other notables included Albert Einstein, P. T. Barnum, department store magnate Marshall Fields, explorer

Richard Byrd, and actresses Lillie Langtry and Mary Pickford. The Fabyans' home, a farmhouse they called the Villa, was extensively redesigned and expanded by Frank Lloyd Wright in 1907, although Colonel Fabyan grew dissatisfied with the haughty architect and kicked him off the project, using his own workers to finish the remodeling. (Now on the National Register of Historic Places, the Prairie-style house is open to the public as a museum.)

Visitors often remarked that the estate was like a self-contained village—lacking only a church and a school. What it did have, besides the Villa and the research complex, were multiple lodgings for workers and guests, a Roman-style swimming pool, a Japanese tea garden, large vegetable gardens, green-houses where roses and other flowers were raised, riding stables, barns, dog-breeding kennels, a chicken ranch, a boathouse and lighthouse along the river, and a screeching, howling, Noah's Ark–like menagerie that included monkeys, bears, alligators, ostriches, peacocks, zebras, and a kangaroo. At one point, the colonel and Mrs. Fabyan needed nearly a hundred people to keep everything running.

A network of paths wound throughout the property, which the Fabyans allowed the public to use, making Riverbank a favorite place for a Sunday afternoon stroll. The estate's windmill was a local curiosity—Fabyan spent $75,000 to have it relocated to his farm and put in working order. Even odder was the Temple de Junk, a storehouse containing a magpie collection of unclaimed railroad freight, which the colonel purchased just for the fun of opening the containers to see what they held. The Fabyans enjoyed three decades together at Riverbank, a prolonged experiment in joyful eccentricity. More than a village, the estate was akin to a college campus, a retreat where innovation and experimentation were encouraged—and there was never a dull moment. A "community of thinkers," Fabyan called his private research institute.

Colonel Fabyan died at Riverbank in 1936 at the age of sixty-nine. In his lifetime, he was responsible for nurturing some of the country's finest scientific minds, although he's often remembered for his project to discredit Shakespeare. That effort may seem half-baked, but it produced the nation's first pool of professional cryptanalysts. Led by the Friedmans, the advances in cryptology emanating from Fabyan's Illinois think tank contributed to the United States' military success in two wars, saving countless lives. Today, Riverbank Laboratories is regarded as the birthplace of modern cryptology and the progenitor of the National Security Agency. That highly secretive organization honored Fabyan's contributions by posthumously awarding him a plaque, now on display at Riverbank. The terse inscription reads: "To the memory of George Fabyan from a grateful government."

Interestingly, the Friedmans returned to the Shakespeare-Bacon controversy in their later years. In their 1957 book *The Shakespearean Ciphers Examined*, they blew large holes in the findings of fierce old Mrs. Gallup. By then, the couple had forty years of experience in cryptology, so it was easy for them to expose their former associate's flaws, which consisted mainly of unproven assertions about what she saw in the type fonts of the original editions of Shakespeare's plays. There was no maliciousness in their demolition of Mrs. Gallup's theories. They even thanked her and Colonel Fabyan for instilling an interest in the subject, the gateway to their life's work. Just for fun, the Friedmans hid their own biliteral cipher on page 257 of their book. The message they encrypted was this: "I did not write the plays. F. Bacon."

If George Fabyan had still been alive, he might well have congratulated the Friedmans on their findings. It's not hard to picture the boisterous, fun-loving colonel slapping them on the shoulder and having a good laugh over the whole affair. And why not? Fabyan expressed his own doubts about Bacon's authorship in a letter he wrote in 1929. The Friedmans' convincing verdict simply added to the world's knowledge—and, as the ever-inquisitive benefactor of Riverbank maintained, "You never get sick of too much knowledge."

FIFTEEN

Sealing the Victory at Gettysburg

HERMAN HAUPT

A SLENDER, STRIKINGLY handsome man in civilian dress stood at the rail of the small steamer as it splashed down the Potomac River south of Washington, D.C. It was the last week of April 1862, and Herman Haupt was on the way to his first assignment as a newly appointed colonel in the Union Army. His destination was Aquia Creek, forty-five miles south of the capital. A military depot had been established where the creek empties into the Potomac, just east of Fredericksburg, Virginia. Haupt's orders were to rebuild three miles of railroad track and two bridges between the depot and Fredericksburg, a key rail link destroyed by the Confederates.

A successful civil engineer, Haupt had built railroads, bridges, and tunnels in several eastern states before the war. In 1851, his book *General Theory of Bridge Construction* was hailed as a definitive work. Now he needed to call on all his talents, and to do it quickly. Union forces under Gen. Irvin Mc-Dowell were languishing near the Aquia Creek depot, unable to support Gen. George B. McClellan, whose 120,000-strong Army of the Potomac was poised to the south on the York-James

Peninsula. McClellan was preparing to march on Richmond in a major Union offensive (the Peninsular Campaign). He was counting on McDowell to stage a diversionary movement, but McDowell couldn't advance until the damaged rail line was repaired.

Arriving at Aquia Creek, Haupt quickly assessed the situation. It was a dispiriting spectacle. The Confederates had not only destroyed the two bridges and three miles of track, they'd also burned the cross ties and hauled off the rails. To make matters worse, Haupt had no dedicated crew to make the repairs. Each day, a different group of soldiers showed up. Haupt spent most of his time training the new men. In addition, heavy rains had softened the rail bed, which Confederate cavalry had ridden over and churned into a quagmire.

Haupt didn't waste time moaning about the difficulties he faced. He set crews to work cutting three thousand new cross-ties. The ties were an assortment of mismatched lengths and thicknesses, but somehow Haupt was able to lay down a level track. With his men working day and night in the driving rain, he repaired the three miles of track in three days.

Haupt then turned to reconstructing the two bridges that had been destroyed, one over Aquia Creek and another over Potomac Creek. He rebuilt the 150-foot-long Aquia Creek Bridge in fifteen hours. The Potomac Creek Bridge was another matter. It had to span four hundred feet, with the deck eighty feet above the water, necessitating an elaborate system of trusses. Building it would have been a challenge for a trained crew, but with the ragtag work squads that Haupt had at his disposal, it was a sobering prospect. The original bridge had taken nine months to build. Haupt completed his new bridge in less than two weeks. Its towering latticework of trusses looked like something a child might fashion out of Tinkertoys, but the supply trains were once again running to Fredericksburg.

General McDowell (a college friend of Haupt's) was pleased with his new man's efforts, and so was President Lincoln. After Lincoln saw Haupt's handiwork firsthand, he remarked to his staff, "I have seen the most remarkable structure human eyes ever rested upon. That man Haupt has built a bridge across Potomac Creek . . . over which loaded trains are running every hour and, upon my word, gentlemen, there is nothing in it but beanpoles and cornstalks."

So who exactly was Herman Haupt—this miracle worker with the piercing gaze and flowing beard? Although he was destined to become a behind-the-scenes hero in the Civil War, Haupt wasn't your normal military man, even with his West Point credentials. Haupt was born in Philadelphia in 1817, the son of a merchant of middling success. His father died when Haupt was a boy, leaving his mother to support six children. When Haupt was a teenager, a congressman helped him win a presidential appointment to the U.S. Military Academy. He completed his studies there in 1835 and was brevetted a second lieutenant in the infantry. He quickly realized that he wasn't cut out to be a soldier. He resigned his commission after only three months to become a railroad civil engineer.

Haupt started out working on railroads in Pennsylvania and Maryland, first as a surveyor, then as a construction engineer. When he was twenty-one, he married Ann Cecilia Keller, the daughter of a Gettysburg pastor. Ann was described as "lively, cheerful and accomplished." Lively indeed—with clocklike regularity, she bore eleven children, seven sons and four daughters. (Like all good railroad families, the Haupts believed in sticking to a schedule.) Haupt and his wife made their first home just west of Gettysburg, on Seminary Ridge—a plot of ground that would be immortalized twenty-five years later.

In 1840, Haupt was hired to help build the York & Wrightsville Railroad in Pennsylvania. On that project, he discovered that none of the railroad civil engineers of the time were properly assessing the strength of the trusses used in bridge construction. Haupt perfected a means of calculating the strength mathematically, information that became the basis for his book on bridges, which established his reputation as an engineering expert.

Over the next few years, Haupt served as general superintendent of the Pennsylvania Railroad and chief engineer of the Southern Railroad of Mississippi. In 1856, he became the chief engineer and contractor for the Troy & Greenfield Railroad and Hoosac Tunnel in Massachusetts—a job that thoroughly gummed up his career. After investing much of his own money in the company, he ran into a thicket of financial and political setbacks that prevented him from completing the tunnel. He ended up battling the state to get his money back. The troubles continued into the spring of 1862, which was when Haupt received a telegram that sent his life on a history-making tangent. The message was from Secretary of War Edwin M. Stanton, asking him to come to Washington immediately. The Civil War was raging, and the North needed him to build and run its military railroads.

Haupt reported to Washington as requested, keeping one eye on the legal mess in Massachusetts (the problems there would dog him for years). Stanton told him he'd only need his services for three or four weeks, since the war would be over in three months (it lasted, of course, for three more years). Haupt agreed to serve as Stanton's chief of construction and transportation— with a few conditions. Although the secretary of war appointed his new engineer to the rank of colonel, Haupt refused to sign his commission papers. He wanted to remain a civilian to be free to attend to his business affairs. He insisted on wearing civilian clothing and on being paid only for his expenses. In addition, Haupt told Stanton that he was a field man, not a desk jockey. He would keep the trains chugging along, but he wouldn't be bothered with paper-shuffling. Stanton reluctantly agreed, making Haupt a unique civilian-soldier—a forerunner of the military contractors common today.

Stanton had picked the right man for the job. For the first time, trains were playing a major role in warfare, with both sides fighting to capture or destroy each other's equipment and control key routes. However, a multitude of problems plagued military rail operations, including conflicting lines of authority, lack of skilled crews, interference from competing military officers and civilian agencies, worn-out equipment and tracks, inadequate telegraph communications, and difficulties with loading and unloading trains. For nearly a year and a half, from April 1862 to September 1863, Herman Haupt overcame every one of those problems. The operational procedures he instituted, and the railroads and bridges he built or repaired, enabled the North to move troops, supplies, and the wounded with an efficiency never before known.

Besides his technical and organizational skills, Haupt possessed a backbone as hard as one of his iron rails. Blunt to the point of rudeness and completely sure of himself, Haupt wasn't afraid to speak his mind to anyone. He pummeled Secretary of War Stanton, Secretary of the Treasury Salmon P. Chase, and Secretary of the Navy Gideon Welles with his (not always welcome) ideas. He presented crisp, businesslike accounts of war developments directly to President Lincoln, sometimes in person. According to Lincoln's private secretary, John Hay, the president appreciated Haupt's candor, contrasting his reports with the "weak, whiney, vague, and incorrect" dispatches he sometimes received.

In August 1862, Haupt was responsible for transporting troops from Alexandria to Manassas, Virginia, where Gen. John Pope was preparing to engage the Confederates. On the eve of the battle (known as Second Manassas to the federals and Second Bull Run to Southerners), Haupt was shocked to learn that Union Gen. Samuel Sturgis had commandeered several trains carrying wounded soldiers—trains that Haupt needed to deliver Pope's reinforcements. When Haupt confronted Sturgis, the drunken general replied, "I don't care for John Pope one pinch of owl dung."

Still chortling at his own remark, Sturgis was taken aback when Haupt whipped out a dispatch from Henry Halleck, the general in charge of all the U.S. armies. "No military officer has any authority to interfere with your control over railroads," it stated. "Show this to General Sturgis, and if he attempts to interfere, I will arrest him." Sturgis looked glumly at the note and replied, "Well, then, take your damned railroad."

Sturgis's meddling had delayed ten thousand men and needed supplies from reaching the front. Haupt did all he could to speed them on their way, but his efforts couldn't change the results of the battle. Pope's forces suffered a disastrous defeat at Manassas. Haupt's tireless efforts to transport the retreating troops to safety earned him the effusive thanks of Secretary Stanton, given in the presence of President Lincoln and his cabinet. The next day, Haupt was promoted to brigadier general, although he again refused to formally accept the military rank or any pay.

Haupt's greatest contributions came during the Battle of Gettysburg. In the first three days of July 1863, Confederate forces under Gen. Robert E. Lee and federal troops led by Gen. George G. Meade converged at the little southern Pennsylvania town in one of the pivotal battles of the war—a bloodbath in which nearly a third of the 158,000 soldiers who fought (over 83,000 Union troops and 75,000 Confederates) were killed or wounded. Haupt knew the area intimately (during the battle, a Confederate battery would be set up in the front yard of his former home on Seminary Ridge). To resupply the Union side, Haupt was forced to rely on a network of small branch lines around Gettysburg, most of them in bad shape. One was the run-down Western Maryland Railroad, a single-track line connecting with Baltimore. It had no sidings, no water towers, and no turntables along the way, and it lacked sufficient supplies of wood for fuel and experienced men to run things. Normally, three or four trains a day were all the route could handle. Haupt needed to move thirty trains daily, in both directions.

Haupt put his construction corps to work. By this time, he had a disciplined, well-trained body of men to assist him, including several hundred former slaves. The men quickly improved the line so it could handle the necessary trains. Haupt then set to repairing nineteen bridges that had been damaged or destroyed between Harrisburg and Hanover, Pennsylvania—another important rail link. Haupt's trains poured in tons of supplies during the battle. When Lee broke off the fight and retreated south, General Meade had a week's stockpile of food and equipment. Haupt's trains also evacuated over fifteen thousand wounded soldiers from the battlefield. By delivering those men to hospitals in Baltimore, Harrisburg, and other cities—where they received better care than they would have in the field—

Haupt saved untold numbers of lives. Under the worst possible conditions, Haupt had worked another miracle.

When the battle at Gettysburg ended, Haupt met with General Meade, another West Point classmate. As always, Haupt gave his own frank opinion of the situation. He pleaded with Meade to go after Lee's forces—crush the South's top general and the war could be ended. Haupt pointed out that Lee's supplies had to be depleted, his men demoralized. He was especially vulnerable at the moment. Meade said that his own troops were too tired to rush off in pursuit. Haupt replied that the Confederates had to be even more exhausted.

Unable to convince Meade to take action, Haupt jumped on a train and headed back to Washington. He briefed Secretary of War Stanton, General Halleck, and President Lincoln on the advisability of pursuing Lee's army while it was in tatters. The three men agreed with the railroad man, but General Meade dithered and Lee escaped. The war would drag on for two more years. Meade's inaction drove Lincoln to tears of frustration. For the rest of his life, Haupt remained convinced that if Meade had acted, the war could have been won right then.

Haupt's own involvement in the war did end right about that time. In September 1863, the governor of Massachusetts, John Andrew—one of Haupt's old adversaries in the legal wrangling over the Hoosac Tunnel project—saw a way to keep Haupt from pressing his case. Knowing that Haupt had refused to sign his commission papers, Andrew leaned on Secretary Stanton to make Haupt commit to military service, which would rob him of his freedom to return to Massachusetts. Stanton went along with the scheme, and when Haupt again declined to sign the papers, Stanton sacked him, despite his invaluable service. (Stanton had a history of getting rid of useful people, especially those with the nerve to stand up to him, which Haupt certainly had.)

When Haupt was booted out, the man who took over the task of keeping the railroads repaired and the trains running was Daniel C. McCallum, Haupt's administrative superior (although Haupt had never paid much attention to him). Haupt had already trained enough assistants to make McCallum's job considerably easier. McCallum had never cared for Haupt. He was jealous of the acclaim Haupt had won and his easy interaction with President Lincoln. When the war was over and McCallum was asked to write an account of all military rail operations, he never once mentioned Haupt's name. An October 1866 article in the *Chicago Tribune* glowingly described the achievements of Haupt and his staff, attributing everything to McCallum. The paper stated that McCallum was the man "to whom all the credit of the energy and systematic operation of [the military railroads] belong"—a grossly unfair assessment.

Haupt's career following his wartime service was a roller-coaster ride. He eventually won a settlement from Massachusetts—for a measly eight cents on the dollar (he lost an estimated $400,000 of his own money; a sympathetic contemporary observed that "he was not only plucked and skinned, but drawn and quartered"). At various times, Haupt served as chief engineer of the Shenandoah Railroad, general manager of the Richmond & Danville, and president of the Dakota & Great Southern. As general manager of the Northern Pacific, Haupt organized that railroad's golden spike ceremony at Gold Creek, Montana, in 1883. Haupt built one of the country's first oil pipelines, and he found time to write several more books, including *Herman's Wooing*, a parody of Longfellow's interminable poem *Hiawatha*. He also wrote a memoir called *Reminiscences of*

General Herman Haupt (he wasn't above using his old military title, even though it was never official). In some of his ventures he made money, but on the whole he struggled financially.

There's little doubt that Haupt's greatest triumphs came during the war years, when almost single-handedly he brought order out of chaos. Before his involvement, the Union's military railroads were all but dysfunctional; after Haupt left the service, the men he'd groomed were able to keep things running smoothly for the duration of the war. His ability to construct and repair railroads and bridges was a thing of myth—it was said that his men could "build bridges quicker than the Rebs can burn them down." Haupt's organizational skills were equally impressive: he had that rare ability of being able to go to the heart of a problem in an instant, and to come up with an immediate solution—a railroader who never idled on a siding for a moment.

Haupt was one of those curious historical personalities who appear at exactly the right time and place to make a difference. There's no disputing that his skill at railroad construction and management helped the North win the war in less time and at less cost in blood and treasure. His impact on the Battle of Gettysburg was equally unequivocal. By delivering tons of vital supplies and evacuating thousands of wounded soldiers, he was key to sealing the Union victory. If he had no other wartime accomplishment than that, he would still be worthy of remembrance—which makes it all the more baffling why Haupt isn't prominently mentioned in history books. But then, master logisticians have never been celebrated like battlefield generals. Still, among those who know the importance of transporting troops and supplies in time of war, Herman Haupt remains a legendary figure.

Haupt outlived every other member of his class at West Point. He died in December 1905 at the age of eighty-eight, suffering a heart attack as he returned home to Washington with his son Lewis after a business meeting in New York. Fittingly, his death came while he was riding a train.

SIXTEEN

Keeping Eisenhower's Invasion Afloat

ANDREW JACKSON HIGGINS

IN THE EARLY hours of June 6, 1944—D-day—an armada of sturdy wooden landing craft wallowed through heavy seas toward the beaches of the Baie de la Seine, a fifty-mile stretch of Normandy coast. The Brits, Yanks, and Canadians aboard the boats gazed apprehensively at the heavy black clouds hanging just above the distant hills, a scene as ominous as an El Greco landscape. The misty air shook from the fury of naval and aerial bombardment, the opening salvos in the Allies' massive amphibious assault on German-occupied France. The World War II offensive was an audacious undertaking, and success was the only option.

As they neared the shore, the landing craft, mostly American-built LCVPs and British-built LCAs—boats holding thirty-six combat troops each—dropped their bow ramps into the choppy, shallow water. Thousands of soldiers leaped into the sea and began the seemingly endless slog through the waist-deep surf. All sense of order was instantly lost as the men flailed about, some of them pulled under by their heavy packs, drowned without ever firing a shot. Thousands more were cut down by artillery and machine-gun fire from the German units dug in among the hills above the beaches.

The worst of the fighting was on Omaha Beach, one of five designated landing areas—and one of two, along with Utah Beach, assigned to American troops. Once ashore, the soldiers on Omaha Beach had to cross two hundred yards of mine-laced open ground, with nothing to shield them from the German barrage. The casualties here accounted for a third of the day's toll of 9,000 Allied troops killed or wounded. But the Allies established a vital foothold at Normandy on that stormy day in June. Some 160,000 soldiers were ferried ashore during D-day. Within two months, hundreds of thousands of additional troops would land on French soil to begin the long, arduous march on Nazi Germany.

The Normandy invasion was the largest and one of the most difficult amphibious operations in history, an assault involving over 12,000 warplanes and 5,000 ships and boats—the majority of those small landing craft. Heroism was commonplace, but a number of individuals stood out, from the officer who headed the operation—Supreme Allied Commander Gen. Dwight D. Eisenhower—to the twelve Americans who won the Congressional Medal of Honor at Normandy.

There was also one unlikely hero, a civilian who was involved behind the scenes. At the time of the invasion, he was in faraway New Orleans, but his contribution to the operation's success was incalculable. General Eisenhower, in fact, singled out him as "the man who won the war for us." The estimable gentleman Eisenhower was referring to was Andrew Jackson Higgins, a cantankerous Louisiana boatbuilder known by some as "The-Hell-It-Can't" Higgins for his self-confident, in-your-face determination. It was Higgins who designed and constructed the shallow-draft landing craft that made the Normandy invasion possible.

Higgins needed all of his feistiness and tenacity to get his landing craft built in the first place. When he originally offered to build the boats for the U.S. Navy, the top brass in Washington, D.C., basically told him to go jump in the ocean, but Higgins kept bulling ahead—the only way The-Hell-It-Can't Higgins knew how to do business. This irascible Irishman with a fondness for bourbon and a hatred of bureaucratic bull never hesitated to bend the rules or take a gamble to get things done. With his wavy brown hair, square jaw, and broad shoulders, Higgins looked like he could take care of himself in a fight. "A.J."—if you knew what was good for you, you wouldn't call him "Andy"—was the sort of cocky tough guy character that Clark Gable played throughout the 1930s and '40s.

Higgins was born in landlocked Columbus, Nebraska, in 1886, the son of a lawyer, judge, and newspaper editor who named his youngest child after one of his favorite presidents. Young A.J. showed an early interest in boats. Before he reached his teens, he refurbished a derelict sailboat, and he later built an iceboat in the family basement (he knocked out a section of wall to remove the finished iceboat while his mother was away shopping). Higgins also showed an early flair for business. At the age of nine, he began mowing lawns. He eventually owned a fleet of mowers and hired other kids to do the work. When he was twelve, he organized a newspaper delivery service, which brought in more than $100 a month—equivalent to $2,500 today. Higgins again hired other kids to do the labor, while he ran things and toted up the profits.

In 1906, the twenty-year-old Higgins moved to Mobile, Alabama, where he farmed, ran a small lumber operation, and met the love of his life, his "barefoot contessa," Angele Leona Cols-son. The two were married in 1908. For the next couple of years, Higgins worked at a variety of jobs, all chosen to prepare him for a career in the lumber industry. In 1910, he moved to New Orleans to manage a lumber-exporting firm. Five years later, he quit to start his own business, A. J. Higgins Lumber and Export Company. Higgins imported hardwood from Central America, Africa, and the Philippines, and he exported native cypress and southern pine. He needed boats to haul his lumber, so he assembled a fleet of sailing ships. Then he needed a shipyard to repair his watercraft and build new ones. Before he knew it, Higgins had become a full-fledged boatbuilder, turning out cargo vessels, tugs, and barges. By 1926, his boatbuilding business had become more lucrative than the lumber trade.

Throughout the late 1920s and early '30s, Higgins worked to develop the vessel that would make him famous—the Eureka boat. He designed the boat to negotiate the swamps and marshes of the Mississippi Delta and the shallow coastal waters of the Gulf of Mexico. Two innovations made the Eureka boat a success. To protect the craft's propeller from the weeds and debris often found in shallow water, Higgins located the prop inside a recessed channel along the bottom of the boat. To enable the vessel to slide onto shore and be backed up without getting stuck, he gave it a rounded, upturned "spoonbill" bow. The highly maneuverable craft could skim through shallow, swampy waterways with ease, making it the perfect boat for Louisiana's oil drillers and fur trappers.

Shallow-draft vessels became the mainstay of Higgins Industries, the dedicated boatbuilding operation Higgins formed in 1930. The company manufactured a variety of watercraft based on the Eureka design, all known for their high quality.

Higgins workboats plied waterways all along the Gulf Coast, as well as in the Amazon, the Persian Gulf, and the Far East. The Army Corps of Engineers, the Biological Survey, and the U.S. Coast Guard became loyal customers, along with another category of boating enthusiast—the rumrunners who flourished along the gulf during the Prohibition era. (Higgins took full advantage of his customers' competing interests. He persuaded the coast guard to use his shallow-draft vessels as patrol boats for chasing rumrunners, who unloaded their cargoes on deserted beaches at night. He then alerted the smugglers to the fact that the coast guard possessed faster boats than they did, resulting in additional sales. With no shortage of chutzpah, Higgins returned to the coast guard and offered to sell them an even speedier model!)

The biggest plum Higgins hoped to land was a contract with the U.S. Navy, which had been experimenting for years with boats designed for beach assaults by the marine corps, whose budget the navy controlled. Higgins made several trips to Washington to try to interest the navy's Bureau of Construction and Repair in his Eureka boat. The navy honchos he met with smiled and nodded and sent him on his way. The rough-talking, no-nonsense gent from New Orleans struck them as a presumptuous upstart.

Then in 1935, the navy announced it would entertain bids for the production of a landing craft. The evaluation of competing prototypes took years, and the navy showed a stubborn bias toward its own design and those of the big East Coast shipyards ("those smart bastards in the East and North," Higgins called them). However, in test after test, the Eureka boat proved to be the superior vessel. And Higgins had an ally in the marine corps, which was convinced that the Eureka boat came closest to fitting its requirements. Finally, in 1940, Higgins won a contract to build 335 boats based on his Eureka design. It was perfect timing. War had just broken out in Europe, and in December 1941, the United States was dragged into the conflict when Japan attacked Pearl Harbor. The navy's new LCVP (Landing Craft, Vehicle, Personnel)—or "Higgins boat," as it came to be called—would prove to be an invaluable weapon.

The thirty-six-foot LCVP was ideal for carrying troops, but the navy also needed a larger boat, or lighter, to carry tanks and other heavy equipment ashore. The navy had designed a tank lighter, but after examining the architectural drawings, Higgins reacted in his typical blunt manner. "This boat stinks," he scrawled across the plans. He then shocked navy officials even further. "I can give you a right nice sample lighter in three days," he announced. When one officer remarked that such a feat could never be done, Higgins fired back his famous reply: "The hell it can't. You just be here in three days." At the appointed time, navy officials showed up at Higgins's New Orleans plant, where a new forty-five-foot tank lighter awaited them. The boat had been designed and constructed in sixty-one hours. The navy immediately ordered fifty of the lighters, later designated as LCMs (Landing Craft, Mechanized).

In addition to landing craft, the Higgins factory built PT boats—fast seventy- to eighty-foot vessels used to harass enemy ships. (Future president John F. Kennedy became a hero while captaining a PT boat in the Pacific.) Higgins would do whatever it took to meet his navy contracts. To produce his first order of tank lighters on time, he was forced to "liberate" some scarce bronze material he needed from a Texas oil well supply depot—with Texas cops pursuing his men as they raced back to Louisiana with the goods. On another occasion, he dispatched a shipment of boats before they'd been painted, placing crews on the train to finish the work en route.

At its peak, Higgins Industries operated eight plants in New Orleans and employed more than twenty thousand workers, who turned out some seven hundred boats a month. With wartime labor shortages, Higgins hired women, African Americans, the handicapped, and the elderly. He exhorted his workers to achieve higher production goals over a public address system, and he hung this inspirational banner over his assembly line: THE GUY WHO RELAXES IS HELPING THE AXIS!

By the end of 1943, Higgins Industries had designed or built more than 90 percent of the U.S. Navy's fleet of 14,000 ships and boats. The company also supplied thousands of boats to other Allied navies. In all, Higgins Industries and its licensees produced 20,094 vessels for the Allied cause. Higgins's major contribution was the LCVP, the troop carriers used so successfully on the beaches of Normandy and in the Pacific. "If Higgins had not designed and built those LCVPs, we never could have landed over an open beach," said General Eisenhower. "The whole strategy of the war would have been different."

After World War II ended in 1945, Higgins continued to build workboats and pleasure craft. When the Korean War broke out in 1950, the federal government again turned to Higgins to manufacture boats for the military. The Korean conflict was still raging when A. J. Higgins died in August 1952 following a brief illness. He was just shy of his sixty-sixth birthday. His family kept the business going for a few years, but financial difficulties forced the sale of the company in 1959. Today, Andrew Jackson Higgins is memorialized at the National World War II Museum in downtown New Orleans, located on Andrew Higgins Drive. Higgins's hometown of Columbus, Nebraska, also honors its native son with the Higgins Memorial, and the state of Nebraska has named a section of U.S. Route 81 south of Columbus after the industrialist.

The U.S. Navy—whose hidebound bureaucracy did all it could to thwart the bull from Louisiana who upset their tidy china shop—finally acknowledged Higgins's invaluable wartime contributions by naming a ship in his honor. The USNS *Andrew J. Higgins*, a fleet oiler, was commissioned in 1987. (The ship has since been decommissioned and was sold to the Chilean navy in 2009.)

Higgins's most enduring legacy is the thousands of lives he saved by providing American troops with an efficient landing craft. Without the Higgins boat, beach assaults would have been far more cumbersome, with soldiers exposed to enemy fire for longer periods of time. The Marines were aware of Higgins's accomplishments. "There would not have been a Normandy or an Okinawa or an Iwo Jima without that boat," said the son of Lt. Gen. Victor H. Krulak, the marine who first suggested the retractable bow ramp for the LCVP.

General Krulak appreciated the fact that Higgins had taken on the military bureaucracy, which Krulak described as "a more formidable battlefield than many the corps has known." Krulak called Higgins "the Marines' kind of man." The scrappy Irish boatbuilder certainly incurred his share of battle scars. He was knocked around by repeated financial wipeouts, federal bean counters, and big-time labor bosses—but he always bounced back. You'd expect nothing less from a guy called The-Hell-It-Can't Higgins.

SEVENTEEN

The Lovely with the Lovely Brain

HEDWIG KIESLER

ONCE UPON A TIME in a fairytale town called Hollywood, there lived a lovely young princess. With her raven hair and regal bearing, she was called the most beautiful girl in the world. Her name was Hedwig Eva Maria Kiesler. In Hollywood, though, that sort of challenging moniker doesn't go over well, so a powerful lord named Louis B. Mayer made her change it. She chose the name Hedy Lamarr.

Miss Hedy Lamarr became a silver screen goddess, appearing in over thirty films. She first made a splash in the 1933 European movie *Ecstasy*—frolicking naked in the woods and contorting her face orgasmically, to the indignation of American censors. In Hollywood, she appeared opposite Clark Gable, Spencer Tracy, and Charles Boyer. Her biggest role was in Cecil B. DeMille's 1949 costume epic *Samson and Delilah*, in which she played strongman Victor Mature's barber. She married six times and got a star on Hollywood Boulevard, which proves she was a big deal in her day. She made her last movie in 1958, then slid into semi-obscure retirement in Florida, popping into the news briefly in 1965 and 1991 when she was charged with shoplifting. Her autobiography, *Ecstasy and Me*, came out in 1966.

That was the Hedy Lamarr everyone knew.

The other, little-known, Hedy Lamarr—the one who proved to be the polar opposite of a flighty, husband-a-month Hollywood actress—had a mind filled with details about military armaments. How she came by that knowledge, and what she later did with it, would make a thrilling movie—although parts of it might be hard to believe.

To know the secret Hedy, you have to go back to her pre-Hollywood life, when she was still Hedy Kiesler. Born in Vienna in 1914 (there's some dispute about the year), she was the only child of a bank director and his concert pianist wife, both members of Europe's Jewish aristocracy. Hedy attended private schools, took piano and ballet lessons, and studied design in finishing school. Afterward, she enrolled in drama classes in Berlin, which led to stage roles and movie parts. When she was nineteen, she landed the part that made her famous, playing the love-starved young wife of a withdrawn older man in the Czech film *Ecstasy*. Following her naked romp in the woods in *Ecstasy*, her life took a fateful turn.

In August 1933, Hedy married Austrian arms manufacturer Friedrich Mandl. Mandl was a wealthy but shady character, willing to peddle weapons to anyone. To get around the restrictions of the Treaty of Versailles, which outlawed the manufacture of armaments in Germany or Austria after World War I, Mandl set up satellite plants in Switzerland, Poland, and Holland. He sold weapons illegally to Hungary in the early 1930s and supplied arms for the Italian invasion of Ethiopia in 1935 and the Spanish Civil War the following year. A supporter of Austria's fascist movement, Mandl invited Hitler and Mussolini to his extravagant parties. (Palling around with Hitler didn't do the half-Jewish Mandl much good; in 1938, Germany confiscated his property and Mandl fled to Argentina, where he once again began manufacturing weapons of war—proving that you can't keep a bad man down.)

Extremely jealous, Mandl tried to buy up every copy of *Ecstasy* to prevent people from seeing his wife naked, but that horse was out of the barn and miles down the road. A control freak as well, Mandl restricted Hedy's movements, often taking her to business meetings and client dinners so he could keep an eye on her. Hedy was a quick learner, and, having nothing better to do, she listened as Mandl discussed weapons with his customers and technicians. She soon knew the intricate workings of Mandl's products—shells, grenades, and military aircraft. Mandl also had an interest in weapons control systems, and Hedy would later put her grasp of that technology to good use.

By 1937, Hedy had reached her limits with Herr Mandl and his fascist cronies. She fled to Paris and got a divorce. Not long afterward, she was in Hollywood, with a new name and a new contract with MGM Studios, both courtesy of movie mogul Louis B. Mayer. The next two decades cemented Hedy Lamarr's fame as an American actress (she became a naturalized citizen in 1953). She had critical success in the film *Algiers* and commercial success in *Samson and Delilah*. Her public persona was that of a glamorous star, but those who knew her well spoke of a humorous, down-to-earth woman who was far more than a pretty face. Though she gladly took the roles of the sultry siren, Lamarr often mocked them, famously stating, "Any girl can be glamorous. All she has to do is stand still and look stupid."

Lamarr's life took another turn in 1940 when she attended a dinner party at the home of actress Janet Gaynor. Lamarr fell into conversation with avant-garde composer and pianist George Antheil, the self-styled "bad boy of music." Born in the United States, he'd spent most of the 1920s in Europe, becoming part of the Paris art scene while writing his percussive style of "mechanistic" music. His first major work, *Ballet Mécanique*, was written for sixteen synchronized player pianos, plus automated bells, xylophones, bass drums, and a siren—all playing over the noise of two whirling airplane propellers. At the Paris debut of his jarring compositions *Airplane Sonata*, *Sonata Sauvage*, and *Mechanisms*, appalled audience members started rioting halfway through the program—to Antheil's complete delight. He loved to cause a scene. He sometimes began his performances by pulling out a revolver and placing it conspicuously on the piano. On several occasions, he injured himself with his wild pounding on the keyboard.

Antheil was a man of wide interests. Since 1935, he'd made a living writing Hollywood film scores. He also found time to pen a mystery novel, write a column for *Modern Music* magazine, churn out a nationally syndicated newspaper advice column, and contribute regularly to *Esquire*, *Coronet*, and other magazines. One of his areas of expertise, strangely enough, was female endocrinology, a topic he and Lamarr discussed. (She asked him how she could make her breasts larger; he recommended glandular extracts.)

Lamarr invited Antheil to dinner at her home, where they talked about the war in Europe. Antheil was keenly interested in the conflict, having just written a pamphlet called *The Shape of the War to Come*, in which he predicted the involvement of the United States in the fighting. Because German U-boats were attacking Allied ships in 1940, the subject of torpedoes came up. Lamarr told Antheil how torpedoes work, having learned about them from Friedrich Mandl. She also mentioned that she'd been thinking about a new technology that could be used to create a more accurate torpedo, something that might interest the U.S. government.

Lamarr explained that conventional torpedoes often went astray because of tricky ocean currents and the evasive actions of their targets. The result was a costly waste of munitions. A torpedo guided by radio signals, on the other hand, would be deadly accurate. But such a torpedo had a major stumbling block: radio signals are easily detected and jammed. Lamarr's solution to that problem was called "frequency hopping"—broadcasting over a random series of frequencies that change at split-second intervals, with the receiver synchronized to follow the frequency changes. Anyone trying to monitor the broadcast would only pick up a series of meaningless blips. Attempts to jam the signals would be useless, since even if an enemy blocked one frequency, that would only disrupt a tiny part of the transmission.

The concept of frequency hopping originated around 1900, when Nikola Tesla was wrestling with the problem of secure transmissions for a radio-controlled submersible boat he was working on. Lamarr had likely heard her first husband discussing the theory with his associates. It was still a revolutionary idea, far ahead of its time. Lamarr's application of frequency hopping to a torpedo guidance system was a significant step in developing the technology.

Antheil started making schematic drawings of the proposed system. It occurred to him that the rapid changes in frequencies could be synchronized with slotted paper rolls—the same way he'd synchronized his sixteen player pianos in *Ballet Mécanique*. He even suggested broadcasting over eighty-eight frequencies, the same as the number of keys on a piano. After noodling with the idea a bit more, Lamarr and Antheil sent a description of the concept to the National Inventors Council, which had recently been set up in Washington, D.C., to gather technical innovations from the general public. The council encouraged the pair, recommending that they develop the idea to the point that it could be patented. With the help of an electrical engineer from Caltech, that's what they did, receiving a patent in August 1942. By then, the United States had entered World War II.

Unfortunately, when Lamarr and Antheil presented their concept to the U.S. Navy, it was rejected as impractical. Antheil thought their chances had been hurt when he pointed out that their synchronization mechanism was essentially a player piano roll: "'My God,' I can see them saying, 'we shall put a player piano in a torpedo.'" The navy politely suggested that Miss Lamarr stick to acting, saying she could help the war effort more by capitalizing on her fame than by playing inventor. Lamarr responded by selling $7 million in war bonds in a single evening—proving the navy right on at least one count.

After their idea was shelved, Lamarr and Antheil went back to their regular lives. They'd simply wanted to help the war effort, but if the military couldn't use their idea, then that was that. The concept of frequency hopping lay dormant until the 1950s, when several laboratories engaged in military research began experimenting with the technology. Engineers developed electronics to synchronize the rapid shifts in frequencies, and they increased the bandwidth of signals with a technique called "spread spectrum," which reduces interference and permits increased traffic over the same frequencies.

In 1962, U.S. Navy ships blockading Cuba used the technology to provide secure communications. Since the 1980s, spread spectrum technology has fueled the explosive growth of the wireless communications industry. It's the innovation behind cellular and cordless phones, GPS devices, and wireless computer networks. The military uses the technology in countless systems, including its multibillion-dollar Milstar defense communications satellites.

Today, every time someone uses a cell phone, they're paying tribute to Hedy Lamarr. But because Lamarr and Antheil's patent on frequency hopping expired in 1959, they never made a cent from the concept, even though later patents acknowledged their work as the foundation of the field. Lamarr once expressed mild displeasure at not receiving anything for her contribution. "Never a letter, never a thank-you, never money," she said. "I don't know. I guess they just take and forget about a person." (She did acquire some stock from a wireless technology developer in 1998, in exchange for a 49 percent interest in her patent rights.)

But people hadn't forgotten about Hedy Lamarr's surprising achievement. A few years before her death in January 2000, she was honored with three significant awards given to technological innovators. In March 1997, she received the Electronic Frontier Foundation Pioneer Award (George Antheil was recognized posthumously; he died in 1959). In August 1997, Lamarr became the first female to receive the so-called Oscar of inventing—the Gnass Spirit of Achievement Award, or "Bulbie" (the bronze award is shaped like a light bulb in homage to Thomas Edison). In 1998, she was given the Viktor Kaplan Medal, Austria's highest award for inventors.

We owe a big debt to the beautiful and brilliant Hedwig Eva Maria Kiesler. As the famous Hedy Lamarr, she lit up the screen with her exotic, sophisticated presence. As the everyday Hedy, she put her mind to the task of aiding her adopted country. Her effort to improve U.S. military capabilities was no showy demonstration of loyalty. Motivated by the same concerns as any other citizen, she stepped down from her Hollywood pedestal and did her patriotic duty without fanfare. On the patent application for the new torpedo guidance system, she unpretentiously listed her married name at the time, Hedy Kiesler Markey. The public had no inkling of what she'd done.

Though she couldn't have known it that evening in 1940 when she sat down to dinner with George Antheil, Hedy Lamarr was pioneering a technology that would usher in a new age of wireless communication. It just took a few decades for the rest of the world to catch up.

EIGHTEEN

Choctaw Code Talker of World War I

SOLOMON LOUIS

CORPORAL SOLOMON Bond Louis huddled in the narrow fortified trench along with other members of Company E, gripping his Springfield rifle with sweaty hands. The young Choctaw Indian had expected the fighting to be bad when he'd enlisted, but the warfare along Europe's Western Front was brutal beyond belief. Louis's outfit, the 142nd Infantry Regiment, had arrived in France in July 1918. Over the following three months, the Americans had seen some of the worst fighting in a war noted for its savagery. Ever since the conflict began in the summer of 1914, the German army and the Allied forces led by France and Britain had been battering each other like punch-drunk boxers, spread out along a line of battle that snaked across Belgium and northeastern France all the way to the Swiss border.

The shrieks of incoming artillery shells assaulted Corporal Louis's ears, their deafening explosions shaking the earth beneath his feet. Just overhead, a curtain of bullets and shrapnel sizzled on the air like high-voltage electricity. Amid the mayhem, Louis stayed alert for any shouts warning of deadly mustard gas, a nearly odorless poison that left its victims blinded and retching for weeks until they finally choked to death, their throat and lungs burned and blistered.

War here was an exercise in futility. Both sides clung fiercely to their bits of wasted terrain, a cratered lunar landscape. The constant bombardment had stripped the soil bare, leaving splintered black tree stumps rearing up like startled witches. Again and again, ranks of exhausted men staggered across this nightmarish battlefield to gain a few yards of ground, only to give it back in the next counterattack. Bodies were scattered everywhere—tangled in coils of razor wire, heaped at the bottom of trenches, lying askew wherever they fell during the pointless charges across no-man's-land, mowed down by the ceaselessly stuttering machine guns.

The Yanks arrayed along the front had come late to the fight against Germany. The first troops of the American Expeditionary Force arrived in Europe in June 1917, under the command of Gen. John J. Pershing. For Solomon Louis, this was a war he could have avoided. Like most Native Americans, Choctaw Indians had never been granted U.S. citizenship (that wouldn't come until 1924). Born in Bryan County, Oklahoma, Louis had attended a boarding school for Choctaw orphans. When the United States entered the war, he wasn't old enough to join the military, but after his friends signed up, he lied that he was eighteen so he could enlist along with them. That wasn't his only impulsive move: during basic training at Fort Sill, Oklahoma, Louis was asked for his next of kin, information gathered from all servicemen in case they were killed or wounded. Since he had no kin that he knew of, Louis sent for a Choctaw girl he'd met at a school football game and married her on the spot.

Corporal Louis's regiment, part of the Thirty-sixth Division, was made up of National Guard troops from Oklahoma and Texas. Besides having a considerable number of Choctaws in its ranks, the 142nd Infantry included members of thirteen other tribes—Arapaho, Caddo, Cherokee, Cheyenne, Chickasaw, Creek, Delaware, Osage, Peoria, Ponca, Quapaw, Seminole, and Shawnee. In all, more than fourteen thousand Native Americans would serve during World War I. (From that time to the present, Native Americans have volunteered at a far higher rate than any other segment of the population. According to Native American veterans, they serve to safeguard their homelands, which, as the original "green" Americans, Native peoples have always held sacred.) For Louis and the other Choctaw soldiers, warfare wasn't a significant part of their heritage, being an agrarian people. In the early 1830s, most of the tribe had been relocated to Oklahoma from their original territory in the southeastern United States—the first Native Americans forced onto the infamous Trail of Tears.

Right now, Louis and his fellow doughboys were negotiating a different sort of trail. In late September 1918, they'd been tossed into the maw of the Meuse-Argonne offensive, part of the last big Allied push of the war. Orchestrated by France's Marshall Ferdinand Foch, the supreme commander of the Allies, the series of advances stretched along the entire Western Front, with regional commands made up of various Allied armies. The bulk of General Pershing's troops, bolstered by French forces, were assigned to the sector between the cities of Nancy and Sedan, a swath encompassing the Meuse River and the Argonne Forest. The fighting here was going badly for the Americans. Over half of their soldiers had never seen combat before, and leadership and logistical problems complicated the effort to capture their main target, Sedan, a vital rail link in the German supply line.

By late October, the 142nd Infantry had reached the town

of Chardeny. The Germans were dug in not far away, among the wooded hills of the Forest Ferme, located along the Aisne River on the western fringe of the Argonne Forest. Intending to attack the German position, the Americans found their efforts compromised by their inability to establish secure communications. The Germans repeatedly tapped their telephone lines, intercepted their radio signals, and captured one out of every four messengers dispatched between field commands. Even coded communications weren't safe. German analysts easily decoded every encryption system the Americans tried. As a result, the Germans were always one step ahead of the Americans, anticipating their troop movements and discovering the location of their supply depots, which they immediately shelled. The frustrated American commanders were desperate for a solution. The remedy, it turned out, was astoundingly simple. It had been right before their eyes—or, more accurately, their ears—all along.

By chance, one of the 142nd's company commanders, a Captain Lawrence, overheard a conversation between Solomon Louis and another Choctaw soldier, Private Mitchell Bobb. The two men were speaking in their native tongue, a so-called obsolete language that Choctaw schoolchildren were forbidden to speak, since it was considered an embarrassing relic that hindered the process of assimilation. As Captain Lawrence listened to the two soldiers yakking away in their mystifying language, he suddenly realized that the Germans would never be able to decipher messages conveyed in Choctaw. The language had twenty-six dialects, and only four or five of them had ever been written down. The Germans would have no vocabulary list or grammar books to consult, and since Choctaw wasn't Latin-based, it would be impossible to extrapolate the language's meaning.

Lawrence asked Solomon Louis how many Choctaw speakers were in his battalion. Louis conferred with Bobb and reported that they knew of eight fluent speakers. "Are there any of them over in headquarters company?" Lawrence asked. "I think that Carterby and Maytubby are over there," Louis replied. The captain telephoned the commanding officer of the 142nd, Col. Alfred W. Bloor, and confirmed that Ben Carterby and Pete Maytubby were assigned to headquarters company. Lawrence asked Colonel Bloor to have the two Choctaws stand by. "I've got an idea that just might get these [Germans] off our backs."

Captain Lawrence wrote out a message in English and asked Private Bobb to deliver it over the telephone in Choctaw. At the other end, Ben Carterby received the message and translated it for Colonel Bloor. *Voilà.* Native American code talking had just been invented. In only a few hours, the eight Choctaw speakers Louis identified were reassigned so that there was one in each field company headquarters. Soon afterward, ten more fluent Choctaw speakers were found and assigned as code talkers, with Solomon Louis heading up the detail. Louis himself was posted to division headquarters, where he could receive messages from the front lines.

The first operational use of the code talkers came on October 26, when the Choctaws transmitted a message concerning Allied troop movements between Chufilly and Chardeny. The Germans were clearly flummoxed by the chattering Choctaws, since the operation came off as planned. The next day, the Americans attacked Forest Ferme. The assault's success was largely due to the element of surprise, again thanks to the use of the Choctaw code talkers. A captured German officer admitted that his analysts had been stymied by the strange "code" they'd overheard. The officer asked about the nationality of the men who'd been speaking on the telephone. "They were only Americans," he was told.

Because the Choctaw language doesn't contain precise translations for many English words, a set of equivalent terms had to be invented for the code talkers' use. Artillery became "big gun" in Choctaw. "Little gun shoot fast" indicated a machine gun. "Arrows" meant ammunition; "stones" meant grenades; "scalps" meant casualties; and "bad air" stood for mustard gas. "One grain of corn" meant the First Battalion, "two grains of corn" the Second Battalion, "three grains of corn" the Third. "Bow" represented a company, "thong" a platoon, and "many scouts" a patrol. Even if the Germans had been able to translate these Choctaw substitutions, they'd have been bewildered. Imagine overhearing a report that "a thong from two grains of corn had inflicted heavy scalps with stones." The eavesdroppers would have been reaching for their schnapps.

The code talkers' effectiveness was beyond question, and though their use came in the waning days of the war, they contributed materially to the success of the Meuse-Argonne offensive, the largest operation involving American troops and the Yanks' biggest victory. The offensive also proved to be the costliest for American forces, with nearly 27,000 men killed and almost 96,000 wounded. Although it was only one part of the final grand offensive all along the Western Front, the Meuse-Argonne campaign was instrumental in the German defeat. Solomon Louis and the other Choctaw code talkers could be justifiably proud of the part they played in the final offensive. Only a few days after the men began conveying telephone, radio, and written messages in Choctaw, the tide of battle shifted, putting the Germans on the run. Within two weeks, the Germans sued for peace, and on November 11, 1918, the war ended.

The Choctaws' commanding officers praised their efforts, assuring them that they'd be given medals for what they'd done, although the men never received any awards. In the tumultuous aftermath of the war, the deeds of a small band of Native Americans were easily overlooked. The 142nd Infantry sailed for home on May 20, 1919. In mid-July, the men paraded through Oklahoma City, and a few days later they mustered out, civilians once more. For decades, few people knew of the code talkers' unique contribution to the war. Military officials had sworn the Choctaws to secrecy to prevent foreign powers from learning about the wartime use of their language, in case it needed to be used again in future conflicts. In some instances, even family members were unaware of what the men had done. (Somehow, Adolf Hitler learned of the Choctaw code talkers and dispatched a team of anthropologists to study Native American languages before World War II, although the abundance of languages and dialects and their complexity made it impossible for the Germans to gain much useful information. During the war, Comanche code talkers referred to Hitler as "crazy white man.")

The secret of the Choctaws gradually emerged, but not until after another group of Native Americans became famous as code talkers during World War II. Following the successful example of the Choctaws, Navajo soldiers used their own native language to thwart the enemy, this time the Japanese. Navajo code talkers facilitated several American victories in the Pacific, including the Marines' hard-fought triumph on Iwo Jima. The Navajos' exploits were declassified in the late 1960s, and the soldiers were honored by President Ronald Reagan in 1982. In 2000, the Navajos received Congressional Gold Medals. Two years later, Navajo code talkers figured in the movie

Windtalkers. As far as the public knew, Navajos were the one and only code talkers.

While Choctaw tribal members and historians were aware of the pioneering role the Choctaw code talkers played in World War I, the U.S. government seemed oblivious to their achievement. In 1986, the Choctaw Nation took the initiative, granting the code talkers medals of valor and erecting a monument in their memory on the grounds of the Choctaw capitol building near Tuskahoma, Oklahoma. In 1989, France made the men knights of the National Order of Merit, one of that nation's highest honors. In 2007, Texas awarded the Choctaw code talkers the Lone Star Medal of Valor and opened a permanent exhibit about them at the Texas Military Forces Museum in Austin.

At long last—after ninety years—word finally trickled in to the federal government that a group of Native American heroes had been overlooked. In 2008, President George Bush signed the Code Talkers Recognition Act into law, authorizing Congressional Gold Medals for the eighteen original Choctaw code talkers. Today, an even greater tribute is being paid to the men: their language—once banned from public schools—is now proudly taught over the Internet and in dozens of elementary schools, colleges, and community centers.

Solomon Louis would no doubt have been thrilled by the long-overdue recognition he and his friends received. Present at the inception of the Choctaw's groundbreaking wartime service, Louis outlived all his fellow World War I code talkers. After settling down in Bennington, Oklahoma, with his wife, Mary, Louis lived into his eighties, passing away around 1982.

The precedent that Louis and his brethren set in 1918 led directly to the full-scale military project that took place during World War II, when individuals from over a dozen tribes, including Choctaws, were utilized as code talkers, many of them recruited and trained specifically for that purpose. Through the use of their mother tongues, hundreds of Native Americans have been able to help the United States win two wars—and all because someone happened to overhear young Solomon Louis chewing the fat with his Choctaw buddy.

NINETEEN

A Thorn in the Side of Convention

ANNE ROYALL

THE BEST STORY told about journalist Anne Royall isn't true, although it fits her character perfectly. According to legend, Royall wanted to interview President John Quincy Adams but had been denied access. Knowing that the president bathed in the Potomac River each morning, Royall supposedly waited until Adams was happily splashing about one day, then she sat on his clothes on the riverbank and refused to budge until he answered her questions.

It's a great anecdote, but Royall didn't need to waylay the president in order to talk with him. The two had become friends soon after Royall arrived in Washington, D.C., in 1824. The apocryphal tale may have gotten started because it represented just the type of resort-to-any-means journalism that Anne Royall practiced. She wasn't intimidated by power or privilege. For more than two decades, she roamed the halls of Congress and haunted federal office buildings, badgering people, charming them, or simply raising hell until she got her stories.

Dubbed "the grandma of the muckrakers," Royall set a new standard for journalistic vigilance in the public interest. She was relentless in sniffing out corruption, fraud, and incompetence. Government officials routinely ducked down corridors or cowered behind closed doors when the little old lady with the green umbrella and the hectoring voice was on the prowl. Her constant, predatory smile revealed a set of gleaming white teeth that seemed poised to take a bite out of something. She was like a fierce old mongoose circling a snake.

The impoverished widow of a Revolutionary War officer, Royall had originally come to Washington to petition Congress for a pension. One of the first important men she met was Adams, who was then secretary of state in the Monroe administration. Adams saw beyond her shabby clothing and took a liking to the small, wrinkled-faced woman with the piercing blue eyes. He backed her petition, and even invited Royall to call on his wife, Louisa, who gave her a new white shawl. Later, Royall visited Adams's father, John Adams, the country's second president, who was living in Massachusetts.

As a child, this irrepressible journalist probably never imagined that one day she'd be hobnobbing with bluebloods. Born in colonial Maryland in 1769, Anne Newport grew up in a log cabin in the wilds of western Pennsylvania. In her book *Letters from Alabama*, she described a childhood of poverty and danger: "I suffered all that human nature could bear, both with cold and hunger. . . . Often running for our lives to the forts, Indians pursuing and shooting at us. At other times lying concealed in brushwood, exposed to rain and snakes, for days and nights without food, and almost without clothes."

The hard life in Pennsylvania took its toll. Anne's father died when she was a young girl. Her mother got married again, to a man named Butler, but he died after a few years as well. Sick and destitute, Anne's mother set off with her three children for a better life in western Virginia. They eventually settled in the Staunton area, where Anne's mother found work in the household of William Royall, a wealthy landowner with a fine home on Sweet Springs Mountain. Anne was sixteen at the time.

Born to an aristocratic family, William Royall had served in the American Revolution under General Lafayette, attaining the rank of captain. He was an educated, generous man, and he gave Anne the run of his considerable library. Suddenly Anne was immersed in the heady world of the Enlightenment. Royall introduced her to the thinking of Voltaire, Thomas Jefferson, and Thomas Paine. A Freemason and a deist, Royall imparted his own liberal views on democracy and religion.

In 1797, Royall asked Anne to marry him. She was twenty-eight; he was around fifty. For the next sixteen years, Anne was the mistress of a lively, cultured household. The Royalls' guests included George Washington, Thomas Jefferson, and a number of foreign dignitaries. William Royall included his wife in all their dinnertime conversations, which no doubt helped her overcome any reservations about her humble origins.

In 1813, William Royall passed away, leaving his estate to Anne. The couple had no children, and after a few years, Anne grew weary of life alone on Sweet Springs Mountain. In 1817, she set off on a journey to Alabama. Except for a brief trip back home in 1819, Anne stayed in Alabama until 1823. That year, her life was turned upside down when William Royall's family broke his will, leaving Anne penniless at the age of fifty-four. The only recourse she had was to go to Washington and petition Congress for a pension as the widow of a war veteran. Even with the backing of John Quincy Adams, Royall lost her plea before Congress. Destitute and alone, Royall had to come up with a means of survival. She decided to become a writer.

For the next seven years, Royall traveled throughout the East—by stagecoach, boat, and foot—cataloging her journeys in ten volumes of nonfiction (and writing one long-winded novel). As she traveled, she peddled her existing books from her trunk and sold her upcoming books in advance by subscription. She journeyed as far west as St. Louis and ventured north into Canada. She braved malaria in New Orleans and a blizzard in Maine. She laughed at seasickness and walked until her shoes fell apart. She encountered cheating coachmen and tavern-keepers, and put them in their place with her sharp tongue. She never made much money from her work— she was sometimes reduced to begging in the streets and often fell back on the generosity of local Masons—but she never lost her love of travel.

In her first published work, *Sketches of History, Life and Manners in the United States*, which came out in 1826, she described the attraction of a life on the road: "To the homeless traveller, no pleasure is equal to that which he feels, when, after paying his fare to a certain place, he takes his seat in the stage. Here at least, he is at home. The thought that he is for the time being, sole proprietor of the small space he occupies, gives him an independence which he feels no where else."

While her books were well known in her time—she sought out publicity wherever she went—they're of little interest today other than to historians. It's hard to slog through them, since she seemed to write about *everything* she encountered— every person she met, every building she saw, every road she traveled, every stream she crossed, everything she heard, felt, smelled, or tasted. It's no wonder she's been called America's first blogger.

Her writing veered from tedious to prescient to charming to

vitriolic to hilarious. You never knew what would pop into her head, and you get the feeling that she exercised little control over the torrent of words that flowed from her pen. It's easy to picture her looking over some particularly wicked piece of invective she'd just written and cackling madly, delighted at the prospect of shocking her readers.

She could loftily opine about public gardens or monuments one moment, then fire off a zinger like this: "The young doctor of Knoxville, in a few words, was a pert little fop, and an ignoramus besides." In *Letters from Alabama*, she described the local soil in loving detail: "From Mount Sterling to Danville, called first rate land, it is generally black as your hat, but in many places, for instance on the margin of creeks, it has a grayish color, and resembles calcined stone, and has a light crumbling appearance; the growth is locust, cherry, and walnut." A few pages away, she took a hatchet to the daughter of one of her hosts, dismissing her as "an awkward lump of mortality." With a straight face, she tweaked an overbearing rube from Norfolk by inquiring about the welfare of the city's "numerous and respectable" Lobster family.

Royall advocated many causes in her writing. She supported public education, scientific research, liberal immigration laws, the rights of women and Native Americans, and public assistance for the old and infirm. She opposed slavery, flogging in the navy, the monopolistic Bank of the United States, and all forms of government corruption. Her grand crusade was for the separation of church and state. She was leery of organized religion, specifically evangelical Christianity. A deist like her husband, she believed in God but rejected the "narrow mind which is attached to a sect or part, to the exclusion of the rest of mankind." She called religious foes "blue skins," "black coats," and

"Holy Willies," and she accused evangelicals of being money-grubbing hypocrites who preached the Bible and lived in sin. She even claimed that she didn't read the Bible for fear it would make her as sinful as Christians.

Naturally such writing infuriated Protestants. At the time, there was a concerted effort among conservative Christians to increase their influence over the government (imagine that). Wherever Royall traveled, she was reviled by evangelicals as a heathen, an infidel. Her books were destroyed, and she was routinely harassed. The worst encounter happened in Burlington, Vermont, in 1827, when a devout, humorless storekeeper named Hecock shoved Royall down some icy steps, breaking her leg and dislocating her ankle. She was confined to her room in Burlington for several months before she was able to return home.

Once Royall got back to Washington, her troubles continued. Ever since she'd moved to Washington, she'd had a running feud with a group of Presbyterians who held their services in a firehouse close to her home on Capitol Hill. Royall claimed that the "Holy Willies" sent their children to pelt her windows with stones at night, and that members of the congregation stood in front of her house praying for her soul. She paid them back with curses and abuse. She got in the face of the congregation's leader, John Coyle, and called him "a damned old bald headed son of a bitch." She wrote that another prominent member of the group, a man she called "Love Lady," was seen in Capital Park "while he was in the act of converting a colored woman." She added demurely, "They were both in a state of nature." She even hinted that one of the men had gotten her hired girl pregnant.

This bickering came to a head in the summer of 1829, when

the congregation filed suit against Royall for being a public nuisance and disturber of the peace. Royall was brought before the Circuit Court of the District of Columbia on the archaic charge of being "a common scold." The trial was a farce, but it attracted a good deal of attention—chiefly for its comic value. One writer likened it to the sort of trial that inmates in an asylum might conduct. Apparently few people other than the dour Presbyterians took the proceeding seriously.

The handful of witnesses who testified against Royall painted her as the devil incarnate. Royall's own witnesses sent the courtroom into peals of laughter. Royall fired off one-liners that would make Don Rickles proud. She commented that one of her judges had a face "that resembles a country road after the passage of a troop of hogs," and that another's had "a good deal of the pumpkin in it." Royall said the trial was so preposterous that it deserved to be commemorated with a painting in the Capitol rotunda.

Even though Secretary of War John Eaton testified on Royall's behalf, the court found the fractious old lady guilty. The traditional punishment for a common scold was the ducking stool, and although one of the contraptions was built down at the Washington navy yard, the court decided that a fine of $10 would do, plus a $50 bond to ensure that Mrs. Royall behaved herself.

Anne Royall probably hadn't seen $10 at one time in years, let alone $60. To her good fortune, two Washington newspapermen paid the fine and Secretary Eaton put up her bond. The notoriety of the trial sparked the sale of Royall's writing, so she set off on another trip to promote her books and gather material for a new work. She returned from her journey in 1831 and completed the last of her travel books, *Mrs. Royall's Southern Tour*. Afterward, she embarked on the next phase of her life. In December 1831, at the age of sixty-two, she launched a newspaper called *Paul Pry*. (Paul Pry was a mischievous, eternally curious character in a contemporary British play by John Poole.)

Like all of her previous publications, Royall's newspaper was a means of earning a living. (Royall had renewed her plea for a pension during every session of Congress but had never been granted any financial support.) The newspaper also provided a platform for Royall's causes. In her first issue, she stated her purpose: "The welfare and happiness of our country is our politics. To promote this we shall oppose all and every species of political evil, and religious frauds without fear, favor or affection. . . . We shall advocate the liberty of the Press, the liberty of Speech, and the liberty of Conscience."

Royall printed the paper in her kitchen, assisted by orphans she'd taken in and a friend named Sally Stack. Each four-page weekly issue contained a mishmash of news and personal opinion, with plenty of venom directed at the pious and at government malfeasance of all stripes—graft, nepotism, and incompetence being favorite targets. Royall ran jokes and frequent letters to the editor with long replies. She interviewed everyone she could in government and reported their views, and if she believed they were up to no good, she printed their names and salaries and told what she thought of them. Royall was the first to expose fraud in the U.S. Post Office and in the handling of Indian lands in Georgia and other southern states, and she took on big bankers and the beef monopoly. Naturally, people began dodging her. One day she called on the commandant of the navy yard, Isaac Hull, a man she'd previously butted heads with. Hull had his servant tell her that he was sick, to which Mrs. Royall replied, "Is there any hope of his death?"

In 1836, Royall ceased publication of *Paul Pry*. She'd riled up so many people that the post office stopped delivering her paper. Royall waited two weeks, then launched a second newspaper called *The Huntress*, which she distributed privately. The name of her new publication more accurately reflected her mission—she was always on the hunt for the enemies of democracy and enlightenment. (During her newspapering years, Royall also wrote a play, a comedy called *The Cabinet, or Large Parties in Washington*. The "Holy Willies" tried to suppress it, but her Masonic friends helped her stage the play.)

Royall continued to fight for the separation of church and state. She advocated the establishment of the Smithsonian Institution. She helped inventor Samuel Morse obtain funds from Congress and stood at his side when he demonstrated his telegraph. She met every president from George Washington to Franklin Pierce, becoming the first journalist to interview and quote a chief executive. Though the circulation of her newspapers was always small, her influence was significant, and when she died in 1854 at the age of eighty-five, Washington and the nation lost a unique voice. At times strident and unreasonable, she was also honest and direct. No one ever questioned where Anne Royall stood. Above all, she never stopped fighting for freedom and human dignity, and she did it in the best journalistic tradition—by holding government officials' feet to the fire. In the process, she invented a new form of no-holds-barred investigative journalism that made what preceded it seem tepid. Still studied in journalism schools, she remains the revered prototype of a relentless government watchdog.

Six years before her death, Royall finally received her widow's pension. In 1848, Congress paid her a lump sum of $1,200. Her creditors and the family of her husband succeeded in claiming the entire amount except for $10. When Royall passed away, she possessed 31 cents and owed $6 in back rent. She lay in an unmarked grave in Washington's Congressional Cemetery until 1911, when a group of admirers erected a tombstone in her honor, a long overdue tribute to a truly original character.

TWENTY

The Man Behind the Checkout Counter

CLARENCE SAUNDERS

WEDNESDAY, SEPTEMBER 6, 1916, was just an ordinary summer day in Memphis, Tennessee. Folks went about their lives as usual, perhaps browsing the new $15 fall dresses that had recently come in down at the Gerber clothing store, or taking a test drive in a new Chevrolet motorcar—only $490 (including electric starter and lights!). Most people had the war in Europe on their mind, reading daily reports filled with unfamiliar names like the Somme, the Carpathians, and Turkish Armenia. But the news wasn't all bad. Ty Cobb had regained his winning form for the Detroit Tigers, which he attributed in advertisements to the miraculous effects of Nuxated Iron tonic.

As ordinary as September 6 seemed, though, it turned out to be a day on which the settled order of things changed forever. Admittedly it was a small change, but it would soon have people wondering why they ever did things differently. That day, thirty-five-year-old businessman Clarence Saunders opened a grocery store, his first, at 79 Jefferson Avenue. Saunders's store bore a curious name, Piggly Wiggly, and it ushered in a new way of retail shopping called self-service. Simple as it was, the novel notion shattered decades of tradition.

Before Piggly Wiggly, Americans stood at the counter of their local grocery, handed a clerk their list, then waited for him to scurry about the store and fetch the items up to the counter, where they were measured out, weighed, wrapped, and tied up with string. Shoppers had been doing that since the days of the earliest frontier towns, when general stores received shipments of goods in bulk—sacks or barrels of sugar, salt, flour, and other staples. All of which made Clarence Saunders's idea so revolutionary: Why not prepackage every item and let customers fetch what they wanted themselves?

In a series of newspaper ads in the Memphis *Commercial Appeal*, Saunders laid out the benefits of this new way of shopping. He did it with a puckish sense of humor that would become his hallmark. "The Piggly Wiggly knows its own business best and its business will be this: To have no store clerks to gab and smirk while folks are standing around ten deep to get waited on. Every customer will be her own clerk, so if she wants to talk to a can of tomatoes and kill her own time, all right and well. . . . Every article in The Piggly Wiggly will be put up in convenient packages ready for sale. . . . Prices!! Go 'Way Honey and Sit Down."

In addition to introducing self-service and prepackaged, individually priced goods, Saunders pioneered other features common to modern retail shopping, including the first checkout counter and the first use of turnstiles to prevent customers from leaving without paying for their merchandise. He organized his store into departments to help customers find what they wanted, and he created floor displays to highlight products, making brand recognition important for the first time. In fact, he originated just about all the basic features of modern supermarkets, other than their extended hours, massive size, and enormous parking lots.

Saunders's ads underscored the economic advantage of his new approach. "Every waste item of expense has been eliminated," he claimed, including telephones, extra clerks, twine and wrapping paper, and delivery charges. To court housewives on a budget, he poked fun at a mythical "High Heel Society of Memphis," made up of wealthy women who had nothing better to do than sit around arguing about the proper height of their heels. "Those whose thoughts run along snobbish lines we don't care to have call to see us," Saunders proclaimed in an ad. "Our appeal is to the practical woman—the woman who is above the reproachful grin of her next-door neighbor, who thinks more of high-heel shoes than she does her family."

Having been in the grocery trade since he was fourteen, Saunders never ran out of clever ways to promote his new enterprise. For his grand opening, he staged a beauty contest that awarded $50 in gold to five women. Prizes included $10 each to the "Lady with the Prettiest Eyes," the "Lady with the Prettiest Hands," the "Lady with the Noblest Face Expression," the "Lady with the Prettiest Red Hair," and the "Most Stylish Looking Lady." Saunders hyped the event by bringing in a cameraman to make a movie during the hour the beauty contest took place—"so if you want to get in the picture," he wrote, "be there by 10 o'clock." He handed out red roses and hired a brass band to set a festive mood. He also promised customers a glimpse of Miss Piggly Wiggly, the "Most Beautiful Girl in the World"—no half measures for Mr. Saunders.

The following day, Saunders took out a full-page ad in the *Commercial Appeal* with photos of the contest winners, beauties whose names glide off the tongue, such as Mrs. N. L. Sledge,

Miss Mildred Ehrman, and Miss Maxine Menke. Suddenly, Saunders was the P. T. Barnum of the canned-fruit aisle. Step right this way and see the lady with the pretty red hair! And people loved it. The garrulous, unorthodox salesman had apparently tapped into a vein of gold: "487 Customers Actually Bought Goods From Us on Our First Day," Saunders boasted in a subsequent ad.

The instant popularity of Piggly Wiggly led Saunders to open a second store in Memphis. In 1917, he patented his design of the "self-serving store." He formed a company and began selling franchises across the country, all built according to his formula. The company took off like Jack's beanstalk. By the early 1920s, the Piggly Wiggly Corporation operated hundreds of stores, with annual sales in the millions. A brash new food mogul had been born. Other chains and independent grocery stores soon switched to their own versions of the self-service concept. In just a few years, the vision of Clarence Saunders had swept the land. He'd certainly come a long way since his start as a $2-a-week general store clerk in Palmyra, Tennessee.

As he grew rich, Saunders undertook the construction of a new house for himself and his family. As with everything he did, Saunders thought big when he planned his new home. He bought 160 acres in Memphis and began building a twenty-two-room mansion made of pink Georgia marble. Locals dubbed the place the Pink Palace. "If I never do anything else," Saunders declared, "I'll give Memphis a landmark—a real showplace of the South."

Nearly a hundred workmen swarmed over the building site, including stonemasons brought in from Scotland. As the cost of the estate topped $1 million, Saunders nonchalantly explained that the place was "being built to stand for a thousand years."

Besides, he could afford it. His fortune at the time was somewhere in the range of $10 million.

Along with its eight bedrooms—some of them thirty-five feet long—the Pink Palace contained a ballroom, a bowling alley, a swimming pool, and an immense banquet hall. And as for those log cabins on the grounds—one for each of the three Saunders boys, Clarence Jr., Lee, and J.T.—well, you had to admit they were a darned cute idea. Unfortunately, the Saunders family never got to spend a single night in the Pink Palace. Before it was finished, the world of the Piggly Wiggly king came tumbling down like a house of straw.

Clarence Saunders's downfall began in November 1922, when Wall Street traders started driving down the price of Piggly Wiggly stock. By early 1923, the price was down to $39, a fraction of its former value. Enraged over this manipulation, Saunders decided to take on Wall Street. He hopped aboard a train and headed for Manhattan—according to some stories with a million dollars in cash stuffed into a valise. In New York, he began buying Piggly Wiggly stock. On his first day in town, he bought 30,000 shares, driving the price up to $77. Eventually, he purchased 196,000 of the corporation's 200,000 outstanding shares—pushing the stock up to $124. Saunders appeared to have won. His profits were in the millions, on paper at least.

Wall Street, however, struck back. The governors of the New York Stock Exchange declared that a corner had been established on Piggly Wiggly, and they delisted the stock. Without a listing, there was no price quotation and hence no market for Saunders's 196,000 shares. As *Time* magazine mordantly observed, "Piggly Wiggly went to the Stock Market and wound up in the stock yard. . . . Mr. Saunders discovered that Wall Street has a cemetery at one end and a river at the other."

Saunders tried desperately to unload his stock, but there were no takers. Defeated, he was forced to pay off the bankers who'd financed his leveraged buying spree—wiping out his vast fortune. "If it had worked the other way," he lamented, "I would have cleared $40,000,000." But it didn't. He was ousted as president of Piggly Wiggly and had to declare personal bankruptcy. The chain was sold off to Kroger, Safeway, and other grocery companies. Saunders had to sell his uncompleted mansion to the city of Memphis (now called the Pink Palace Museum, it houses a replica of Saunders's original store).

The Piggly Wiggly stock fiasco would have driven lesser men into despondency, but Saunders was determined to bounce back. After a court fight, he won the right to use his own name in new business ventures. In 1924, he started a second grocery chain, which he named, in his typically wacky fashion, the Clarence Saunders Sole Owner of My Name Stores, commonly known as Clarence Saunders Stores. By 1929, the chain included four hundred food markets in eighteen states. The former Piggly Wiggly king was on his way back to the top.

The success of his new chain brought Saunders a second fortune, and he built another grand estate in Memphis, this one called Woodland. He took up golf and constructed a private course on his property, where he favored an odd style of game— playing at top speed with little or no conversation. To promote his new stores, Saunders started a professional football team, the Clarence Saunders Sole Owner of My Name Tigers (pity the poor cheerleaders). Thanks to Saunders's spare-no-expenses approach, the team did well, even defeating the champion Green Bay Packers 20–6 in 1929.

Everything was working out for Saunders until the stock market crash of 1929 and the Great Depression, which drove him into bankruptcy for a second time and kept him on the ropes for years. In 1937, he laid the groundwork for yet another comeback with the design of a completely new type of grocery store, which he called Keedoozle, a play on "Key Does All." Keedoozle was built on the concept of self-service but with a new wrinkle: total automation. In essence, the entire store was an elaborate vending machine. Customers picked up a key as they entered and inserted it into the display for each item they wanted to buy. Their merchandise was dispatched directly from the stockroom to the checkout counter on a conveyor belt. "I'll be back in the million-dollar class within a year," Saunders predicted at the outset of his latest venture. While the idea sounded good, the equipment needed to make the system work proved impractical, and Keedoozle fizzled.

Saunders soldiered on. During his last years, he developed plans for another automated store he called Foodelectric, the first of which was scheduled to open in the fall of 1953, two blocks away from his original Piggly Wiggly. Before Foodelectric opened for business, though, Saunders suffered a heart attack. He died on October 14, 1953, at the age of seventy-two.

To say that Clarence Saunders was unconventional is an understatement. Even he wondered if he hadn't been a tad crazy when he came up with the funny name for his original store. "The fellow that got up that name must have a screw loose somewhere," one of his early ads suggested. But as usual, Saunders's nuttiness represented a carefully calculated business strategy. Pressed on why he'd chosen such an unusual name, Saunders replied, "So people will ask that very question."

Today, more than six hundred grocery stores in seventeen southern and midwestern states carry the Piggly Wiggly trademark, with its striking image of a jolly laughing pig. It's an appropriate logo. Piggly Wiggly: once you hear the name, you never forget it—and it always brings a smile to your face. We can thank Clarence Saunders for giving us that bit of whimsy, along with a revolutionary advancement in convenience in the way we live.

TWENTY-ONE

An Idea that Bloomed to Perfection

ELIZA SCIDMORE

IN 1885, TRAVEL writer Eliza Ruhamah Scidmore looked around her hometown of Washington, D.C., and had one thought: Yuk! The city was as ugly as a baboon's backside. That may come as a shock to modern visitors, especially anyone lucky enough to be in Washington at the peak flowering of the city's 3,700 ornamental cherry trees, when clouds of white and pink blossoms turn the grounds around the Washington Monument and Jefferson Memorial and other pockets of the city into a visual poem.

In Scidmore's day, however—in fact, ever since the capital was founded—Washington had been, quite honestly, an eyesore. The place drew a steady stream of criticism for its aesthetics. One early congressman said it was a city that "so many are willing to come to and all so anxious to leave." A half century after Pierre L'Enfant presented the plans for the capital in 1791, Washington was still an unfinished conception, with few attractive buildings and livestock roaming the muddy streets. Charles Dickens called it the "City of Magnificent Intentions." The Capitol dome wasn't completed until 1863, and the construction of the Washington Monument dragged on until 1884. As for beauty, citizens could content themselves with sweeping views of the Potomac—if they overlooked the miasmic marshlands along the river.

Those foul-smelling marshes were suspected breeding grounds for malaria and yellow fever. Beginning in the 1880s, army engineers dredged mud from the river channel to fill in the marshes—in the process creating the Tidal Basin and the peninsula that now forms East and West Potomac Parks. The problem of the fetid wetlands had been addressed, but unsightly heaps of reclaimed soil were left along the riverbank.

That stretch of raw land gave Eliza Scidmore an idea. While traveling in Japan, she'd been moved by the beauty of cherry trees in bloom—and by the reverence the Japanese people showed for the flowers. To the Japanese, the brief, transcendent beauty of the cherry blossoms is a symbol of the fleeting quality of human life ("Life is short, like the three-day glory of the cherry blossoms," one proverb goes). Called *sakura* in Japan, the ornamental trees have inspired poets and painters for centuries. Viewing rituals and festivals have grown up around the flowers. Some devotees even follow the progression of the blossoms from southern Japan, where the trees can bloom as early as January, to the north, where the show can continue into May.

Scidmore envisioned the reclaimed area along the Potomac covered with cherry trees, which she called the "most beautiful thing in the world." Of all the people who played a part in bringing the cherry trees to Washington, Scidmore deserves the most credit. Hers was the original inspiration. As the *Washington Post* put it, "she painted the town pink."

It would take three decades for Scidmore's plan to come to fruition, but she never abandoned the idea, which says as much about her personality as it does about her affinity for cherry trees. Scidmore committed herself wholeheartedly to everything she did, a trait that contributed to her success as a writer. During her career, she turned out a half-dozen travel books on Alaska and Asia, as well as a historical novel based on the Russo-Japanese War. Her first book, *Alaska, Its Southern Coast and the Sitkan Archipelago,* caught the attention of the directors of the National Geographic Society. Two years after the society's founding in 1888, Scidmore joined the organization and became a regular contributor to its new journal, a rare achievement in a period dominated by male writers—made further remarkable by the fact that Scidmore took her own photographs to accompany her stories. Over a period of twenty-four years, she wrote seventeen articles and served as the society's correspondence secretary, foreign secretary, associate editor, and first female board member.

Born in Madison, Wisconsin, in 1856, Scidmore (pronounced *Sid*-more) was the daughter of two missionaries whose travels to Japan and China inspired a lifelong fascination with Asia in both Eliza and her older brother, George. (George spent thirty-eight years in the Far East as a career diplomat; at the time of his death, he was the U.S. consul general to Japan.) After attending Oberlin College for a year, Scidmore moved to Washington, D.C. She launched her writing career by covering society news for the *New York Times* and the *St. Louis Globe-Democrat.* A trip to Alaska resulted in a series of newspaper articles that were gathered into her first book.

Scidmore first traveled to Japan after her brother was posted there in 1884. She later visited China, India, Ceylon (Sri Lanka), Java, and the Philippines, often in the company of her brother, whose diplomatic status gave her access to places denied to other travelers. She wrote about her experiences for

Harper's Weekly, Outlook, Century Magazine, Asia, and *Cosmo-politan,* as well as *National Geographic.* Travel in the late 1800s and early 1900s was still an exotic affair, and Scidmore's stories had the cachet of adventure. Her discussions of Asian history, religion, and politics no doubt boosted intercultural understanding, although her writing was colored by the colonialist outlook of her time. Describing Singapore, she gushed "what a marvel of a place British energy has raised from the jungle in less than half a century." Still, her appreciation for Asia was genuine—she lived in Japan for extended periods, was a member of the Japan Society in both London and New York, and lectured on Asian culture at scholarly conferences. She decorated her Washington apartment with Asian art and antiques, including the Empress Dowager's throne from Beijing's Summer Palace.

Scidmore's first love was always Japan—forever symbolized by the spring rituals associated with the cherry blossoms. Scidmore launched her cherry tree campaign in Washington when she returned home from her first visit to Japan. She presented her idea to the military engineer in charge of the capital's public buildings and grounds. Scidmore brought along photographs and postcards of Japanese cherry trees in bloom, hoping they would be persuasive. She was listened to politely and sent on her way.

That setback occurred in the first year of Grover Cleveland's first term as president (1885–1889). During each administration that followed, Scidmore renewed her appeal to a succession of "amiable army officers," as she called them, none of whom "grew excited or was convinced." When Benjamin Harrison took office in 1889, Scidmore approached Col. Oswald H. Ernst. "Nothing happened," lamented Scidmore. She pleaded with Ernst's successor, Col. John M. Wilson, again producing her photographs of the blooms in full glory. Wilson, at least, offered a reason for rejecting her proposal. He said that such a scheme would result in boys climbing into the trees after the ripe cherries and breaking all the limbs. "We would have to keep the park full of police day and night." When Scidmore explained that the trees bore no fruit, Wilson was incredulous. "What good is that sort of cherry tree?" he snorted.

After two decades of being the lone advocate for the cherry trees, Scidmore finally found an ally in Dr. David Fairchild, a plant explorer with the Department of Agriculture (his wife, Marian, was the daughter of Alexander Graham Bell). In 1906, Fairchild imported 125 ornamental cherry trees to test their hardiness in the Washington area. When the trees proved suitable for the region, Fairchild presented saplings to each school in the District of Columbia, and he suggested that cherry trees be planted along the city's streets. He also echoed Scidmore's idea of planting the trees around the Tidal Basin. Soon, though, Scidmore had a more powerful supporter. In 1909, William Howard Taft moved into the White House. Taft and his wife, Helen, had both traveled in Japan and were acquainted with its traditions. Scidmore wrote a note to the first lady asking for her help "in getting an avenue of Japanese cherry trees planted in Potomac Park." She received this reply two days later: "I have taken the matter up and am promised the trees." (Helen Taft was seldom hesitant: when Teddy Roosevelt asked her husband whether he wanted to become president or be appointed to the Supreme Court—Taft's dream job—Helen told William to forget about the judicial robes—*she* wanted to be first lady.)

Mrs. Taft's involvement brought a swift resolution to Scidmore's twenty-four-year-long campaign, although several more years would pass before significant numbers of cherry trees were

in the ground. At Mrs. Taft's request, ninety trees were purchased from a nursery in Pennsylvania. That was far fewer than
Scidmore envisioned. Just then, however, fate intervened: Dr.
Jokichi Takamine, the Japanese chemist who discovered adrena-
line, happened to be in Washington at the time. When Takamine learned of the first lady's interest in cherry trees, he offered
her two thousand plants as a gift from the city of Tokyo. The
trees were duly shipped, but when they arrived in Washington
in January 1910, inspectors found that they were diseased and
infested with insects. The trees had to be burned. Dr. Takamine
was unruffled, observing that the United States' first president
had "set the example of destroying cherry trees." He immediately placed an order for three thousand new plants.

In February 1912, a shipment of 3,020 replacement trees
left Japan, arriving in Washington disease- and insect-free. On
March 27, Mrs. Taft and the wife of the Japanese ambassador,
Viscountess Chinda, planted a pair of the trees on the northern
bank of the Tidal Basin. Eliza Scidmore was present at the simple ceremony. It took a few years to finish the landscaping along
the Tidal Basin, in East Potomac Park, and at other spots around
the capital, but when the work was done the city had been transformed. Each spring since that time, a profusion of color has
softened the severe lines of Washington's granite and marble
buildings and monuments. From a distance, the trees' puffy blossoms look like popcorn or tufts of cotton candy clinging to the
branches. Up close, each bloom is an exquisite arrangement of
shapes and hues—delicate white petals with hints of pink in the
predominant Yoshino species, and thick, vibrant pink blossoms
in the Kwanzan variety (there are ten other species of cherry
trees in Washington as well, although in smaller numbers).

It was Scidmore who recommended that Yoshinos be planted

close to the Tidal Basin so their blooms would reflect in the water, providing a double dose of beauty. Two-thirds of the 1,800 Yoshinos included in the 1912 shipment were arrayed around the basin, planted "as closely as currant bushes in a kitchen garden," Scidmore wrote. Their reflected colors play lightly on the water, a soft-focus, gently undulating image that painters struggle to capture and even photographs don't do justice to.

The gift of the cherry trees was meant to symbolize the friendship between Japan and America. When that relationship was shattered by World War II, someone chopped down four of the trees (not the only attack on record—in 1999, apolitical beavers felled several of the trees). To prevent further vandalism during the war years, the trees were referred to as "Oriental" flowering cherries, and the annual Cherry Blossom Festival was suspended until 1947 (civic groups sponsored the first official festival in 1935, although the celebration's roots go back to 1927, when schoolchildren reenacted the 1912 tree-planting ceremony).

In 1952, Washington's cherry trees provided a symbol of healing between Japan and the United States. Because of the war, the grove near Tokyo that had provided Washington's first cherry trees was in decline. To help restore the grove, the National Park Service supplied the Japanese with budwood from the Yoshino trees planted around the Tidal Basin. Today, an estimated 50,000 cherry trees add a living counterpoint to the gleaming office buildings and flashing neon of Tokyo, where the trees flower at approximately the same time as those in Washington, D.C.

Because of the relatively short life span of ornamental cherry trees, a program of replanting has been ongoing in Washington for decades. In 1965, Japan presented the United States with an additional 3,800 Yoshinos, many of them placed around the Washington Monument (the first two were planted by Lady Bird Johnson and Mrs. Ryuji Takeuchi, wife of the Japanese ambassador at that time). Just over a hundred of the trees from the 1912 plantings are thought to survive today. Among them are the two Yoshinos planted at the Tidal Basin by First Lady Helen Taft and Viscountess Chinda. Those historic trees are located a few hundred yards west of the John Paul Jones Memorial, at the end of Seventeenth Street. Nearby are two bronze plaques commemorating the planting ceremony.

Nowadays, huge crowds pour into Washington to see the cherry trees in bloom and attend related events. Tourists often miss the blossoms at their peak, since the time of blooming is so unpredictable, depending entirely on the happenstance of weather. That fact plays havoc with the Cherry Blossom Festival, which has grown into a two-week round of parties and cultural exhibitions, along with the traditional parade and crowning of the Cherry Blossom Queen. The staging of the festival coincides with the trees' average date of peak blooming—April 4 (the peak occurs when 70 percent of the Yoshino blossoms are open). However, the trees can explode with color anytime from mid-March to mid-April, depending on the temperatures. Many's the year that the flowers have come and gone before the celebration commences, their evanescent beauty withered by frost or whisked away by gusty spring winds and showers. Even under ideal conditions, peak bloom lasts only a few days.

The most fortunate spectators are Washington's office workers, who have their own traditions regarding the cherry trees. Every spring, word spreads quickly as the flowering trees approach their peak. ("Have you been down to see the cherry blossoms?" is probably the most frequently asked question in the city at that time of year.) On those few glorious days, buildings empty out at lunchtime as government drudges, high-powered attorneys, sales clerks, and office workers alike make the pilgrimage to see the flowers. Spreading out their blankets beneath the laden boughs (and uncorking or uncapping their favorite beverages), they enjoy a lunch hour that seldom lasts just sixty minutes. The nation's capital is never at its most productive in the afternoons during cherry blossom time.

Visitors who make it to Washington when the cherry trees are in bloom should utter a silent thank-you to Eliza Scidmore. If not for her, the city would be a far less congenial place. Her vision and persistence led to a spectacle of nature that millions of people have enjoyed. Probably only a few of those spectators have ever heard of Miss Scidmore (she never married). Scidmore spent her last years in Geneva. When she died in 1928 at the age of seventy-two, she requested that no services be held for her. She wanted to be cremated and asked only that her ashes be distributed in the "most seemly way." Despite her request, her friends got together to pay tribute to her memory. The government of Japan—which once gave Scidmore an award for her depiction of the country in her writing—requested that her ashes be interred in Yokohama. She lies there now, surrounded each spring by the "most beautiful thing in the world."

TWENTY-TWO

Dispenser of Beauty and Truth

MADAM C. J. WALKER

SARAH BREEDLOVE'S workaday world was a slice of domestic hell. The twenty-one-year-old daughter of former slaves spent every day but Sunday washing and ironing for white families in St. Louis, Missouri. It was hot, backbreaking labor, but the $1.50 or so she earned each day kept a roof over her head and allowed her to feed herself and her three-year-old daughter, Lelia. The job didn't do much for her health, though, considering the polluted air in the downtown area where she lived. The coal-fired furnaces in the city's many riverfront factories spewed clouds of sulfurous soot, a witch's brew that stung the eyes and lungs and withered leaves on the trees. On the back porch of Breedlove's rooming house, the foul air was made worse by the caustic fumes from lye and bleach wafting up on the steam from her washtub.

Every Monday, Breedlove picked up a week's worth of soiled laundry from each of her clients. By Saturday, she had to have everything ready for delivery back to the owners, spotless, starched, and ironed—which meant that her days were a monotonous routine of stooping over a tub with her arms immersed in sudsy water, her skin burned raw by the harsh lye soap. Each night, she had to wield a hot, heavy flatiron to press out the wrinkles in the clean laundry. Though Breedlove's life was hard, it was typical for an uneducated African American female in 1889. And the young woman knew there were worse things than being a laundress, something she was reminded of whenever she hurried past the saloons and bordellos near her Wash Street rooming house.

What separated Sarah Breedlove from all the other poor black women toiling away at menial, low-paying jobs was her unshakable determination to improve her life—along with the fact that she did. In the course of the next three decades, this downtrodden washerwoman would turn herself into one of the wealthiest women in the United States. It was an astounding accomplishment for someone who began life in abject poverty, and who had two major obstacles to overcome in being both black and female. But Breedlove inherited a fighting spirit from her parents, who endured the degradation of slavery followed by the never-get-ahead life of tenant farming.

Owen and Minerva Breedlove had six children—four sons and two daughters. Sarah, their younger daughter, was born in December 1867, just two years after the end of the Civil War. Although Owen and Minerva had been emancipated by President Lincoln, freedom didn't bring much change. As sharecroppers in Delta, Louisiana, they still lived in the same one-room shack as before, still sweated in the same cotton fields. Their hard-scrabble existence took its toll. They both died in their midforties, when Sarah was still a child.

After her parents' deaths, Breedlove moved to Vicksburg, Mississippi, where she lived with her older sister, Louvenia, and her husband. Forced to earn her keep, Breedlove did laundry for white folks, just as her mother had done before her. The girl was robbed of her childhood and an education by the twin scourges of poverty and discrimination. She grew up subjected to the horrors of shootings and lynchings perpetrated by white bigots battling the civil rights initiatives of Reconstruction. In the postwar years, African Americans in the South were murdered with impunity, their deaths warranting only a passing mention in local newspapers—of no more importance than the announcement of a pilfered vegetable patch or a missing cat. Breedlove also faced terrors at home, where she was abused by Louvenia's husband. When she turned fourteen, she escaped from her sister's household, running away with a man named Moses McWilliams. Three years later, she gave birth to Lelia, her only child.

Breedlove kept hoping for a better life for her family, but tragedy struck again when her husband died three years after Lelia's birth. A widow at twenty, with a young daughter to care for, she decided to join her brothers in St. Louis, where they ran a barbershop. After making the journey up the Mississippi River, Breedlove spent the next several years struggling to earn a living. She got married a second time, to a no-good layabout who left her for another woman. Still toiling over a laundry tub, Breedlove did her best to provide for Lelia, pushing her to get an education and proudly seeing her enrolled in Knoxville College in 1902.

Around that same time, Breedlove began going out with a man named Charles J. Walker. "C.J." was a snappy-dressing salesman who radiated confidence and ambition. With fresh inspiration to better herself, Breedlove began attending night school. She also took a new interest in her appearance. For one thing, she wanted to improve the look of her hair, a mundane decision that changed the direction of her life.

During the previous few years, Breedlove's hair had become brittle and was beginning to fall out, a common problem with poor black women owing to inferior diet, lack of hygiene, or the use of harsh grooming products. Embarrassed by her appearance, Breedlove usually kept her short, wiry hair covered. She experimented with every treatment she could find, but none of them improved her condition. Then she met St. Louis beautician Annie Turnbo Pope, whose ministrations worked wonders. Breedlove was so impressed that she went to work for Turnbo Pope, selling her "hair grower" preparation door to door to supplement her income.

Things had begun to look up for Breedlove by 1904, the year that St. Louis hosted the World's Fair, a showcase for the latest technological advances—everything from automobiles to electricity. Excited by the possibilities of the new century, Breedlove resolved to make a fresh start for herself. She moved to Denver to be near her sister-in-law and her four nieces. Breedlove continued selling Turnbo Pope's hair grower while working as a cook and laundrywoman. Before long, however, she began to experiment with producing her own hair restoration remedy.

It's likely that Breedlove based her formula on Turnbo Pope's preparation, although she denied that. (Breedlove definitely copied Turnbo Pope's sales methods, and a long and testy rivalry developed between Breedlove and her former boss, whose Poro brand was a huge success.) Describing the origins of her balm, Breedlove said that she had a dream one night in which "a big black man appeared to me and told me what to mix up for my hair. Some of the remedy was from Africa, but I sent for it, mixed it, put it on my scalp, and in a few weeks my hair was coming in faster than it had ever fallen out." (According to A'Lelia Bundles, Breedlove's great-great-granddaughter and biographer, the tale was simply good marketing. It combined three strong appeals to an African American clientele—divine intervention, a black source of inspiration, and a nostalgic tie to African herbal remedies.)

In Denver, Breedlove became convinced that her future would be dedicated to hair care. She was now spending five days a week making and selling her hair grower and only a couple of days doing laundry. The African American beauty market was expanding as social and economic opportunities for urban blacks increased after the turn of the century. Many black women wanted to have the long hair associated with beauty in white women, an image drilled into them by magazine illustrations of narrow-waisted Gibson Girls, their lengthy tresses piled atop their heads. It was clear that Breedlove's preparation—a mixture of coconut oil, petrolatum, beeswax, copper sulfate, precipitated sulfur, and violet extract—improved scalp condition and hair growth (especially when supplemented with more frequent shampooing), but the budding businesswoman still had to make it in the marketplace. In addition to the word-of-mouth promotion she received from satisfied customers, she started advertising in the *Colorado Statesman*, a Denver newspaper for African Americans. In her late thirties, Sarah Breedlove was establishing a name for herself.

Toward the end of 1905, the jaunty C. J. Walker reappeared in Breedlove's life, following her to Denver from St. Louis. In January 1906, the two were married. Always a promoter, C.J. was helpful in building the reputation of his wife, who adopted the impressive moniker of Madam C. J. Walker. Later that year, Madam Walker's daughter—recently trained as a beautician—joined them and went to work for her mother. Madam Walker herself had become living proof of her treatment's effectiveness.

A photograph appeared in the *Colorado Statesman* showing her luxuriant hair, elegantly coiffed into a Gibson Girl look.

Even though she traveled to towns all over Colorado to promote her treatment, Walker knew that her prospects were limited unless she could expand into other regions. In the fall of 1906, she made a swing through several southern and eastern states, giving demonstrations and setting up a mail-order business for her hair restorative, which she sold as "Madam C. J. Walker's Wonderful Hair Grower." Put up in tins, the product bore an illustration of Walker with flowing tresses falling onto her shoulders. The road trip proved so successful that Walker closed up shop in Denver to focus on building mail-order sales.

For the next year and half, Walker was on the road, moving from town to town in midwestern, southern, and eastern states. At each stop, she introduced herself to the black community, put on demonstrations, and trained local representatives who could then provide restoration treatments—using, of course, Madam C. J. Walker's Wonderful Hair Grower. She also took mail orders from individuals for her miracle cure in a can. During her first year on the road, she took in an average of $300 a month—in a period when a white factory worker earned about $60 a month. Walker's income had jumped to ten times what she'd made as a laundress.

By 1907, requests for Madam Walker's hair preparation were pouring in from as far away as California. The product Walker had once stirred up in a tub in her room had become a national brand. For two years, Walker ran her mail-order operation out of Pittsburgh, where she also opened a beauty college. Her annual sales kept growing: over $6,600 in 1908; nearly $8,800 in 1909. She trained hundreds of representatives, feeding the demand for her products, which by then included Vegetable Shampoo and Glossine hair oil. In 1910, Walker started scouting locations for a new permanent headquarters and factory. She settled on Indianapolis because of the city's central location and excellent rail and highway connections.

To raise her company's profile, Walker assumed a larger role in business and civic affairs. In the summer of 1910, she attended the biennial conference of the National Association of Colored Women, a group that backed women's suffrage and opposed discrimination. Having joined the organization in 1904 while still a St. Louis laundress, Walker was now the most prominent businesswoman in attendance. Her income in 1910 would approach $11,000—an amount equivalent to $250,000 today. The next year, she took her business to a new level by incorporating it as the Madam C. J. Walker Manufacturing Company of Indiana. The washerwoman had turned corporate mogul.

As Walker's business acumen increased, so did her social conscience. She felt a kinship with the millions of black people fighting daily to earn a living. In Indianapolis, she donated $1,000 to build a YMCA for black youths, and she supported homes for the indigent and the elderly. A believer in the power of education (she made a point of surrounding herself with bright, educated people), she became a benefactor of the Florida school for African American girls founded by Mary McLeod Bethune, an institution that became Bethune-Cookman College. She set up scholarships for black women at Alabama's Tuskegee Institute and gave to Palmer Memorial Institute in North Carolina. She also donated generously to the National Association for the Advancement of Colored People.

One of Walker's most meaningful contributions was the empowerment of African American women to earn a decent living. Her company not only taught black women how to sell and use

Walker products but also how to run their own salons. Walker would eventually train more than twenty thousand "hair culturists" all over the country. Women who previously labored as domestics or farmworkers could earn more in a week than they'd made in a month in their old jobs. "You have opened up a trade for hundreds of colored women to make an honest and profitable living," one graduate wrote in thanks.

Walker organized her agents into a union, encouraging each local group to engage in service work and to campaign for racial equality. She offered cash prizes for groups that contributed the most to worthy causes. She held national conventions, bringing her agents together for additional training and inspirational talks. The conventions gave agents a chance to share their personal stories, and they also allowed Walker to strengthen ties with her representatives, making them even more loyal to the company. It was a clever business strategy. If only Walker had been as savvy in her personal life.

After making the best of things for six years, Walker finally saw it was time to divorce the fun-loving C.J., who'd turned into a big-spending goof-off and philanderer. The company continued to prosper after C.J.'s ejection. In the first four months of 1913, sales came to $11,000—roughly the same amount it had previously been taking in annually. Walker introduced her line of products into Central America and the Caribbean. As her wealth grew, she diversified her holdings by purchasing real estate in Los Angeles, Chicago, New York, and other cities. She also stepped up her involvement in social causes, speaking out against lynchings and racial discrimination. Inevitably, she came to regard Indianapolis as too small a stage. In 1916, she moved in with Lelia in an opulent four-story, twenty-room town house in New York City's Harlem district.

Harlem was then in the midst of a transformation from a white neighborhood to a predominantly black area. For years, African Americans had been fleeing the rural South in pursuit of political freedom and economic opportunities in Northern cities, the phenomenon known as the Great Migration. The concentration of talented businessmen, intellectuals, civil rights activists, musicians, writers, and artists would soon make Harlem the black capital of the country and lead to the halcyon period known as the Harlem Renaissance, a time of high aspirations and hope for blacks. From the late 1910s through the Roaring Twenties—until it was crushed by the Great Depression—the Harlem Renaissance produced an outpouring of African American creativity. The likes of Duke Ellington and Billie Holiday dazzled audiences nightly at the Savoy Ballroom, the Apollo Theater, and the Cotton Club, and black writers such as Langston Hughes and Zora Neale Hurston earned national reputations. To her great good fortune, Madam C. J. Walker was there at the outset of it all.

Walker loved entertaining almost as much as she loved business. The Harlem town house she shared with her daughter quickly became a central focus of black artistic and intellectual life. With her company's income having skyrocketed to over $100,000 a year (equal to nearly $2 million today), Walker could afford to host lavish parties. In addition to her soirees, she provided financial assistance to black activists, writers, and artists. Her largesse continued after she built a thirty-four-room Italian Renaissance–style villa at Irvington-on-Hudson, a few miles north of Manhattan—not far from estates owned by the Rockefellers and other patrician families.

The mansion, which Walker named Villa Lewaro, was finished in June 1918. The proud mistress of the house didn't get to enjoy her new home for long. Walker had developed high blood pressure and kidney disease. Five months after celebrating her fifty-first birthday, she passed away, on May 25, 1919. Newspapers across the country and in Europe reported her death. Articles put her net worth at over $1 million, which would have made her one of the country's first self-made female millionaires—and in 1919, $1 million was a staggering sum, equivalent to over $12 million today. (Her estate reportedly came to between $600,000 and $700,000, and the value of her company would have been well over $1 million at the time of her death.)

Sarah Walker's rags-to-riches story is one of the most remarkable in American history, given the challenges she faced. After starting out trudging the furrows of a Louisiana cotton field, she ended up walking with the giants of her day. In her business and civil rights activities, she worked alongside Booker T. Washington, W. E. B. DuBois, and other black luminaries. She was probably the only woman ever to go from the washhouse to the White House, having called on Woodrow Wilson in 1917 as part of a delegation hoping to persuade the president to actively oppose violence and discrimination against black people.

Walker wasn't without her detractors. She was criticized for profiting from the desires of black women to make themselves more acceptable by masking their own racial traits and mimicking the appearance of whites. The pursuit of straight hair and lighter skin has long been a hot-button issue for African Americans, although A'Lelia Bundles, who once cringed at the accusations directed at her ancestor, discovered a different story when she began work on Walker's biography: "While Madam Walker was alive the Walker Company never sold skin bleaches and the words 'hair straightener' never appeared in her ads." Madam Walker's own words on the subject were unequivocal: "I have always held myself out as a hair culturist. I grow hair."

Walker's company remained in business for nearly seventy years after her death before being sold in the mid-1980s. Her estate in Irvington-on-Hudson and her company's headquarters in Indianapolis have both been designated National Historic Landmarks (the latter was refurbished as the Madame Walker Theatre Center in the 1980s). In 1998, the U.S. Postal Service honored Walker with a commemorative stamp.

Describing her career, Walker once said, "I got my start by giving myself a start." She proudly declared to an audience of black businessmen, "I am a woman who came from the cotton fields of the South. I was promoted from there to the washtub. Then I was promoted to the cook kitchen, and from there I promoted myself into the business of manufacturing hair goods and preparations." It was a simple, clear-eyed assessment of her life, but it failed to do her justice. Her great-great-granddaughter points out that as one of the "pioneers of the modern cosmetics industry," Madam Walker "fostered self-esteem, glamour and power among several generations of African American women."

In other words, Madam Walker's true legacy wasn't her accumulated wealth. It was the impact her success had on her race in general and on the lives of black women in particular. What the groundbreaking entrepreneur actually sold in those little tins of Wonderful Hair Grower was inspiration.

PART III

HUMANITARIANS

TWENTY-THREE

Defender of the Defenseless

GRACE ABBOTT

AMERICA, 1911: In New York's Greenwich Village, a fourteen-year-old Italian girl leans over her sewing machine in the hot, cramped Triangle garment factory, stitching together women's blouses for hours on end. Row after row of young seamstresses fill the ninth-floor sweatshop to capacity, their machines clattering like a plague of angry locusts. In Pittston, Pennsylvania, crews of Polish, Greek, and Croatian boys, some as young as ten years old, labor in the hellish maw of the Hughestown Borough coal mine. For up to sixteen hours a day—their faces and lungs blackened by coal dust—they chip away at immense piles of rock like prisoners on a chain gang, separating anthracite from slate.

In cities across the land, millions of women and children toil in grim anonymity. They work in glass factories, canneries, and textile mills, earning a meager dollar or two a day. They roam the streets selling newspapers or shining shoes for pennies. Still others earn beggarly wages on the nation's farms. Often recent immigrants, they arrived in this country with hopes of realizing the American dream. What they encountered was the American nightmare—the stark reality that in early twentieth-century America, life for the least among us meant endless, low-paying, often hazardous drudgery. More fortunate Americans, mostly earlier-arriving Anglo-Saxon Protestants, often ignored the plight of the latest influx of immigrants—the non-English-speaking, non-Protestant "undesirables" from southern and eastern Europe. As for employers, they claimed they were doing the poor a favor by giving them any kind of job, no matter how difficult or dangerous. If the workers didn't like it, they could always quit—and starve, which was truly their only option.

Those were the facts of life in the early 1900s, before the existence of effective labor laws. It was an era when many bosses preferred female and child employees since they could be paid less and were easier to run roughshod over than grown men. The circumstances of workers were only marginally different from indentured servitude or outright slavery—in some southern textile mills, children as young as five worked eleven-hour shifts. Slowly, labor unions and organizations such as the National Child Labor Committee began to disrupt the system of impoverishment and exploitation that existed in America's workplaces. The struggle dragged on for decades. Like the heartless taskmasters in Dickens's *Oliver Twist*, factory owners fought to keep their shops free from regulation of any sort, while most federal legislators seemed content with the status quo. It wasn't until 1938 that the situation was permanently rectified. That year, the federal government passed the landmark Fair Labor Standards Act, which established a nationwide minimum wage, overtime pay, and standards for the employment of minors.

The crusade to end America's shameful labor practices featured a long list of dedicated individuals, but a few names stand out. Social worker and political philosopher Jane Addams—the first American woman to win the Nobel Peace Prize—founded

Chicago's Hull House to aid the poor and later helped found the Juvenile Protective Association to champion children's rights. Union firebrand Mary Harris Jones organized a historic children's march on President Theodore Roosevelt's New York home, giving young mine and mill workers a chance to plead for the simple right to go to school. Documentary photographer Lewis Hine captured children at work in mines and sweat-shops, his searing images bringing home the horrors of child labor to the American public. Another member of this honor roll of reformers was an unassuming midwestern schoolteacher named Grace Abbott, a woman whose concern for the welfare of women and children propelled her into pioneering roles in government and education.

Between 1908 and 1939, Abbott ran the Immigrants' Protective League of Chicago, headed the U.S. Labor Department's Children's Bureau, and taught the first generation of social service administrators. Abbott directly improved the lives of millions—by providing mothers with guidance on maternal health and child care, by developing new policies to combat juvenile delinquency, and by lending her impassioned voice to the struggle against child labor. With her soulful blue eyes and placid demeanor, Abbott looked harmless enough, but she was relentless when it came to standing up for the disadvantaged. With equal aplomb, she could rustle up emergency housing for a harried immigrant family, shoo underage children out of a barroom, or hold her own against obstreperous Washington congressmen.

During her illustrious career, Abbott helped write the Social Security Act of 1935 and shaped key parts of the Fair Labor Standards Act. She was the first person chosen to represent the United States on a committee at the League of Nations. She was the first woman to receive widespread support for nomination to a presidential cabinet post. In a 1931 nationwide poll run by *Good Housekeeping*, she was named one of the twelve greatest living American women, an honor she shared with Jane Addams, Willa Cather, and Helen Keller. In 1935, *Parents Magazine* presented her with a gold medal for outstanding service to children. Perhaps her greatest accolade was bestowed by the *New York Times* in 1930, during her tenure as head of the Children's Bureau. In an article entitled "Guardian of the Children of America," the newspaper called Abbott a mother to all 43 million of the nation's young.

A prolific communicator—in print, on the radio, and in film—Abbott tirelessly promoted her belief that women, children, and immigrants should be treated with fairness and equality, a spirit of generosity rooted in her pioneer Nebraska upbringing. Abbott was born in 1878 in Grand Island, not far from the Overland Trail. She later claimed that she came into this world already believing in equal rights and social justice, thanks to her Quaker mother—a teacher, abolitionist, pacifist, and feminist.

Grand Island may have been isolated, a place where lonesome prairie winds rustled the corn and sandhill cranes ghosted above the creeks and cottonwoods, but the Abbott household made up for it with its liveliness. Abbott's lawyer father invited Grace, her older sister Edith, and their two brothers to attend local court sessions to witness the law in action, and the whole family engaged in spirited political debates. The Abbott children were encouraged to get the best educations possible, although family financial difficulties made that a challenge. The girls began their college educations in Nebraska. For a time, both taught high school in Grand Island. Eventually, the Abbott sisters ended up at the University of Chicago, where Grace would earn a master's degree in political science.

To help pay for her studies, Abbott took a job with the Juvenile Protective Association. She moved into Hull House, a hotbed of social activism situated among Chicago's worst tenements—"a beautiful place for people who lived in an area of the city where nothing else was beautiful," wrote Abbott's sister, who soon joined her at Hull House. Living and working in the trailblazing settlement house with Jane Addams and other reformers added real-world experience to Grace's university education. Her talent for administration caught the attention of the founders of the city's new Immigrants' Protective League. In 1908, the organization hired her as its first director. Over the next nine years, Abbott dedicated herself to the protection of immigrants. She led the push for a state law to safeguard newcomers from fraudulent employment agencies and unchartered "immigrant banks." She fought literacy tests designed to disenfranchise immigrant voters. She promoted compulsory education for immigrant children and followed up with home visits to ensure that youngsters were in school. She even traveled to eastern Europe to get a better understanding of the predominant immigrant groups at that time.

Abbott's work led to the publication of her first book, *The Immigrant and the Community*, which appeared in 1917. In it, she argued for government policies directed at speeding assimilation and overcoming prejudice. Her views weren't universally embraced, but her writing drew a national audience. The year her book came out, Abbott accepted a job as the director of the Child Labor Division of the U.S. Children's Bureau, the federal agency dedicated to improving the lives of all young Americans. (The bureau was the brainchild of New York public health advocate Lillian Wald, who observed that if the government could have a department dedicated to the welfare of the country's farm crops, it ought to have one "to look after the Nation's crop of children.")

Abbott's new job made her responsible for administering the country's first federal child labor law—the Keating-Owen Child Labor Act of 1916. The law banned the sale of products produced by factories employing workers under the age of fourteen, mines employing workers under sixteen, and any business that required workers between fourteen and sixteen to work at night or for more than eight hours a day or six days a week. Although the Child Labor Act was a major step forward, the Supreme Court overturned the law not long after its adoption. The most monstrous crime imaginable—stealing a childhood— was allowed to continue.

Another child labor bill was passed at the end of 1918, but it too was nullified by the Supreme Court. Child labor opponents then attempted to advance their cause with a constitutional amendment, but it failed to receive enough support. The amendment's enemies argued that it would give the federal government too much power. Some even claimed that the attempt to abolish child labor was a communist plot. The Supreme Court's decisions and the foes of a constitutional amendment sentenced the country's youth to two more decades of exploitation. (The Fair Labor Standards Act of 1938 survived a Supreme Court challenge and is still in effect today.) Abbott blamed the failure to end child labor on "the selfish interest in the exploitation of children by the few and the patient toleration of injustice to children by the many."

In 1921, Abbott became chief of the Children's Bureau, a position she would hold for thirteen years. If Abbott felt thwarted by the slow progress of child labor reform, at least her office gave her the opportunity to improve the health of mothers and their children—and thus the nation as a whole. As she wrote in 1922, "Care of the mother and the child from birth is the foundation on which a national program for real physical fitness must be built." At the time, maternal and infant mortality rates were far higher in the United States than in most other industrialized nations. Only 20 percent of women received proper prenatal care. (The United States still has twice the maternal death rate of the United Kingdom and four times the infant mortality rate of Japan.) Abbott's most powerful tool to remedy this situation was the Sheppard-Towner Act of 1921, the first federal legislation aimed at improving maternal and child health care.

The modest level of funding allocated by the Sheppard-Towner Act paid for prenatal checkups, education of new mothers in infant and toddler care, nurse home visits, and instructional bulletins. The law was a resounding success, and all but three states (Connecticut, Massachusetts, and Illinois) took advantage of the programs it sponsored. As a result, maternal deaths dropped 12 percent and infant mortality fell by 16 percent. Even so, in 1929, Congress killed the Sheppard-Towner Act. The view that health care wasn't the responsibility of government prevailed, largely because of intense lobbying by the American Medical Association, which invoked the always potent specter of socialism. With shocking suddenness, the most effective program administered by the Children's Bureau imploded. It couldn't have come at a worse time—just as the nation was sliding into the Great Depression. As one prominent supporter of the Sheppard-Towner Act marveled, the federal government seemed content to spend more on the health of hogs than on the health of children.

Despite such setbacks, Abbott forged ahead. She represented the United States at a spate of international labor and child welfare conferences, and she served on the League of Nations' council combating traffic in women and children. In 1930, Abbott received an outpouring of support from influential citizens who felt she should be appointed secretary of labor. Her backers included the entire Nebraska congressional delegation, the American Federation of Labor, numerous industrial leaders, and a prestigious collection of university professors. Had she been appointed to this cabinet-level position, it would have been a first for an American woman, but President Herbert Hoover—no great friend of the Children's Bureau—chose William N. Doak instead. (Frances Perkins would become the first female cabinet member when President Franklin D. Roosevelt made her head of the Labor Department in 1933.)

As the only social worker running a major federal agency when the Depression struck, Abbott was able to help shape the responses to the financial crisis. She sought federal aid for dependent children of the unemployed, focused attention on childhood malnutrition, and looked for ways to curb the rise in juvenile delinquency and youthful transients. Abbott's friend and mentor Jane Addams said that Abbott brought a maternal sensibility to her job, enabling her to accomplish the seemingly impossible feat of "endearing the federal government to millions of its citizens."

By 1934, Abbott was ready to escape the "Washington traffic jam," as she called it. She had persevered through five presidential administrations. Abbott accepted a professorship in the University of Chicago's School of Social Service Administration, the country's first university graduate program in social work. It was a genuine homecoming, since Edith Abbott—a respected educator, social worker, and author in her own right—was the dean of the school. Grace also took over the editorship of the

Social Service Review, the leading publication on social welfare policy and practices, which Edith had cofounded.

Abbott remained a consultant to the Children's Bureau for a token payment of $1 a year, a fee she earned thousands of times over. Recruited as an advisor to FDR's Committee on Economic Security—the group responsible for drafting the Social Security bill—Abbott took the lead in shaping the legislation's maternal and child welfare provisions. She made an even greater contribution, possibly the most significant achievement of her life, by leading the lobbying effort that persuaded a reluctant Congress to pass the controversial welfare bill. Afterward, Abbott was asked to serve as one of the three original board members to administer the new law. Unable to accept because of health problems, she continued advocating for women and children in her writing, which included *The Child and the State,* a two-volume work that appeared in the same year that saw the passage of the Fair Labor Standards Act—whose child labor provisions she had proposed.

In Chicago, Abbott shared a home with her sister. (The two never married, having dedicated themselves early in life to their respective careers.) Already suffering from tuberculosis, Abbott was diagnosed with multiple myeloma in 1938. She died the following year at the age of sixty, leaving behind a legacy that continues to influence American life. William Chenery, the editor of *Collier's Weekly,* said of her, "Perhaps no one in America did more to put an end to the exploitation of immigrants than did Grace Abbott." Americans are far better off today thanks to Abbott's contributions to the Social Security and Fair Labor Standards Acts and her precedent-setting stewardship of the Children's Bureau. (In 1946, the Children's Bureau was transferred from the Labor Department to the Social Security

Administration; its functions are now part of the Department of Health and Human Services.)

Abbott's parents chose a fitting name for their second daughter: grace was a quality this selfless advocate for social justice possessed in abundance. Even though she was the federal government's most powerful female administrator for a time, she never abandoned her mother's Quaker teachings of living with humility and simplicity. In Washington, she rented a modest furnished apartment near the National Zoo and ate most of her meals in the building's unpretentious café. She still wore the plain dresses of a prairie schoolteacher, and when opponents derided her as a meddling old maid who had no right telling people how to raise their children, she just smiled and kept up the struggle to do "what one could."

Edith Abbott recorded a revealing observation her sister once made about their Nebraska home: "Grace used to say that a small Western town was the most honestly democratic place in the world. There were no people who were rich, and the poor we all knew as individuals. They were people who had had one misfortune or another, people whom we should try to help." Grace Abbott never lost that spirit of neighborly helpfulness. She took it with her from the dusty streets of Grand Island to Chicago's tumbledown tenements to the corridors of power in Washington, D.C.

As a child, Abbott was said to have been as fearless as her brothers, always ready to venture "beyond bounds." It was a trait that stayed with her all her life. At a time when men were thought to be mentally superior and females were expected to remain at home, Abbott demonstrated the important role that women could play in government and higher education. Her accomplishments earned her the admiration of everyone from paupers to presidents. Three years after her death, a World War II liberty ship was named in her honor.

Abbott was proud to serve in the federal government. Unlike today's cash-and-carry officeholders, she refused to take advantage of her contacts for personal profit. For Abbott, government employment was strictly a means of serving those whose needs were greater than her own. She was convinced that national social programs such as those run by the Children's Bureau could be more effective and more consistent than individual state initiatives or private charitable efforts. And she never abandoned her belief that spending public money to help the disadvantaged is every bit as justifiable as using it to rescue corporations in times of trouble.

Abbott was adamant that every American, especially children—"our greatest national asset," she called them—had the right to proper health care. She pointed out that paying for a child's health care with public funds is no different than paying for public education with tax dollars—both are necessary to fully developed bodies and minds. It outraged her that the wealthy received better health care than the poor—a demonstration of moral poverty in the richest nation on Earth.

Americans are still sparring over the causes Abbott championed. Whenever state or federal legislators need to balance the budget, it's often the health and welfare of women, children, or immigrants that suffer first. Even more disturbing is the fact that sweatshops continue to exploit poor and immigrant workers in the United States. Recent Labor Department studies indicate that two-thirds of the garment factories in Los Angeles and New York pay less than the minimum wage and routinely violate overtime laws. In Los Angeles, 98 percent of the garment factories have serious health and safety issues. As always, the weak make easy targets.

Grace Abbott dedicated herself to turning that ugly fact on its head by attempting to make the defenseless one of our first priorities. She knew that by being our brother's keeper, we lift ourselves—lift humanity—to its highest level. Fairness and equality were causes she believed in, fought for, and, in many cases, achieved. Like any good mother, Abbott never stopped loving and nurturing every one of her children.

TWENTY-FOUR

The Man Who Fed Asia

HENRY BEACHELL

THE HEAT WASN'T bad at this early morning hour, only in the low 70s. It was the humidity that was the killer—a clothes-soaking 90 percent. Things would dry out a bit in the afternoon, although by then the mercury would push well into the 90s. Here on the tropical island of Luzon, the largest in the Philippines, you never got away from the heat and humidity. In the rainy season, there were daily downpours that turned the countryside into an impressionistic watercolor of blurred greens and browns. Newcomers tried to dodge the weather, but the locals simply worked right through it, as they always had. This was rice-growing country, and the year-round steam-bath conditions helped explain its productiveness. The island's two-thousand-year-old Banaue Rice Terraces attested to the longstanding importance of rice to the Philippine culture.

Hank Beachell, a lean, gray-haired, fifty-seven-year-old American, appreciated the significance of rice to Filipinos. He knew that billions of people in Asia and other areas of the world depended on rice as their main food staple. Rice ranks as the world's second-largest grain crop, after corn, although since corn is often grown for fodder or nonfood uses, rice is more important to human nutrition. Beachell had been studying this valuable cereal grain all his adult life. He'd spent thirty-two years with the U.S. Department of Agriculture, researching and improving rice cultivation in the United States. After his retirement in 1963, he'd come to the Philippines to continue his work at the International Rice Research Institute (IRRI) in Los Baños, a resort and academic center forty miles southeast of Manila. Los Baños was home to the University of the Philippines, as well as several research facilities dedicated to the study of agriculture, forestry, and life sciences.

Funded by the Ford and Rockefeller foundations and the Philippine government, the nonprofit IRRI had been established in Los Baños in 1960. As the institute's chief rice breeder, Hank Beachell directed a team of scientists from over a dozen countries. Their goal was to help subsistence farmers by developing strains of rice that could increase yields without damaging the environment. Rice cultivation is labor-intensive and requires abundant water, since fields are traditionally flooded to control weeds that might harm young seedlings. Weed competition can reduce a rice crop by a third or more. The main alternative to flooding is pesticides, which carry the risk of pollution. For the scientists at IRRI, finding a way to grow more rice with less water and fewer chemicals was the Holy Grail, but they were racing against time. Throughout Asia, poor nations struggled to feed their exploding populations.

The evolution of rice had already come a long way since Asian farmers first cultivated the slender grass around five thousand years ago. Some historians believe that rice was originally domesticated in India, while others think it occurred in China. Just two species account for nearly all cultivated rice, *Oryza sativa,* originating in Asia and now grown all over the world, and *O. glaberrima,* which originated in Africa. Rice cultivation reached Europe in the Middle Ages, and European explorers, in turn, introduced it to the New World. Of all the regions in which rice is an important food source, none depends on it more than Asia, where more than 90 percent of the world's rice is grown and consumed.

As the sun rose over Los Baños, Hank Beachell carefully examined the rice plants growing in the research center's experimental plots. Even when he was a college student, Beachell was known for his ability to judge and grade grain crops. This morning, one particular specimen caught his eye, the third plant in row 288. He noted the plant's short, thick stem, a semi-dwarf characteristic that helped it avoid "lodging," a problem common to varieties with taller, weaker stems. (When fertilizer is added to increase yields, thin stems can't support the weight of the heavier seed heads and the plants fall over, ruining the crop.) Tagged IR8, this plant was a hybrid that Beachell had developed from a cross of a semidwarf variety from China and a taller, pest-resistant Indonesian strain.

Beachell smiled as he stood over the sturdy little plant—with good reason. IR8 possessed just the traits he'd been looking for: it responded well to fertilizer, resisted most pests and diseases, matured early, and produced a heavier yield than traditional varieties of rice. A milestone in the history of agriculture, this single plant would become the progenitor of the first widely planted strain of "miracle rice," a line of hardy, high-yielding varieties that literally saved hundreds of millions of people from starvation. IR8 would fuel a green revolution in rice farming that paralleled advances in wheat cultivation triggered by the work of American agronomist Norman Borlaug. This new strain of rice more than doubled the average yields of traditional varieties of rice, which normally produced only one or two tons per hectare (2.5 acres). IR8 routinely produced yields of four or five tons per hectare, and when fertilized with nitrogen it yielded an astounding ten tons per hectare. In the years immediately after IR8 came into widespread use, farmers throughout Asia increased their incomes and improved the nutrition of their countries, and Hank Beachell was the man they could thank for it. It was quite an accomplishment for a modest midwestern farm boy.

Born near Waverly, Nebraska, in September 1906, Henry Monroe Beachell grew up working on his family's wheat farms. As a kid, he built models of farm machinery, and in school he took two years of vocational training in agriculture. It was no surprise, then, that when Beachell reached college age he went off to study agronomy at the University of Nebraska. Following his undergraduate work, he earned a master's degree in plant breeding and genetics at Kansas State University, finishing school just after the start of the Great Depression. Beachell had hoped to spend his career breeding improved varieties of wheat, but jobs in that area were scarce. When a research position opened up with the U.S. Department of Agriculture, Beachell jumped at it. The job, however, entailed research on rice, not wheat—a quirk of fate that sent Beachell's life in a new and immensely productive direction.

During his three decades with the USDA, Beachell worked at the agricultural research station of Texas A&M University, in Beaumont. There he developed nine new strains of high-yielding rice. For more than fifteen years, those nine varieties represented some 90 percent of the long-grain rice grown in the United States. Beachell helped form a private organization to fund ongoing rice research at Texas A&M, and he was instrumental in establishing the Rice Quality Laboratory, the first U.S. rice-testing facility. Over the years, Beachell's reputation spread beyond the United States. Foreign agricultural experts came to Beaumont to confer with him, and he began consulting internationally. After his retirement from the USDA, it was a logical step for Beachell to make the transition to the International Rice Research Institute.

Beachell's development of the miracle rice IR8 was just one of his accomplishments during his years in the Philippines. From the first, he recognized that the new strain wasn't perfect. It was susceptible to certain pests and diseases, and the grain it produced had some undesirable qualities. One Filipina complained to Beachell that the cooked rice scratched her throat. However, given the ever-present threat of famine in Asia, Beachell and his colleagues rushed IR8 into distribution despite its shortcomings. Bellies needed filling, so the variety's high yields and overall hardiness outweighed everything else. Beachell knew that IR8 was a foundation he could build on. Continuing to experiment with other hybrids, he produced a string of improved varieties—IR20, IR22, IR24, and IR28.

In addition to his plant-breeding prowess, Beachell was a first-rate teacher. At IRRI, he mentored an impressive roster of international students, one of whom would carry on his work with far-reaching results. Indian agronomist Gurdev Singh Khush came to the Philippines in 1967. In 1972, when Beachell faced mandatory retirement at Los Baños, Khush took over his position as chief plant breeder. In 1976, Khush crossbred IR8 with thirteen other varieties to produce IR36, a semidwarf variety that was more resistant to pests and diseases than IR8 and which matured two months sooner than traditional varieties,

allowing many areas to grow two crops a year. IR36 also produced the slender grains of rice that most Asians preferred. The
strain quickly became one of the world's most widely planted
food crop varieties, and Khush later improved on it with new
generations of miracle rice.

Although Hank Beachell had left IRRI in good hands, the
sixty-five-year-old scientist wasn't ready to rest on his laurels.
From the Philippines, he moved on to Indonesia, where over
the next ten years, he produced a 100 percent increase in that
country's rice crop. In 1982, he returned to Texas and became a
consultant to RiceTec, Inc., a company specializing in rice technology and consumer products. In 1997, he collaborated with
Cornell University and the USDA to set up a genetic seed bank
to preserve rice cultivars, whose varieties are seemingly endless.
The International Rice Genebank, maintained by IRRI, today
holds the seeds of more than 100,000 strains of rice (researchers
believe the world's total exceeds 140,000 varieties). In addition
to domesticated rice, twenty species of wild rice grow around
the world, which breeders sometimes use to incorporate desir-
able traits into new hybrids. Back when IRRI began its work,
it collected seeds from over 10,000 varieties of cultivated rice,
which provided the deep pool of genetic material used to develop IR8.

Beachell remained active in his field until he was ninety-
five. He told a newspaper reporter that he kept working because
he enjoyed helping people earn a living. Maybe that had something to do with his having lived through the Great Depression,
when simply earning enough to feed your family was exhaust-
ing. Beachell died in 2006 at the age of one hundred. In the
years before his death, he received two honorary doctorates and
was formally recognized by the governments of Korea and Japan

for his achievements in agriculture. The American Society of Agronomy cited him as "the individual most responsible for the Green Revolution in rice." In 1996, he and his colleague Gurdev Singh Khush shared the World Food Prize, a prestigious award presented to those who've made major improvements in the world's food supply. (Beachell used his prize money to establish scholarships at the University of Nebraska, Kansas State, and Texas A&M.)

The impact of the green revolution begun by Henry Beachell, Norman Borlaug, and other plant researchers has been profound, although the new generations of food crops do have their drawbacks. They depend heavily on pesticides and inorganic fertilizers, which too often have poisoned the environment. Critics claim that planting only miracle grains threatens genetic diversity. Improvements intended to aid subsistence farmers have been taken to undreamed of levels by mammoth corporate farming operations. Perhaps the most controversial development in agriculture is the genetic modification of crops, a practice fraught with unknowns. Some of these issues are being addressed by the sustainable agriculture movement, which stresses water and soil conservation, less reliance on synthetic fertilizers, environment responsibility, and the encouragement of small-scale farming.

Beyond all of these considerations lies a more fundamental question: Can food production keep up with the planet's expanding population? Although the population growth rate has slowed since peaking in the early 1960s, Earth's current population of 6.8 billion is still expected to top 9 billion in the next thirty to forty years—a 32 percent jump in the number of people to feed by midcentury. Even if the green revolution is able to keep pace, there'll be an environmental price to pay:

any large-scale intensification of farming will increase the emission of methane, carbon dioxide, and nitrous oxide—gases that contribute to acid rain, the depletion of Earth's ozone layer, and global warming. Complicating the expansion of agriculture is the fact that most of the world's best farmland has already been developed. Each year, farmers struggle to create more arable land by burning forests, scrublands, and grasslands. Their activities generate a staggering amount of air pollution, releasing nearly as much carbon dioxide into the atmosphere as that produced by the burning of fossil fuels.

The challenges to agriculture are formidable, but wherever the green revolution leads, it's impossible to fault its pioneers. Men like Hank Beachell and Norman Borlaug wanted to feed the world's hungry and reduce human misery—which they did. They knew that hunger is a major cause of civil unrest, war, and terrorism, and that improving a country's ability to feed its people is the best way to maintain a peaceful, stable world.

The many honors that Henry Beachell received in his lifetime were well deserved. He no doubt appreciated all of them, although it's a good bet that for this one-time Nebraska farm boy, his greatest reward was the sight of an impoverished rice farmer standing in his paddy and smiling over a bumper crop. It's estimated that rice feeds over half the human beings on Earth. By more than doubling Asia's rice output, Beachell became one of the few people in history who could honestly say that his life's work touched billions. His tough, bountiful new type of rice was truly a miracle of biblical proportions.

TWENTY-FIVE

America's Joan of Arc

INEZ BOISSEVAIN

THE YOUNG WOMAN in the gold tiara and flowing white cape rode a spirited white horse named Grey Dawn. With her dark hair, regal bearing, and classic beauty, the rider looked like Helen of Troy perched astride Pegasus, or Joan of Arc in the vanguard of French forces at Orléans. Joan of Arc was a better comparison, since twenty-six-year-old Inez Milholland was at the head of an army herself, one about to launch itself into battle. The scene of the conflict was the nation's capital, the date March 3, 1913—the day before Woodrow Wilson's inauguration as the twenty-eighth president. Leading a contingent of more than five thousand activists, Milholland was literally in the forefront of the women's suffrage movement in the United States. As she and her fellow soldiers marched down Pennsylvania Avenue—their placards demanding the long-overdue right to vote—they were spat on, taunted, even attacked by their fellow citizens, at least those who happened to be born male. The right for women to vote struck many men as absurd. Everyone knew that men ran things. A woman's place was in the home. Why couldn't these noisy women just keep quiet and get dinner on the table like they were supposed to?

If Milholland hoped to find a sympathetic reception from the new Democratic president, she was disappointed. After he took office, Woodrow Wilson treated the issue of women's suffrage like a sleeping rattlesnake: he gave it a wide berth. That didn't stop Milholland from continuing her efforts. The resistance she met was just another obstacle to overcome in a lifetime of struggling for the disenfranchised and the disadvantaged. No doubt the angry men along Pennsylvania Avenue thought that the crazy suffragist on the white horse would just ride away and things would continue as they were, but they didn't know Inez Milholland. She was willing to fight to the death for her beliefs, which, tragically, is exactly what she did. Before she died, Milholland touched innumerable lives with her passion and commitment to social justice. She also earned a reputation for feistiness among the bohemians and swank set of New York City.

Milholland had activism in her blood. Born in New York in 1886, she was the daughter of John E. Milholland, a writer who championed numerous progressive causes in his articles and editorials for the *New York Tribune*. He believed in pacifism, prison and election reform, federal aid to education, civil rights, and women's suffrage. In 1909, he helped found the NAACP and served as its first treasurer. In a midcareer transformation, John Milholland went from newspaperman to businessman by developing the underground pneumatic tube system used to deliver mail in New York City at the turn of the century. He grew rich from his companies in the United States and Europe, allowing him to send his children to the best schools in New York, London, and Berlin. Although she grew up wealthy, Inez Milholland absorbed her father's social conscience. An early member of the NAACP, she too was a pacifist and an advocate of equality and fairness throughout society. Her dream was to live in a world where everyone had as much as she was blessed with.

Milholland got a chance to put her convictions to the test at Vassar College, where she enrolled in 1905. The tall, blue-eyed, brown-haired beauty hit the exclusive women's school like a tornado. She starred in school plays and became a top athlete, setting records in basketball and track and captaining the field hockey team. In her spare time, she worked with Poughkeepsie's poor children. She also made a name for herself as a campus agitator. To protest the impractical fashion of extremely long hair for women, she grew her own hair till it hung below her fanny. She annoyed the school's administrators with her speeches on socialism and women's rights. Her fellow students were mesmerized by her Greek-goddess looks and vibrant personality. She got the Vassar ladies so fired up about women's rights that two-thirds of them joined her suffrage club. When Harriot Stanton Blatch and other prominent suffragists visited town and were forbidden to appear on campus, Milholland organized a meeting in a cemetery across from the college. Students sat among the tombstones to listen to the speakers. Vassar officials probably threw themselves a party when Milholland finished her BA in 1909.

From Vassar, Milholland moved on to law school at New York University, one of the few major programs in the country to admit women at the time. In New York, she not only continued her activism, she stepped it up. During a Fifth Avenue parade for President William Howard Taft, Milholland rented a room along the route and leaned out the window shouting "Votes for women" through a megaphone, then she made a speech to the crowd below. When women shirtwaist workers went on strike in the city, Milholland stood shoulder to shoulder with the picketers and was arrested along with them (unlike the less fortunate strikers, she was quickly bailed out by her parents). Newspaper reporters gaped at her, one of them calling her "the most beautiful girl who had ever bitten the wrist of a policeman."

Getting herself jailed fit right in with Milholland's studies at NYU, where she specialized in labor law. She earned her degree in 1912 and went to work as a law clerk at the firm of Osborne, Lamb & Garvan. Once she passed the New York bar exam, she was assigned to investigate conditions at the infamous Sing Sing prison. Milholland surprised prison officials by meeting alone with male inmates, something administrators discouraged. She learned firsthand about the facility's inhuman conditions, information she put in a report that led to landmark reforms.

Milholland gave her time to several progressive organizations. In addition to the NAACP, she joined the Women's Trade Union League, the Equality League of Self-Supporting Women, and the National Child Labor Committee. In 1913, she joined the newly established Congressional Union for Woman Suffrage, one of the most active groups in the fight for a constitutional amendment granting all women the right to vote. Her affiliation with the Congressional Union was the reason Milholland happened to be riding a white horse through the streets of Washington, D.C., the day before Woodrow Wilson took office. In her first suffrage parade, two years earlier, Milholland had carried a banner emblazoned with the words FORWARD THROUGH THE DARKNESS, FORWARD INTO LIGHT. After the Congressional Union changed its name to the National Woman's Party, the group adopted those words as its slogan.

Like her father, Milholland promoted her ideas with her pen. She wrote occasionally for *Harper's* and for the popular literary, political, and muckraking journal *McClure's*. She also became associated with the socialist magazine *The Masses*. The editor of *The Masses* was Max Eastman, a rakishly handsome intellectual who'd been a founder of the Men's League for Women's Suffrage in 1910. Like Milholland, Eastman was part of the bohemian culture in Greenwich Village, a collection of avant-garde writers, artists, poets, and other left-leaning radicals. Eastman was charming and worldly, and he and Milholland found themselves circling each other with looks of mutual admiration. Although they tried, their romance failed to ignite. Eastman later confided that the beautiful, athletic young firebrand didn't like "my lazy-bashful drawl or my languid way of slumping into a chair." Nevertheless, Milholland helped Eastman obtain financing to keep *The Masses* going, and she defended the publication when it was sued for libel in 1913.

Eastman wasn't the first of Milholland's suitors. Years earlier, while sailing home from Europe aboard the Cunard liner *Lucania*, Milholland met inventor Guglielmo Marconi, who was just gaining fame for his wireless telegraph. The impetuous Italian quickly fell in love, which, according to his daughter's 1962 memoir, "he tended to do with fair regularity." Marconi proposed to the seventeen-year-old American beauty, and she accepted, although the romance was never serious and Marconi soon broke it off. It wasn't until after her affair with Eastman that Milholland met the man she would marry, Eugen Boissevain, a liberal-minded, free-spirited Dutch importer who encouraged the independent Yankee to continue her activism and her law career—a rare male attitude for the period. The couple fell in love aboard another Cunard liner, this time the *Mauretania*. (The British shipping line must have put a special potion in its punch.) Asserting her freedom as a "new woman," Milholland was the one who proposed. The two were wed in London in July 1913.

Shortly after her marriage, the new Mrs. Boissevain had

another cause to take up—international peace. Not long after the outbreak of World War I in 1914, she assumed the role of freelance war correspondent and traveled to Italy. Although she wasn't allowed to visit the front, Boissevain wrote a series of pacifist articles that angered the Italian government. She was ultimately kicked out of the country. Undeterred, she sailed aboard Henry Ford's "Peace Ship," an ocean liner chartered by the automobile maker in December 1915 to carry American pacifists to Europe, where they hoped to negotiate an end to the war. Several countries took part in the group's peace efforts. Unfortunately, the warring nations weren't in the mood to cooperate, and the European conflict would drag on until the end of 1918.

When Boissevain returned home from Europe in 1916, she threw herself into her work for the National Woman's Party. She agreed to visit a dozen western states that had already given women the vote. Her job was to convince women in those states to support a federal women's suffrage amendment. Boissevain's speechmaking itinerary was taxing, which exacerbated a lingering illness originally attributed to infected tonsils. In reality, she'd developed pernicious anemia, a decrease in red blood cells caused by the body's inability to absorb vitamin B12. Victims suffer from fatigue, loss of appetite, and a number of other symptoms. Today the disease is easily treated with vitamin injections, but in 1916, it was usually fatal. The only treatment consisted of blood transfusions.

Despite her illness, Boissevain refused to cut back on her grueling schedule. In the middle of a speech in Los Angeles, she collapsed onstage and was rushed to the Good Samaritan Hospital. She lingered for ten weeks, at times giving the appearance of making a full recovery. On November 23, the *New York Times* ran a brief article stating that Boissevain had shown "permanent improvement." Three days later, the paper reported her death at the age of thirty.

After Boissevain died, the National Woman's Party issued a poster depicting her as the heroic maiden in white sitting on a white horse, her banner fluttering overhead with the exhortation "Forward into Light." Framing the portrait was the inscription "Inez Milholland Boissevain, Who Died for the Freedom of Women." The suffrage movement had many other important leaders, but Boissevain made the ultimate sacrifice. The last words she uttered in public, directed at Woodrow Wilson, became a rallying cry for the National Woman's Party: "Mr. President, how long must women wait for liberty?"

President Wilson did come to support women's suffrage, but only out of political necessity. Before he changed his stance, members of the National Woman's Party picketed the White House for several months in 1917. Braving inclement weather and harassment by unruly mobs, the women were eventually arrested and jailed. When the prisoners went on a hunger strike, they were beaten and force-fed. Embarrassed by the negative publicity over the harsh treatment of the picketers, and hoping for the support of women for his decision to enter World War I, Wilson endorsed women's suffrage in January 1918. Even so, Congress failed to pass a proposed amendment. It wasn't until after the war that the measure was approved—and it still needed to be ratified by thirty-six states to become law.

It's hard to believe that well into the twentieth century half the population remained disenfranchised, that the automobile, the airplane, and the radio would all have been invented while women occupied essentially the same position in society they'd held in 1776. Finally, on August 18, 1920—four years after Inez Boissevain collapsed on a Los Angeles stage—Tennessee became the thirty-sixth state to ratify the amendment that granted women throughout the country the right to vote. The Nineteenth Amendment to the Constitution was a reality. By her direct actions and by her example, Boissevain played a major role in winning women the vote, one of the most far-reaching accomplishments in the history of our country.

Although Boissevain will always be associated with the women's suffrage movement, her activism on behalf of workers, prisoners, children, and African Americans, along with her efforts to end international conflict, earned her a place of honor among the champions of human dignity. With the empathy of an innocent child, she once declared that she could never "be happy while others are not." Bringing comfort to all of humanity may have been unattainable, but it was an aspiration worthy of Joan of Arc.

In her marriage and her career, Boissevain overcame the limitations imposed by traditional female roles, making her one of the twentieth century's first liberated women. On Christmas Day 1916, suffragists gathered for a memorial service in her honor in the U.S. Capitol's Statuary Hall. The young martyr was buried near the Milholland family's country estate in Lewis, New York, in the Adirondack Mountains—at the foot of the newly rechristened Mount Inez.

TWENTY-SIX

A Saint's Unassuming Assistant

JOSEPH DUTTON

JULY 29, 1886, was another glorious day in paradise. Warm breezes swept across the Kalaupapa Peninsula, a green triangle of land jutting into the Pacific on the north side of Molokai. The foaming white surf edged the shoreline like a pearl choker. Inland, a fortress wall of two thousand foot sea cliffs sealed off the peninsula from the rest of the island, fifth largest in the Hawaiian chain. People on Molokai went about their daily round of tending their crops and livestock or fishing the bountiful offshore waters. Here on the Kalaupapa Peninsula, however, life was different. Since 1866, this isolated flatland had been inhabited by several hundred souls destined to spend their lives in exile. Kalaupapa was the home of Hawaii's leper colony.

For thirteen years, the lepers on Molokai had been cared for by Belgian priest Damien De Veuster. Before his arrival, the colony was a lawless place, with inadequate shelter and no permanent doctor, its residents largely left to fend for themselves. Father Damien had treated, comforted, and shared the privations of these sick and friendless people, and he'd truly become one of them, contracting leprosy himself in 1876. Damien had built schools, decent residences, and a church. Most important of all, he had restored hope and human dignity to the unfortunate outcasts.

On this sparkling July day, Father Damien gazed toward the sea. He sat in his buggy near the peninsula's small wharf, a thickset, bespectacled man in a shabby black cassock and wide-brimmed hat. An interisland steamer had dropped anchor and sent its rowboat ashore. Climbing out of the boat was a stranger, a middle-aged man, slender and erect, with a bushy, graying beard. He approached the priest, patting the flanks of the aged white horse that pulled his rig.

"You are Father Damien?" the man asked.

When the priest acknowledged who he was, the man said, "I am Joseph Dutton, a lay brother, and I have come here to help you carry on your good work."

Father Damien searched the stranger's face and replied, "I need you. Jump up here alongside me and we will ride over to the settlement."

Although Joseph Dutton showed up that day unannounced and unexpected, he was sincerely welcome. For the next three years, until Father Damien's death at age forty-nine, Dutton served as the priest's right-hand man, and for the following forty-one years, he carried on Damien's work with selfless devotion. Dutton's path to Molokai was long and convoluted—half a lifetime filled with duty, then disillusionment, and, ultimately, the search for redemption. Dutton needed Father Damien as much as the saintly priest needed him.

Born in Stowe, Vermont, in 1843, Dutton grew up in Janesville, Wisconsin, where his family had moved when he was four. He received his early education from his schoolteacher mother, not entering public school until he was twelve but going on to attend Milton College. As a young man, he joined the local military corps, the Janesville Zouaves. When the Civil War broke out, the cadets formed a volunteer company, which became part of the Thirteenth Wisconsin Volunteer Infantry. Dutton was made regimental quartermaster sergeant and later commissioned a lieutenant. He never fought in any major battles, recalling that his regiment mostly just marched around. After the war, however, Dutton got his fill of death. For two years, he worked for the federal government disinterring the bodies of soldiers and reburying them in newly established national cemeteries.

In 1866, Dutton married, but the union was unhappy and soon ended in divorce. His failed marriage and the gruesomeness of his job pushed Dutton into a state of debauchery that lasted for the next ten years. While he was previously a moderate drinker, his consumption of whiskey became "fierce and reckless," as he described it. Toward the end of his "degenerate decade," he calculated that he'd consumed a staggering fifteen barrels of whiskey.

Despite his drunkenness, Dutton was still able to function. In 1868, he joined a friend he'd met in Tennessee to help him run—of all things—a distillery. Two years later, he moved to Memphis, where he worked for the next fourteen years. It was during this period that Dutton swore off alcohol. He also began thinking about taking religious vows. Raised an Episcopalian, he spent a year studying Catholicism. In 1883, on his fortieth birthday, he joined the Roman Catholic Church, having become convinced that although Episcopalianism could make him respectable, Catholicism would give him a better chance to make amends for his past life. He marked his conversion by changing his Christian name from Ira to Joseph, in honor of Saint Joseph, who, he said, had led him "straight into the arms of the historic

Church to enjoy its great penitential system. . . . I was disposed to be a new person, Joseph Dutton, a servant of our Lord."

In the year following his conversion, Dutton entered the Trappist monastery of Gethsemani in Kentucky (later the refuge of writer Thomas Merton). Dutton relished the discipline and hard work at Gethsemani, where he slept on a three-foot-wide wooden bench in a six-by-six-foot cell. But after twenty months, he left without taking his vows. He hungered for a place where he could engage in humanitarian work. He traveled to St. Louis, then to New Orleans. It was in New Orleans that he first heard about Father Damien and his efforts on Molokai. Dutton visited Notre Dame University to learn more about Father Damien from professor Charles Warren Stoddard, who'd written an article about the Catholic priest. Convinced that he'd found his life's work, Dutton journeyed to San Francisco and booked passage aboard the ship *Eureka*. He arrived in Honolulu on July 22, 1886.

Dutton sought and received permission to go to the leper colony from the Hawaiian board of health, although he refused to accept any pay for his work there. "I was square with the world," he wrote. "I did not owe a single cent. . . . I wanted to serve some useful purpose during the rest of my life without any hope of monetary or other reward." Dutton even refused the monthly $50 military pension he'd earned. He never wavered in his vow of poverty, although years later he directed that his pension be paid to the Sisters of the Good Shepherd in Memphis.

One week after arriving in Honolulu, Dutton stepped ashore on Molokai to begin his new life. He climbed into Father Damien's buggy, and the two men set off for Kalawao, home to some five hundred afflicted Hawaiians. As they rode along, Damien revealed that he'd asked for Catholic brothers to be assigned to Molokai, but the Hawaiian mission had none to spare. The priest addressed the new arrival as Brother Dutton, a name he would proudly answer to for the next forty-five years. Damien enthusiastically described his ambitious building plans for the settlement. Already suffering from an advanced stage of leprosy, he meant to use what time he had left to good advantage. "He was full of plans that morning," Dutton wrote, "talking of what he wished for his lepers, the dreams he had always had."

Dutton quickly assumed a heavy workload, never refusing to do anything asked of him. Damien charged him with the upkeep of the settlement's two churches. Dutton spent most of his time assisting Dr. Arthur Mouritz, a physician who'd arrived in the colony two years earlier. Each day, Dutton washed and dressed the sores of the lepers, becoming as proficient as Dr. Mouritz himself. In addition, Dutton was Father Damien's companion, nurse, secretary, and household manager. He became the colony's sanitary engineer, architect, and landscaper. He ran the settlement's small post office. Eventually, he took over the Baldwin Home for Boys, one of two facilities for leper children without families, the other a girl's home in the town of Kalaupapa across the peninsula.

When Father Damien died in 1889, Dutton assumed the role of informing the world about the martyred priest's life and ongoing work. For the next four decades, Dutton kept up a voluminous correspondence, his address book crammed with more than four thousand names. Aside from prompting donations, Dutton's letters unintentionally revealed his own years of devoted service. Though he discouraged personal tributes, his work came to the attention of many high-ranking Americans. He received letters from President Warren G. Harding and fellow Vermonter Calvin Coolidge. Mrs. Woodrow Wilson sent Dutton the bouquet she'd carried at her husband's inauguration. President Theodore Roosevelt paid Dutton an even greater honor.

In 1908, the Great White Fleet—a convoy of sixteen U.S. Navy ships—was sailing around the world in a demonstration of American military power. As the fleet passed Hawaii, Roosevelt ordered it to divert its course and steam past Molokai's Kalaupapa Peninsula. When Dutton's orphan boys spotted the ships offshore and spread the news, the old man hurried down to the beach, where he hoisted the U.S. flag. The "Fleet sighted the flag and headed straight for it," Dutton wrote. "The Sixteen big Battle Ships formed lines right in our front—and made the evolutions for the entire settlement."

Though Dutton vowed never to leave Molokai, he changed his mind in 1917 when the United States entered World War I. Then in his seventies, Dutton volunteered to form a company of Civil War veterans to fight at the front as an example for young Americans. Not surprisingly, his offer was rejected. Still wanting to contribute, Dutton sent his old binoculars to the War Department, hoping they'd be of some use, which they were—the navy issued the binoculars to one of its battleships (they were later returned with a certificate attesting to their use). Dutton viewed the conflict in Europe as a way of reengaging members of the Kalaupapa colony with the outside world. At his urging, the community bought $3,000 in war savings stamps and donated almost $6,000 to the Red Cross for relief efforts.

War may not have dislodged Brother Dutton from his tiny cottage on the grounds of the Baldwin Home for Boys, but failing health finally did. In June 1930, when he was eighty-seven, he traveled to Honolulu for treatment of an eye problem and other ailments. He didn't want to go, but others talked him into the trip. It was the first time since 1886 that he'd left the settlement. He never returned alive to his beloved Molokai. He died in Honolulu on March 26, 1931—one month short of his eighty-eighth birthday.

Dutton was always far too modest to compare himself to his mentor, Father Damien, and he demurred when others did, but for the last half of his life, he was every bit as worthy. In October 2009, Father Damien was canonized for his heroic work and self-sacrifice on Molokai. The Belgian priest spent sixteen years among the lepers. Joseph Dutton spent forty-four. Dutton was imperturbable, a gentle, patient being whose every word and deed represented another small step on his personal road to salvation. One particularly revealing photograph shows him sitting in a chair, a frail old man with snowy hair and beard. A young leprosy patient snuggles against his side, smiling shyly. Dutton's thin arm is wrapped protectively around the girl, a gesture of infinite tenderness. Though never more than a lay volunteer, Dutton had the heart and soul of a saint. Few have ever labored as long, and with so much love in their heart, for their fellow man.

Dutton's extraordinary legacy includes not just what he accomplished on Molokai but also what he represented to the world at large. By living among the lepers for over four decades with no ill effects, he was living proof that the centuries-old fear of the disease was unfounded. Doctors now know that leprosy is not highly communicable, and that only 4 to 5 percent of the planet's population is susceptible to infection. Dutton's efforts to reengage the colony's members with life outside their confines foreshadowed modern treatment protocols that followed the development of sulfone drugs in the 1940s. The new drugs effectively conquered leprosy (now known as Hansen's disease). With only a few treatments, patients are no longer infectious and can live normal lives within their community.

After his death, Dutton was buried in Kalawao at St. Philo-
mena Roman Catholic Church. In addition to his Molokai
gravesite, he is memorialized by the Brother Dutton Elementary School in Beloit, Wisconsin, and the Blessed Sacrament
Church in his birthplace of Stowe, Vermont. The lives of Father
Damien and Joseph Dutton are part of the story told today at
Kalaupapa National Historical Park, created in 1980 to preserve
the memories of the frightful era when no effective treatment
existed for leprosy. "Brother Dutton" is still revered by the few
remaining residents of the Kalaupapa colony, who've chosen to
remain in their longtime home. For them, the compassion of
the once broken man who came to live among Hawaii's outcasts
will never be forgotten.

TWENTY-SEVEN

A Life's Labor of Love

GERTRUDE ELION

THE YOUNG WOMAN in the white lab coat sat amid an array of beakers and flasks filled with mysterious potions, like a sorcerer's apprentice in a medieval workshop. Brushing back a wayward lock of her fiery red hair, twenty-five-year-old Trudy Elion dipped a thin strip of paper into a nose-crinkling green liquid. She waited for the damp test strip to change color, then held it against a chart to check the pH reading, making a notation on her clipboard.

An industrial chemist, Elion worked as a quality control agent in the Brooklyn plant of the Quaker Maid Company, the food-processing arm of the giant A&P grocery chain. There weren't many women chemists in 1943, so Elion felt lucky to have a job, although her role at Quaker Maid wasn't exactly what she'd hoped for. As a child, she'd been inspired by Marie Curie, the Polish-born French scientist whose pioneering studies of radioactivity earned her a pair of Nobel Prizes. Elion hoped to make scientific discoveries of her own one day, but at Quaker Maid, she was given the lowly task of testing the acidity of pickles. She also made sure the berries that went into jams weren't moldy and that the egg yolks used in mayonnaise were fresh. Madame Curie she was not.

By the end of her career, however, Elion would be regarded as an equal to the famous scientist. During a half century on the leading edge of biochemical research, Trudy Elion developed breakthrough drugs used to treat leukemia, bacterial and viral diseases, malaria, gout, and transplant rejections, and her work led to the AIDS drug AZT—none of which might have happened if Elion hadn't vowed to find a cure for cancer while she was still a teenager.

When Elion was fifteen, her beloved Russian grandfather, who had lived near her family since Elion was three, died a painful, lingering death from stomach cancer. Visiting her grandfather in the hospital, Elion was shocked by how much he'd changed from the ravages of his illness. "Nobody should suffer that much," she said. Right then, she knew she had a goal to which she would devote herself. "I was highly motivated to do something that might eventually lead to a cure for this terrible disease." Elion's career became a labor of love, one that saved the lives or improved the quality of life of untold numbers of patients—and continues to do so even now. Elion has been called one of the twentieth century's great humanitarian scientists, but her life was more than a series of triumphs in the laboratory. She also overcame the rigid gender bias that had kept women out of scientific research. Trudy Elion simply refused to think of herself as a woman scientist. She was a scientist. Period.

Gertrude Belle Elion was born in New York City in 1918, the daughter of immigrants. Her father, Robert, had come to the United States from Lithuania when he was twelve. Her mother, Bertha, had emigrated from Russia at the age of fourteen. Until Trudy was seven, the family lived in a Manhattan apartment next to Robert Elion's dental office. In 1925, the family moved to the Bronx, where Trudy and her brother, Herbert, enjoyed a happy childhood, playing in nearby parks, roaming the Bronx Zoo, and attending public schools. Young Trudy often accompanied her father to the Metropolitan Opera, which instilled in her a lifelong love of music.

An exceptional student, Trudy finished high school when she was fifteen. "I was a child with an insatiable thirst for knowledge," she recalled. In 1933, she enrolled in New York's Hunter College to study chemistry. By then, her family's finances had been wrecked by the Great Depression. Fortunately, Hunter College was free at that time. Otherwise, said Elion, "I might never have received a higher education." She was elected to Phi Beta Kappa and graduated summa cum laude in 1937.

Elion wanted to go on to graduate school but couldn't afford it, so she decided to work for a while and save some money. In spite of her academic accomplishments, Elion had a hard time finding employment in her field. "There weren't many jobs," she said, "and what jobs there were, were not for women." To her surprise, several prospective employers told her they wouldn't hire her because she was too good-looking. They were afraid she'd distract the male employees.

It's difficult to picture laboratory workers as leering Lotharios, their libidos seething among the test tubes, and it's even harder to imagine someone in a funky white smock causing their passions to flare like the flame of a Bunsen burner. Of course, there's no denying that petite, brown-eyed Trudy Elion was easy to look at. She bore a faint resemblance to singer Joan Baez. "I guess I was kind of cute," she admitted years later, "but I can't imagine that I would have been a distracting influence."

In desperation, Elion attended secretarial school for a few

weeks—and hated it. She found a short-term job teaching bio-chemistry to nurses. When that ended, she agreed to work for a New York chemist for free, just to get the experience. The chemist finally started paying her $20 a week, and she was able to save enough to enter graduate school. She enrolled at New York University in 1939. After her first year of classes, she began working days as a high school chemistry and physics teacher, completing the research component of her degree at night and on weekends. She received her master's in organic chemistry in 1941, the lone female in her class.

While she was at NYU, Elion met a young man named Leonard Canter, a student at City College who hoped to become an investment banker. The two fell in love and made plans to marry. A photo taken in 1940 shows Elion and Canter lying on a blanket in a park. Elion is on her back, her arms around Canter's neck as he leans over her. Their casual intimacy reveals everything about their relationship. Not long after the picture was taken, Canter contracted subacute bacterial endocarditis, a strep infection of the heart. He died in 1941—two years before penicillin became widely available, a drug that would have saved his life. Elion was shattered, and while she had a few other beaus over the years, she never married. Coupled with the death of her grandfather, the loss of her fiancé increased her dedication to science.

Laboratory work was still hard to find when Elion finished her graduate studies, so she continued teaching high school. It was only after the United States became embroiled in World War II that jobs once denied to women became available, which is how Elion ended up testing the acidity of pickles for A&P. She grew bored with that before long and looked for something more challenging. She found a job as a pharmaceutical researcher

at a Johnson & Johnson lab in New Jersey. To her disappointment, the job lasted only six months. Then, in 1944, Elion got
the biggest break of her career. She landed a job with the Burroughs Wellcome pharmaceutical company in Tuckahoe, New
York. Elion was hired as an assistant to biochemist George H.
Hitchings, who was attempting to develop a new class of drugs.
It was the beginning of a relationship that lasted the rest of Elion's career.

Hitchings was a rare specimen for his time. He was completely gender-blind. "His other assistant was a woman," noted
Elion. "He was one of these unusual people that didn't care
whether it was a man or a woman, and gave us equal opportunity." (The original female assistant told Hitchings he shouldn't
hire Elion—because she was too well dressed! The woman
thought Elion wouldn't want to soil her hands.) Hitchings was
equally liberal when it came to academic credentials. He put
more stock in a person's abilities than in the letters appended
to his or her name. After Elion got the job with Hitchings, she
started working on a PhD at Brooklyn Polytechnic Institute.
Since she could only attend school at night, her progress was
slow. When the school demanded that she quit her job and attend full time, she went to Hitchings for advice. "You don't need
to get a doctorate," he told her. "You can do it all without." And
she did, like a budding Marie Curie.

Hitchings allowed his new protégée to progress as rapidly
as she could. "From being solely an organic chemist, I soon became very much involved in microbiology and in the biological
activities of the compounds I was synthesizing," Elion recalled.
"I never felt constrained to remain strictly in chemistry, but was
able to broaden my horizons into biochemistry, pharmacology,
immunology, and eventually virology."

Hitchings had intrigued Elion with his revolutionary new approach to developing drugs. Traditionally, pharmacologists relied on trial and error: they might tweak an existing drug to see if it produced a different result or test random compounds to find out how they performed against common pathogens or conditions. It was all very hit and miss. Hitchings, on the other hand, set out to create drugs with specific properties, which could be aimed at specific illnesses—in other words, to design drugs rather than stumble upon them. Through his study of how the body's cells work, Hitchings became convinced that he could attack diseased cells by interfering with their growth cycle, a radical new concept in pharmacology.

In the 1940s, the double-helix structure of DNA, or deoxyribonucleic acid, had yet to be discovered. However, it was known that nucleic acids contain four chemical bases: adenine, guanine, cytosine, and thymine (it's these four chemicals that encode a cell's genetic information). Since nucleic acids are required for growth in all living things, including cancer cells, bacteria, and viruses, Hitchings hoped to create artificial chemical bases—"rubber donuts," he called them—that would fool diseased cells into incorporating them into their DNA, inhibiting their ability to divide and multiply. The trick was to create compounds that interrupted DNA synthesis in abnormal cells without damaging healthy cells. In 1945, Hitchings proved that nucleic acids would accept artificial chemical bases when he successfully introduced a thymine substitute into test cells—"the key discovery from which everything else stems," he said.

Using Hitchings's model, Elion succeeded in developing several new rubber donuts of her own. In 1948, she created a compound called diaminopurine, which blocked the reproduction of leukemia cells—a landmark achievement. However, the compound turned out to be too toxic. Two years later, she synthesized thioguanine. While the drug was effective against leukemia, it too had problems. Shortly afterward, Elion created a compound called 6-mercaptopurine. Following toxicology tests and clinical trials in childhood leukemia patients, the drug was put on the market as Purinethol. The drug worked quite well, although patients frequently relapsed. Elion spent years trying to improve Purinethol, which is still used in combination with other drugs to treat leukemia. Her quest to improve Purinethol led her to create another milestone drug.

In 1957, Elion synthesized a compound called azathioprine—the first drug to stop the body's immune system from rejecting foreign tissue. Marketed as Imuran, the new drug permitted kidney transplants from unrelated donors for the first time. Previously, kidney transplants had only been successful between close relatives, such as identical twins. Elion's new drug restored the lives of thousands of patients debilitated by kidney disease and paved the way for other types of organ transplants.

Elion had a host of breakthroughs in this period. She developed pyrimethamine, an effective antimalarial drug. She created trimethoprim, a drug that's still used to treat bacterial infections of the urinary tract as well as gastrointestinal infections and some types of pneumonia. In the 1960s, she modified 6-mercaptopurine to produce allopurinol (Zyloprim), a drug used to treat gout. Elion's many successes earned her a growing recognition at Burroughs Wellcome. In 1963, she was made the head of the chemotherapy division. Four years later, she took over the department of experimental therapy, the first woman to head a major research arm of the company.

In 1970, Burroughs Wellcome moved its laboratories to North Carolina's Research Triangle Park, the sylvan setting of Duke University, North Carolina State, and the University of North Carolina at Chapel Hill. After settling into her new home, Elion led an attack on a problem that had stumped pharmacologists for years—viruses. In a classic "aha" moment, her team came up with acyclovir, the first successful antiviral medication. The drug had a strange and unexpected effect on these puzzling maladies, which include the herpes virus, a common and persistent infection. When it comes in contact with acyclovir, the herpes virus converts the drug into a substance that's toxic to its own cells, essentially killing itself. Marketed as Zovirax, the miracle drug became Burroughs Wellcome's biggest seller. In addition to bringing relief to herpes sufferers, Zovirax is effective against shingles and several other viral diseases.

By the 1980s, Elion was reaching the end of her active tenure at Burroughs Wellcome. In her prolific career, she'd accumulated over forty patents for her pharmaceutical innovations. Although she officially retired in 1983, the team she'd led in the discovery of Zovirax continued her work to create azidothymidine, or AZT, the first drug to successfully delay the development of the AIDS virus in HIV patients. With typical modesty, Elion refused to take credit for AZT, although its discovery was only possible thanks to the groundwork she'd laid.

Elion may have retired at sixty-five, but you wouldn't have believed it if you tried to keep up with her. Retained as a scientist emeritus at Burroughs Wellcome, she consulted frequently on ongoing projects. She became a research professor of medicine and pharmacology at Duke and an adjunct professor of pharmacology at UNC (an avid basketball fan, she must have been conflicted when those two rivals took to the court). She assisted the World Health Organization in its fight against tropical diseases. She served on the National Cancer Advisory Board, consulted with Congress on issues of scientific research, and lectured at universities at home and abroad. In her free time, she loved to return to New York and attend the Metropolitan Opera with old friends.

Elion's life was full in her retirement years, but the best was yet to come. On Monday, October 17, 1988, at six thirty in the morning, Elion received a telephone call while she was getting dressed. "Congratulations," a strange voice said, "you've just won the Nobel Prize in Medicine." Elion thought it was a joke and told her caller she didn't think he was one bit funny. The caller, it turned out, was a radio reporter who'd just read a press release sent from Stockholm announcing that year's winners of the prestigious prize. Elion still didn't believe the man, but after receiving a stream of congratulatory calls, she realized it was true. She and George Hitchings were being honored for their pioneering work in developing the line of drugs that had come to be called antimetabolites (drugs that inhibit the metabolism of diseased cells). The Nobel committee also cited their improvement in research methodology, noting that their ability to design drugs was founded on an understanding of the "basic biochemical and physiological processes" of cells rather than guesswork.

The Nobel Prize had rarely been given to researchers at pharmaceutical companies, or to scientists without a PhD, making Elion's prize even sweeter. Elion felt that she and Hitchings made a great team, one that endured for forty years. Whenever they encountered a research challenge, they would talk it out. By the time they arrived at a solution, it was impossible to tell whose idea it was. "It was very much a meeting of the minds," said Elion. She also counted herself lucky to have worked for Burroughs Wellcome (now GlaxoSmithKline). Founded as a research organization, the company generously supported that aim with its profits. (Today, the London-based Wellcome Trust is one of the largest private charities in the world, spending hundreds of millions of dollars each year on biomedical research.)

Before she died in 1999 at the age of eighty-one, Elion was showered with additional awards. She received several honorary doctorates, including one from Brooklyn Polytechnic Institute, the school that told her she had to quit her job at Burroughs Wellcome in order to complete her PhD. (Elion chuckled over that particular honor, calling it poetic justice.) She was elected to the National Academy of Sciences and inducted into the National Women's Hall of Fame, the National Inventors Hall of Fame (the first female honoree), the Engineering and Science Hall of Fame, and the Women in Technology International Hall of Fame. While the recognition was nice, Elion said that her greatest satisfaction came from having fulfilled the vow she'd made when she was fifteen years old—to do all she could to alleviate suffering caused by disease.

"When you meet someone who has lived for twenty-five years with a kidney graft, there's your reward," said Elion. She received numerous testimonials from people thanking her for saving their lives or the lives of loved ones. She once referred to the "satisfaction that you get from having someone come up and say, 'My child had acute leukemia and your drug saved him.' Or, 'My little girl had herpes encephalitis, and she is now cured.'" Those encounters were the highlight of Elion's career. "What greater joy can you have than to know what an impact your work has on people's lives?"

Gertrude Elion attained the peak of her profession despite the many impediments she faced. She rose above her early financial difficulties, overcame widespread gender bias, and endured the professional skepticism that she and Dr. Hitchings encountered when they sought to create a totally new type of drug.

Throughout her long career, she refused to be frustrated by the false leads and blind alleys inherent in the slow and methodical process of biochemical research.

Elion might have stopped at any point along the way and said, "This is enough. I've done all I can." We should all be thankful that she kept going. In 1991, President George H. W. Bush presented Elion with the National Medal of Science, the nation's highest honor in science. The president said that Elion's work had "transformed the world," which was no overstatement. Today, millions of people lead longer, healthier lives because of Trudy Elion, a woman whose intellectual curiosity was matched only by her concern for her fellow human beings.

TWENTY-EIGHT

The Mayor Who Just Wanted to Be Fair

GOLDEN RULE JONES

SUMMER GUSTS RATTLED the cornstalks in the hilly fields outside Collinsville, New York, a dusty upstate village lost somewhere between the Adirondacks and Lake Ontario. Distant rumbles signaled an approaching late-afternoon thunderstorm. Ten-year-old Samuel Jones returned his tools to a tumbledown shed at the end of another day of toil—one that stretched from 4:00 a.m. till sundown. Sam's work as a laborer here on a neighbor's farm didn't pay much, a meager $3 a month, but in 1856 it was enough to help keep his family from starvation. His father could barely make ends meet with his jobs as a stonemason and tenant farmer, so young Sam had been forced to go to work. Things had been tough ever since the Joneses immigrated to the United States from Wales in 1849, when Sam was three years old. Though he'd only had time to master the bare basics of arithmetic in school and never studied grammar, Sam was a smart boy. He'd set his goals higher than grubbing in the soil for someone else.

When Sam Jones turned fourteen, he found work in a sawmill, which paid considerably more than he'd earned as a farm laborer. For three summers, he was a helper in the engine room of a steamboat plying the Black River. It was a hot and dirty occupation, but it taught him some basic mechanical skills. At nineteen, Jones landed his first job in the oil business, an industry he would be associated with for the rest of life. Jones went to work in the oil fields of western Pennsylvania, the birthplace of the American oil industry. Commercial oil drilling was only a few years old, launched in 1859 with the landmark Drake well near Titusville, Pennsylvania. Jones's career grew along with the expansion of the oil business. He became a jack-of-all-trades around an oil rig, spending time as a driller and pipe liner, running pump engines and dressing tools. He learned the ropes, kept his eyes open for advancement, and saved all the money he could.

After five years, Jones had accumulated enough money and knowledge to go into business on his own. It was the beginning of a career that would make him a wealthy man, but even after he became rich, Jones would never forget his early struggles. He'd spent enough time out of work or sweating at low-paying jobs to make him acutely aware of the difficulty working men faced in providing for their families. That intimate personal knowledge colored everything he did—in business and eventually in politics—until the end of his days. Before he died, Samuel M. Jones would become known throughout the country as an exceptional human being—a rare man of wealth and power who cared more about other people than he cared about money. His guiding principle wasn't complicated. He simply adhered to the Golden Rule: he did unto others as he would have them do unto himself. It was a humane creed of fairness and generosity that had the power to transform society—and scare the stuffing out of businessmen and politicians.

Jones prospered during his early years of running his own company. In 1875, he married a young woman from Pleasant-ville, Pennsylvania, named Alma Bernice Curtiss. The couple had three children, one of whom died in infancy, a blow that Jones took hard. He was even more distraught when Alma died in 1885. Seeking a change to lift his grief, Jones moved to northwestern Ohio, where oil deposits had just been discovered. Jones sank the first major well in the Lima area, one that produced six hundred barrels of oil a day. In 1887, he became a founder of Ohio Oil, a hugely successful company that at one time pumped half of all the oil produced in Ohio and Indiana. In 1889, industry giant Standard Oil bought out the Ohio Oil Company, leaving the already comfortable Samuel Jones a rich man.

In 1892, Jones married Helen Beach and moved to her hometown of Toledo, a city of over eighty thousand in far north-western Ohio, just inland from Lake Erie. Served by railroads and canals, Toledo had become a booming industrial and commercial center in the second half of the nineteenth century. Its factories produced everything from furniture to railroad equipment. Several thriving glass companies, including the Libbey Glass Works, made Toledo famous as the "City of Glass." Thousands of immigrants poured into the area late in the nineteenth century, drawn by the lure of manufacturing jobs. It was an ideal place for an entrepreneur the likes of Samuel Jones. Deciding that his future lay in making tools for the oil industry, Jones experimented with new types of drilling equipment. In 1894, he patented a new kind of iron pumping rod, used to lift oil out of the ground, and he formed a company to produce it, along with other drilling gear. He gave his new enterprise the unpo-etic name of the Acme Sucker Rod Company. It may have had an ugly-duckling moniker, but the business became a beautiful swan under Jones's inspired management.

The labor conditions Jones put in place were fifty years ahead of their time. His company's credo was downright shocking: the most important objective, he said, was "making men"; making money was secondary. Unlike most employers of his day, Jones believed in paying his workers a decent wage. All he asked was that they work hard in return and, as he did, follow the Golden Rule. He shunned the use of child labor, instituted an eight-hour workday, granted everyone a week's annual paid vacation, and awarded Christmas bonuses equal to 5 percent of a person's salary. He subsidized a cooperative insurance program. He held company picnics, concerts, and lectures so he could mix with his employees and get to know them as individuals. He built Golden Rule Hall as a meeting place and dining facility, with meals at less than cost. He constructed Golden Rule Park and Playground for the use of workers and their families. He formed a thirty-piece Golden Rule Band, paying for the members' uniforms and instruments with company profits that he claimed were "the product of our common toil." A believer in the gospel of love espoused by Jesus, Jones wrote inspirational songs for the band about peace and brotherhood (he was a bit of a proto-hippie).

Jones was confident that even society's outcasts—the "worthless and drunken," to use his words—could be productive if given a chance. He was convinced that the way to encourage honorable behavior was by allowing people to earn the self-respect that comes from honest work, and he ran his company on that theory. "We ignored the well-established rule of business in inquiring into every man's history before giving him employment," he wrote in his book *The New Right: A Plea for Fair Play Through a More Just Social Order.* (The "new right" he was referring to was the right to work.) "We simply took him in and assumed for the time being that he was a man, and undertook, so far as we knew how, to treat him as a brother."

Jones was a strong supporter of trade unions, crediting them with helping to build the country. He wrote that unions "have done much to free little children from the sweatshops and factories" and "to relieve underpaid men and women." He encouraged his workers to join unions and walked alongside them in Labor Day parades. In his book *Letters of Love and Labor*—a collection of letters he wrote to his employees in the summer and fall of 1901—Jones went further, maintaining, "I am for something more and far beyond trade unionism; that is, I am for Equality, Brotherhood, for all." It must have seemed like softheaded idealism to some people, but Jones's policies worked. Acme Sucker Rod Company employees were incredibly dedicated, and the company thrived.

Because of his square dealing with his employees, people began calling the innovative Toledo businessman "Golden Rule" Jones. With his lively blue eyes and genial expression, the brawny, mustachioed former roustabout came across as disarmingly frank whenever he spoke in public, always talking from the heart in direct, simple language. In 1897, he caught the attention of the local Republican political machine. When the party nominating convention was unable to agree on a candidate to run for mayor of Toledo, Jones was tapped as a compromise candidate. The Republicans didn't realize what they'd let themselves in for. After eking out a victory (he won by 534 votes), Jones immediately initiated a series of reforms that would have Toledo fat cats chomping through their cigars. How dare the man actually try to accomplish the things he'd promoted in his campaign!

Just as he'd done at the Acme Sucker Rod Company, Jones ran the city government according to the Golden Rule. He implemented an eight-hour workday for city workers and established a minimum wage. He built playgrounds, free kindergartens, and public baths. He did everything he could to eliminate cronyism and patronage and to prevent hidden financial interests from taking over public works projects. Stories about the crusading mayor appeared in newspapers across the country. A teetotaler himself, he provoked a controversy by refusing to shut down the city's saloons on Sundays as called for by blue laws, saying that workers needed a place to socialize after a hard week of labor.

Jones's attitudes toward crime caused a sensation: he believed that most wrongdoing resulted from society's exploitation and persecution of the poor. He made Toledo's cops exchange their skull-crunching billy clubs for less lethal canes. His position as mayor allowed him to serve as police judge, a role he gave new meaning to—becoming perhaps the world's first judge who was reluctant to pass judgment. One month, he dismissed every case he presided over, using each as an occasion to preach about the corrupting influence of social injustice.

Needless to say, Mayor Jones quickly lost the support of establishment politicos. In 1899, after being bounced at the Republican nominating convention, he ran for reelection as an independent. He won 70 percent of the votes—more than twice as many as the Republican and Democratic candidates put together. He called his victory "the triumph of principle over party." Jones won again as an independent in 1901 and 1903. The powerful and the privileged kept wishing that Golden Rule Jones would go away, but working people cheered him on.

The charismatic progressive broadened his crusade in 1899,

making a speaking tour along the East Coast. He contributed articles to journals advocating reform, and he published his life story, personal philosophy, and political views in *The New Right*, including his beliefs that business was the root of all political corruption and that political parties should be abolished so that nonpartisan policies could unite the country. Given his ambitious agenda to serve public rather than private interests, Jones naturally suffered setbacks during his career. In 1899, he ran for governor of Ohio and carried just two counties, and throughout his seven years as mayor of Toledo, he fought unsuccessfully to convert the city's utilities to municipal ownership (he believed that wealthy stockholders shouldn't benefit from essential public services). He was still pushing for that change when he died unexpectedly in office in 1904 at the age of fifty-seven.

Jones came along at a time when the country's rapid industrialization sparked a surge in immigration and urban growth. At the turn of the century, the people jammed into the nation's cities faced a variety of woes—poverty, drunkenness, crime, disease, high unemployment, greedy factory owners, political corruption, racism, class divisions. Between 1880 and 1900, Toledo was the fastest-growing city in the United States, and it had every urban problem imaginable. As mayor, Samuel Jones dealt with those difficulties with the classic tools of the Progressive Era (the period of active social reform that lasted from the 1890s to World War I). Jones believed that education, full employment, honest (nonpartisan) government, and safe, clean living conditions could overcome the worst urban conditions. He pushed through enough of his policies to make Toledo a model of reform for the time.

Because of his efforts to improve the lives of working people and his campaign for city ownership of utilities, Jones was labeled a socialist by his enemies. He did want to start a revolution, but it was a peaceful revolution within each individual, one that would remake society by fostering more caring men and women. If Jones had been a minister, people would have held him up as an exemplar of piety, but instead of talking about Christian values one day a week, he chose to put them into action seven days a week as a charitable businessman, one who stood out because of his lack of the greed gene. He believed that making money was worthwhile only if it helped workers prosper, and he denounced the compulsion to get rich at the expense of others. His business practices were shaped by his belief in the innate goodness of every human being, which sounds overoptimistic, although his own unflagging generosity brought out the best in his employees.

Jones's public career underscored an ancient truism: so much of life comes down to the battle between those who are compelled to aid the disadvantaged and those who aren't. "Civilization," he wrote, "is measured by the amount of sympathy we have for the helpless and unfortunate." Throughout his time in office, Jones donated his entire salary to charity. He was an idealist and a humanitarian who never strayed from his code of conduct. In public service, as in business, he treated everyone he met just as he wanted to be treated—with the honesty and kindness of a kinsman. When he ran for reelection in 1899, before he became an independent, he issued this statement: "I am a Lincoln Republican. I believe in the people as he believed in them, and trust them as he trusted them. I have been the mayor for all of the people, high and low, rich and poor, black and white, employed and unemployed." Those assertions sound a lot like the platitudes we hear from every candidate around election time, but with Golden Rule Jones, they happened to be true.

The visionary social welfare policies that Jones advocated slowly found national acceptance. The eight-hour workday, the minimum wage, and paid vacations have become so firmly entrenched that it would be hard to imagine modern life without them. We may take such benefits for granted now, but without the pioneering efforts of generous spirited men like Samuel Jones, those measures would never have been enacted, and the United States would be a far less hospitable place in which to work and live.

TWENTY-NINE

Healer of the Fallen

JONATHAN LETTERMAN

AS ALWAYS, THE flinty Stonewall Jackson went about his work with the intensity of an avenging angel. In the waning days of August 1862, Gen. Robert E. Lee had dispatched Jackson's corps of Confederate troops north from Richmond with orders to suppress the enemy. On August 27, Jackson's forces overran a Union supply depot at Manassas Junction, thirty miles west of Washington, D.C. The rebels enjoyed a rowdy feast before setting fire to the place. The next day, the Confederates attacked a column of federals on the nearby Warrenton Turnpike.

Jackson's mission was to draw out Union Gen. John Pope's Army of Virginia before it could rendezvous with the Army of the Potomac. The plan worked. Pope closed on Manassas, convinced that Jackson was an isolated target waiting to be taken. Pope should have known better—Manassas held nothing but bad luck for the North. The year before, the Union suffered a humiliating defeat on these same verdant fields in the Civil War's first major land battle. But Pope was confident of victory. What he didn't know was that a second Confederate corps had secretly converged on Manassas—28,000 troops led by Gen. James Longstreet. Even as Pope attacked Jackson's position on the afternoon of August 29, Longstreet lay in wait. When Pope renewed his assault the next day, Longstreet threw his men into the struggle, sending the Union troops reeling toward Washington.

By the end of the Battle of Second Manassas (Second Bull Run to the Confederates), over 22,000 soldiers had been killed or wounded—nearly 14,000 of them federal troops. The bodies of the dead were strewn about the battlefield like broken dolls, cloaked in shrouds of buzzing black flies. Scattered among them, wounded soldiers unable to walk or crawl cried out for water and medical attention. Their shrieks and moans increased as the days wore on. A full week would pass before all of the Union injured were removed from the battlefield and transported to hospitals—grisly proof of the army's appalling inefficiency in dealing with casualties.

Miraculously, the outlook for soldiers wounded in battle changed just two weeks later. On September 17, 1862, Union and Confederate forces clashed again at Sharpsburg, Maryland, in the Battle of Antietam, a massive though mostly inconclusive conflict pitting Lee's Army of Northern Virginia against the Army of the Potomac, commanded by Gen. George B. McClellan. After twelve hours of fighting, some 23,000 men (over 12,000 Union soldiers and more than 10,000 Confederates) had fallen—the bloodiest single day of combat in American history. In stark contrast to the delays experienced at Manassas, every injured Union soldier was evacuated from the Antietam battlefield within twenty-four hours.

The author of this dramatic turnaround was a lanky, bearded Donald Sutherland look-alike—Maj. Jonathan Letterman, a thirty-seven-year-old military surgeon who'd been named the medical director of the Army of the Potomac three months earlier. Letterman's genius revealed itself the moment he took up his new duties. He immediately instituted revolutionary improvements in battlefield casualty management, and at Antietam, his reforms began to pay off. Letterman's innovations were so farsighted that they're still used today, earning him the title of "The Father of Battlefield Medicine."

To speed the evacuation of wounded soldiers, Letterman created the Union Army's first ambulance corps. He set up a uniform system of first-aid stations and field hospitals that brought order to the formerly chaotic, inconsistent treatment of the wounded. He also made sure that medical units received the necessary equipment and supplies. And long before the triage system of medical evaluation was employed in World War I, Letterman instituted standards for prioritizing treatment based on the severity of injuries and the likelihood of survival. Thanks to his efforts, thousands of soldiers survived who might otherwise have died from their wounds.

Letterman brought more than a dozen years of experience to his wartime role. Born in 1824, he was the son of a prominent Pennsylvania surgeon. He grew up in the town of Canonsburg and graduated from the local Jefferson College in 1845. After graduating from Philadelphia's Jefferson Medical College four years later, he immediately applied for a commission as an army surgeon. Early in his military career, Letterman hopscotched all over the country. He was posted to army forts in Minnesota and Virginia. In Florida, he served with future Confederate Thomas J. Jackson—before the man acquired his famous nickname for standing as firm as a stone wall at the Battle of First Manassas. In New Mexico, Letterman gathered specimens for the fledgling Smithsonian Institution and wrote a detailed account of the Navajo tribe and their homeland that was published in the scientific organization's 1856 report of the board of regents.

Stationed in California when the Civil War began, Letterman returned east at the end of 1861. The following May, he became the medical director of the Department of West Virginia, followed quickly by his appointment as medical director of the Army of the Potomac, which came with a promotion to the rank of major. Letterman was given the authority to make whatever changes he felt were necessary to improve the fighting condition of General McClellan's men. At the time, the Army of the Potomac was in a sorry state, with thousands of sick or wounded troops. Letterman recognized that many of the soldiers were suffering from scurvy, which he quickly cured with increased rations of fresh vegetables. Other problems weren't so easy to fix.

Letterman and his fellow Civil War doctors had to cope with a scale of battlefield casualties that no one could have anticipated. The Battle of Second Manassas alone produced twice as many casualties as the entire Revolutionary War. The shocking carnage resulted from a combination of improved weaponry and outdated military tactics. Generals on both sides still employed the mass charges of the Napoleonic era, yet in the face of newer weapons, that sort of head-on assault was suicidal.

Before the war, the most common infantry weapon was the smoothbore musket, which was only accurate inside seventy-five yards. Since it took nearly half a minute to reload a musket between shots, charging soldiers faced a limited number of volleys before they covered the short distance to an enemy's defensive position. After 1861, most Civil War soldiers carried the .58 caliber Springfield musket, which had rifling (spiral grooves) inside its barrel that imparted a stabilizing spin on a bullet, making the weapon accurate at distances of five hundred yards or more. The

Springfield's longer range meant that charging soldiers were exposed to far more volleys as they closed on the enemy, greatly increasing their chances of being hit. With the odds stacked so heavily against them, it was common for units to lose a third or more of their men in a frontal assault.

Over 90 percent of Civil War battle injuries came from gunshots, most of those from the ugly half-inch chunk of metal fired from the Springfield musket—the minié ball, a soft lead bullet that could shatter bones and punch a fist-size hole in a man. Two other brutally effective projectiles were canister shot and grape shot—cannon shells filled with dozens of small iron balls. When the shells were fired, their casings broke apart, spraying the iron balls into oncoming soldiers in a wall of death, like a giant sawed-off shotgun. Close-range victims of canister shot or grape shot virtually disintegrated. (The war's least effective weapons were swords and bayonets. Less than 1 percent of all casualties were inflicted by edged weapons, which is understandable, given that so many soldiers were cut down by muskets or cannons before they could get close enough to be stabbed.)

The extreme numbers and unusual severity of battlefield casualties taxed the woefully understaffed army medical corps all through the war. In 1860, the U.S. Army had just over a hundred doctors to treat its 16,000 soldiers. Although the medical corps grew to more than 10,000 surgeons by the end of the war, the ratio of doctors to soldiers actually went down, since the Union Army had swollen to well over 2 million men by 1865. (Confederate doctors faced an even more daunting situation, with just 4,000 doctors to treat more than 1 million soldiers.)

Besides having too few doctors, the army had to rely on physicians with rudimentary skills. Basic medical procedures hadn't changed much in generations (one historian likened the

Civil War years to the "medical Middle Ages"). Doctors usually received only cursory training, often at unregulated two-
year medical schools. Most new doctors had never dealt with
gunshot wounds or performed surgery of any sort. Their real
training came on the job—hacking on the unfortunate soldiers
who ended up on their operating tables. Thankfully, chloroform
had come into wide use a few years earlier, and morphine and
opium were available to ease soldiers' pain.

Since most Civil War doctors weren't qualified to operate on
serious wounds to the head, chest, or abdomen, those injuries
were considered fatal and usually left untreated, other than to
give the victim painkillers. The most frequent wounds by far
were injuries to the extremities, making the amputation of limbs
the most common surgical procedure (even Stonewall Jackson
had to have an arm amputated after his own men mistakenly
shot him at the Battle of Chancellorsville). A practiced "saw-
bones" could remove a mangled arm or leg in ten minutes, using a variety of fearsome knives and saws. In the heat of battle,
the typical field hospital looked like a scene from *The Texas
Chainsaw Massacre*, with surgeons spattered in gore and body
parts tossed onto grotesque piles. Amputations were so prevalent
that civilians became accustomed to the sight of veterans returning home with an empty sleeve pinned to their uniform or limp-
ing on crutches with a flapping pant leg.

Unaware of the relationship between bacteria and infections, Civil War doctors used the same surgical instruments
over and over without bothering to sterilize them, leading to
postoperative infections that included blood poisoning, tetanus,
and gangrene. Despite the lack of surgical hygiene, nearly three
out of four amputees survived, but there were still plenty of other
ways to die. The close quarters and general squalor of military

life exposed soldiers to an extensive list of contagious and infectious diseases. Of the 360,000 Union soldiers who died in the war, around 220,000 of them succumbed to illnesses such as chronic diarrhea, dysentery, typhoid fever, pneumonia, tuberculosis, smallpox, malaria, and measles.

The deadly mix of injury and illness was exacerbated by the haphazard organization of the army medical corps in the early part of the war. When Jonathan Letterman took over as medical director of the Army of the Potomac, the delivery of medical services appeared to have been planned by the Keystone Kops. Medical personnel had no ambulances, forcing them to borrow wagons from the quartermaster corps—vehicles that were needed to haul munitions and other supplies. There were no dedicated stretcher-bearers either (although regimental musicians sometimes doubled as medics). For the most part, the wounded had to rely on friends to carry them to safety, which took able-bodied soldiers away from the fight. Worst of all, there was no coordinated hierarchy for treating the wounded. Physicians from different regiments operated in a hodgepodge of tents, houses, and barns, delivering a wildly uneven quality of care (and sometimes refusing to treat soldiers from other units). Adding to these shortcomings, doctors ran out of critical supplies far too often.

Letterman knew that the key to saving injured soldiers was getting them immediate help. The first shortfall he addressed was the lack of reliable transportation. His plan for the Army of the Potomac's new ambulance corps, which General McClellan approved, called for a fleet of wagons that would only be used for transporting the injured. The plan also required each regiment to assign stretcher-bearers who would have no combat duties. Next, Letterman organized the treatment of casualties into three stages: battlefield first-aid stations for stop-gap measures, nearby mobile field hospitals for surgery and other emergency procedures, and more distant general hospitals for follow-up care. That simple three-tiered system remains the blueprint for modern battlefield medicine (the Mobile Army Surgical Hospital made famous in the 1970 movie *MASH* and the subsequent TV series was the ultimate expression of the army field hospital of Letterman's day). Finally, Letterman organized a dependable system to provide surgeons with the medical equipment and supplies they needed.

Letterman's comprehensive revamping of the Army of the Potomac's medical corps continued to prove its value after the Battle of Antietam. The new system's biggest test came at the Battle of Gettysburg, which took place July 1–3, 1863, in southern Pennsylvania. The most famous battle of the war involved over 158,000 soldiers—some 83,000 Northern troops led by Gen. George G. Meade and 75,000 rebels commanded by Gen. Robert E. Lee. The Union victory produced a staggering 51,000 casualties (23,000 federals and 28,000 Confederates). Letterman's ambulance corps fielded 1,000 horse-drawn wagons manned by 3,000 drivers and stretcher-bearers. Remarkably, the medical workers were able to clear the wounded from the battlefield by July 4.

More than 20,000 soldiers required continuing medical treatment after the battle, including a substantial number of gravely wounded Confederate troops who were left behind when Southern forces withdrew. Before they could be transferred to permanent hospitals in Harrisburg, Philadelphia, Baltimore, and Washington, the injured were quartered at a large temporary hospital called Camp Letterman, which consisted of some four hundred tents spread over the Pennsylvania countryside.

(Today, a memorial tablet marks the location of Camp Letterman along Route 30, just east of Gettysburg.) Besides medical care, Camp Letterman provided hot meals and cots with clean sheets—luxuries to the average soldier. More than three dozen female civilian nurses assisted military personnel in caring for the wounded, and family members were allowed to visit their loved ones. In contrast to the savagery that had taken place on the battlefield, Camp Letterman was an oasis of humanity.

Six months after the Battle of Gettysburg, Letterman abruptly ended his association with the Army of the Potomac. He asked to be relieved from his position because of a change in the political fortunes of his good friend and superior William Hammond, the army's surgeon general. An outspoken advocate of medical reforms throughout the army, Hammond had rubbed too many important people the wrong way. (For one thing, he wanted medical inspectors to be appointed based on merit, not for their political associations—an idea that didn't sit well with Washington power brokers.) When Hammond was removed from office, Letterman stepped down as well. Fortunately for the common soldier, the changes that Letterman fostered were kept in place. In March 1864, the Army of the Potomac's model of casualty management was extended throughout the military.

After he left the Army of the Potomac, Letterman served for a few months as the medical inspector of hospitals in the Department of the Susquehanna. Then in December 1864, he resigned his army commission and moved to San Francisco, where he practiced medicine and won election to the office of coroner. In 1866, he published his Civil War memoirs, *Medical Recollections of the Army of the Potomac*. Letterman began suffering health problems soon after the death of his wife, Mary, in 1867. He died in March 1872 at the age of forty-eight. (In 1911, the army hospital at San Francisco's Presidio was named in his honor.) Letterman is now interred at Arlington National Cemetery. His headstone bears the following tribute: "Medical Director of the Army of the Potomac, June 23, 1862, to December 30, 1863, who brought order and efficiency into the Medical Service and who was the originator of modern methods of medical organization in armies."

In human terms, Letterman did much more than what's indicated in that simple epitaph. He touched thousands of lives— from his own time right up to the present. Thanks to Letterman's innovations, soldiers struck down on the field of battle are given the best chance possible to survive their wounds. Those chances are much better today, but even in Letterman's era, countless lives were saved through the more efficient system of medical care he devised.

The sight of Civil War surgeons at work was a nightmarish spectacle. They toiled amid the screams of the wounded, the explosions of cannons and rattling of musket fire close at hand. Their bare arms glistened with sweat and blood as they bent over the operating table for hours on end. The sheer numbers of mutilated bodies laid before them could cause surgeons to adopt a mechanical, seemingly heartless manner, which led people to call them butchers, incompetents—accusations that Major Letterman said were "wrong, and do injustice to a body of men who have labored faithfully and well."

Battlefields everywhere are emblazoned with memorials commemorating the deeds of fighting men, but few make note of the heroic accomplishments of those who struggle to save lives rather than take them. The skills of the military surgeons of the 1860s may have been primitive by today's standards, but

Civil War physicians were acutely aware of their patients' fear and pain. Even though they were working under atrocious conditions, these healers of the fallen did the best they could to ease soldiers' suffering. And in that worthy endeavor, they had no greater ally than Jonathan Letterman.

THIRTY

Warrior with a Conscience

HUGH THOMPSON

NOT MANY AMERICANS caught up in the Vietnam War could appreciate it, but they were surrounded by some of the most beautiful scenery on Earth. The slender crescent of Vietnam unfurls like a thousand-mile scroll along the eastern margin of the Indochinese peninsula, suspended below the ponderous bulk of China and abutted on the west by Laos and Cambodia. Everywhere you look, the Vietnamese countryside bursts with greenery, from the misty, jungle-clad Truong Son Mountains that run nearly the length of the land to the palm-fringed beaches and tranquil lagoons that edge the indigo South China Sea.

Scattered about the former kingdom, ancient temples, tombs, and citadels stand cloaked in vines and a patina of mystery. Ramshackle fishing junks bob on the island-dotted waters of Ha Long Bay in the north. Far to the south, rice-laden sampans skim the Mekong Delta's sweltering maze of silty brown waterways. In every town and city, dainty, shockingly beautiful young women float down the street in their colorful silk *ao dais*. In the larger cities, three-wheeled pedicabs glide silently along at the pace of an earlier age, while the graceful French colonial architecture speaks of gin and tonics and languid, velvety nights.

Some of the best views of Vietnam are from the air, which is where twenty-four-year-old army pilot Hugh Thompson, Jr., gained his impressions of the country. Looking down from the glass bubble of his OH-23 Raven helicopter, Chief Warrant Officer Thompson could see the pastoral soul of Vietnam in the omnipresent fields of rice—the glistening mirrors of flooded paddies signaling new plantings, the luminescent green of growing fields, and the tawny, nodding stands of mature plants awaiting harvest. From a couple of thousand feet up, the land resembled a living patchwork quilt, stitched together by the dark borders of dikes and irrigation ditches and speckled with the tiny figures of farmers going about the same tasks of planting, weeding, and reaping that had occupied their ancestors for centuries—2,000-year-old rituals that made the 192-year heritage of Thompson's own country seem like a blip in comparison.

Thompson arrived in South Vietnam in late December 1967, when the United States was still optimistic about preventing a communist takeover of the tiny Southeast Asian nation. At the end of the French Indochina War, in 1954, Vietnam had been divided into two parts by the Geneva Accords, with the North ruled by communists and the South a nominal republic. Even though Vietnamese fighters had defeated the French after nearly a century of colonial rule—and booted the Chinese out following a thousand years of occupation—American generals were sure they would prevail over the North Vietnamese and their southern communist allies, the Viet Cong. After all, the United States had never lost a war.

Hugh Thompson was committed to doing his part. Born in Atlanta in 1943, he grew up in Stone Mountain, Georgia. In

1961, Thompson joined the U.S. Navy. After finishing his four-year hitch, he returned home to civilian life. Two years later, he joined the army to learn how to fly. Following his training as a helicopter pilot, he shipped out to Vietnam, where he volunteered for reconnaissance missions. "My job was to recon out in front of the friendly forces and draw fire, tell them where the enemy was, and let them take care of it," he said. At times, Thompson flew his OH-23 so low that he could smell the earthy, humid scent of the jungle through the chopper's open doors. His craft was like a worm on a hook, tempting any Viet Cong lurking below to snap at it. Reconnaissance was a daring job, and Thompson excelled at it.

On the morning of March 16, 1968, Thompson and his two crewmen—door-gunner Larry Colburn and crew chief Glenn Andreotta—climbed into their tiny scout helicopter at Chu Lai Air Base, a short distance outside the port city of Da Nang, in central Vietnam. They were headed south to Quang Ngai Province, a rural area dotted with farming villages and rice paddies—and a known sanctuary for Viet Cong guerrillas. Three companies of soldiers from the Americal Division were being airlifted in to sweep the area. The troops were told that the only Vietnamese they'd encounter would be Viet Cong. The VC were usually active at night, laying booby traps and mines that caused heavy American casualties. The guerrillas also returned to their home villages after dark to visit their families, melting back into the countryside in the morning. Most towns and hamlets in the South had mixed loyalties, so it was hard to distinguish friend from foe, a problem that plagued American forces throughout the war.

Thompson's chopper was to provide aerial reconnaissance for Charlie Company, the unit assigned to attack the hamlet of

My Lai 4, one of a cluster of settlements in an area called Son My. At around 7:30 a.m., the assault commenced with artillery fire. As soon as the shooting started, My Lai's seven hundred residents scattered in a panic. Helicopter gunships raked the surrounding fields with rockets and machine-gun bursts just before the troop carriers landed.

The 105 soldiers of Charlie Company quickly took up defensive positions, expecting to come under attack from the Viet Cong. To their surprise, there was no enemy fire. Any guerrillas who'd been here had disappeared. Only unarmed civilians remained. From the air, Hugh Thompson spotted one man running from the village with a weapon. "That was the only enemy person I saw that whole day," he said.

The troops began firing at the fleeing civilians, who sought refuge wherever they could—in their homes, in makeshift bunkers, in the surrounding jungle. A group of villagers ran toward the road leading to Quang Ngai City. The soldiers shot them all—old people, women, children, babies. One atrocity followed another. Women and girls were raped and sodomized with rifles and bayonets. Several elderly women praying at a temple were all shot in the back of the head. Tottering old men had their throats slashed or were bayoneted like practice dummies. One man was thrown down a well and a grenade tossed in after him. The soldiers gathered about eighty villagers in the town plaza and gunned them down. In this moment of mass insanity, the troops even killed the villagers' dogs, cows, chickens, and water buffalo. It was as if all bonds to humanity had been severed and some dark force had emerged.

Hugh Thompson and his crew recoiled at the sights below. "Everywhere we'd look, we'd see bodies," Thompson recounted. At first, the men couldn't comprehend what was happening.

Thompson radioed the two helicopter gunships flying with him that day. "It looks to me like there's an awful lot of unnecessary killing going on down there," he reported. Spotting a wounded woman on the ground, he flew his chopper near her. He watched in disbelief as an officer approached the woman, prodded her with his foot, then stepped back and executed her. A member of Thompson's crew identified the man as Capt. Ernest Medina, Charlie Company's commander.

Thompson saw several dozen villagers sprawled in an irrigation ditch just east of the village. When he set his chopper down and got out to see if he could assist the wounded, he was accosted by Lt. William Calley, one of the company's platoon leaders (and a man so obtuse that Captain Medina openly referred to him as "Lieutenant Shithead"). Thompson asked Calley why unarmed civilians were being killed. The lieutenant told him to get back in his chopper and mind his own business. Thompson climbed back into his helicopter and lifted off. He and his crew heard gunfire as the wounded were riddled with bullets. Calley was in the thick of the killing. According to one account, a toddler crawled from the ditch and tried to run away. Calley grabbed the boy, threw him back in the ditch, and shot him.

Thompson was both furious and filled with shame. Were these Americans or Nazis? he wondered. As they flew around the hamlet, Thompson and his crew noticed three Vietnamese being chased by a group of soldiers. The villagers ducked into a bunker. At that moment, Thompson made the most important decision of his life. He was going to stop the soldiers from killing those people. He set his chopper down between the villagers and the Americans and leaped out. Approaching the ground troops, he told them to hold their fire while he attempted to coax the villagers out of the bunker. Thompson then gave his crew a startling order. Glancing at the soldiers, he said, "If the squad opens up on them, shoot 'em." Door-gunner Larry Colburn hefted his M60 machine gun and took a deep breath, praying it wouldn't come to that.

The soldiers eyed Colburn cradling his weapon and decided to leave Thompson alone. Inside the bunker, Thompson found nine Vietnamese villagers huddling together in terror—two women, a couple of old men, and five kids. Thompson realized he couldn't fit them all in his helicopter, which was built for a crew of three. He radioed his two gunships, knowing that what he was about to ask them was against military regulations. "Can you shuttle some of these people out of here before they get killed?" he shouted.

One of the gunships landed and took on passengers while the other hovered overhead. After the gunships had flown the villagers to safety, Thompson and his crew lifted off and made another pass over the irrigation ditch where the mass executions had taken place. Thompson's crew chief, Glenn Andreotta, saw some movement below. Thompson landed the chopper and Andreotta hopped out. Climbing down among the mangled bodies, he lifted a blood-spattered child from the carnage. The young boy had been clinging to his dead mother. Though he hadn't been hit by the gunfire, he was in shock. The men loaded him into the helicopter and made a beeline for the hospital at Quang Ngai City. As their chopper pounded its way southward, the three Americans sat in silence, tears streaming down their faces.

Once the little boy was safely in the hands of the nuns at Quang Ngai, Thompson and his crew returned to their landing zone. Still boiling with anger, Thompson confronted his platoon leader about the war crimes taking place at My Lai. He threatened to rip the wings from his fatigues and never fly again if it meant having to be a party to such senseless violence. "It wasn't war," he said years later. Thompson repeated his description of the massacre to his commanding officer, who took Thompson's charges seriously and informed Lt. Col. Frank Barker, Jr., head of the task force conducting the Quang Ngai operation. Barker immediately radioed Captain Medina to stop the killing. Thompson had helped to end the massacre, but by then My Lai had been devastated.

In the days ahead, Thompson gave his account of what happened at My Lai to his brigade commander. As a result, planned attacks on other villages in the area were called off, saving additional civilian lives. Afterward, Thompson resumed his normal recon missions. Given the danger of his assignment—to act as bait to draw out enemy fire—it's not surprising that his helicopter was repeatedly hit. He had several choppers shot out from under him, and the last crash broke his back. He was evacuated to Japan to recuperate, ending his service in Vietnam.

Thompson kept waiting to hear that the perpetrators of the My Lai massacre were being called to account. The army, however, went into cover-up mode. An official report said that about twenty civilians had been inadvertently killed in the fighting. Reliable estimates place the actual number at just over five hundred. Almost two years passed before the truth leaked out. At that point, Thompson was called to Washington and interviewed by Pentagon officials and a congressional committee. Subsequent investigations produced a flurry of military trials, all of which came, more or less, to nothing, although reports about the brutality of My Lai helped galvanize opposition to the war.

Of the dozens of soldiers and officers who took part in the My Lai massacre, only Lt. William Calley was ever convicted of a crime. Capt. Ernest Medina managed to evade all responsibility.

Viewed as a scapegoat by many, Calley was sentenced to life in prison. President Richard Nixon reduced Calley's punishment to three years of house arrest. Calley spent a total of three days in a military stockade. In other words, no one ever really paid for the atrocities committed at My Lai. The inhabitants of that tiny hamlet had gotten up in the morning hoping to be allowed to tend their fields in peace. What they received was unspeakable savagery visited upon them by men who were supposedly in their country to save it. It's hard to understand how anyone could have engaged in the horrors of that day in 1968. To strike down women, children, and old people when it was clear they posed no military threat can only be viewed as an act of blind prejudice—the common denominator of all atrocities.

To their credit, several soldiers in Charley Company refused to be a party to the barbarity that took place at My Lai—even though Lieutenant Calley threatened some of them at gunpoint to try to force them to comply with his order to shoot the villagers. After the massacre, Captain Medina told one soldier who'd refused to participate that he'd better keep quiet about what he'd seen. The butchery so sickened the young enlistee that he considered assassinating every officer associated with the massacre after he got out of the army.

More than 3 million Vietnamese died in the war. Over half of those were civilians. In light of those figures, the ten lives spared by Hugh Thompson and his crew may seem insignificant, but saving even one life would have set them apart from the men who participated in the violation of My Lai. During the long, grueling years of the Vietnam War, there were countless instances of heroism on the part of Americans. Nearly 250 U.S. servicemen received the Congressional Medal of Honor for acts of bravery above and beyond the call of duty. Hugh Thompson's act of courage was just as noteworthy, perhaps even more so, given that he had to go against norms of conduct that were accepted by many of his fellow soldiers. Thompson could have simply walked away and no one would have faulted him, but that was impossible. "These people were looking at me for help and there was no way I could turn my back on them," he said.

The glaring lesson of My Lai is that orders don't always equate with duty. When obedience lapses into insanity, the bravest and most loyal among us are those who follow their conscience, even if that means being labeled a coward or a traitor. After My Lai, Hugh Thompson had to endure being ostracized by his fellow servicemen, along with the slurs and death threats of those who thought he was unpatriotic. One congressman even told him he was the only one who deserved to be punished over the massacre.

Thompson stood tall through all of that, secure in the knowledge that he had been loyal to his country's ideals. By choosing to intervene in the slaughter of defenseless noncombatants, Thompson made a stand for universal human values. Years after the massacre, he said, "I truly pray to God that My Lai was not an everyday occurrence. I don't know if anybody could keep their sanity if something like that happens all the time." Thompson said he had only one regret about what he'd done at My Lai. As he lay in his bunk that night, thinking of the atrocities he'd witnessed, he felt sorry that he hadn't been able to save more lives. He vowed that if he ever had a similar experience, he would act faster and do more to protect the helpless.

Hugh Thompson remained in the military until 1983. In 1998, thirty years after the events at My Lai, he and his old door-gunner, Larry Colburn, returned to Vietnam and were reunited with Pham Ti Nhung and Pham Thi Nhanh, the two women who were among the group of villagers they had saved. That same year, the U.S. Army finally recognized the heroism of Thompson and his crew. All three men were awarded the Soldier's Medal. (Glenn Andreotta's was given posthumously—he was killed in Vietnam three weeks after the My Lai massacre.) At the presentation ceremony, held at the Vietnam Veterans Memorial in Washington, D.C., the three men were praised for having "set the standard for all soldiers to follow." Their actions at My Lai are now cited in American and European military training manuals as examples of ethical wartime behavior. Thompson also received the prestigious Courage of Conscience Award, which recognizes the world's great humanitarians, and he was asked to speak about his experience in Vietnam at the U.S. Military Academy.

In 2001, Thompson and Colburn were reunited with Do Hoa, the boy they'd pulled from the bloody irrigation ditch outside My Lai. The two Americans were hoping that he'd been too young at the time to recall the obscenities that had taken place in his village, but the now forty-two-year-old Vietnamese man—who called both of his saviors "Poppa"—remembered it all, a memory no human being should have to bear. Thompson and Colburn were amazed to learn that, after two days, Do Hoa had left the hospital where they'd taken him and walked back to his village to help bury his parents.

Hugh Thompson acted without hesitation at My Lai, despite knowing that he could have been killed there or court-martialed for what he did. He was willing to pay the ultimate price for his convictions, and for that, he deserves our admiration. The people Thompson rescued certainly revered him. As he helped the frightened villagers onto the waiting helicopter gunship, one of the old men in the group, his back bent from years of labor, bowed to this American stranger who dared to defy his fellow soldiers. It was a simple message transcending spoken language, a heartfelt thank-you from one human being to another.

In January 2006, Hugh Thompson died of cancer at the age of sixty-two. Larry Colburn was at his side.

Afterword

ONE THING BECAME apparent in the course of assembling this roster of memorable Americans: this is by no means a definitive collection. In archives and libraries across the country, the yellowing pages of old books and newspapers are filled with references to unheralded men and women whose lives were noteworthy—lives brimming with drama, adventure, and accomplishment. For every celebrated general astride a white horse there is a forgotten foot soldier who struck the blow that turned the tide of battle. For every famed inventor or scientist who captures the public imagination, there is a man or woman of signal achievement laboring in the shadows. Their stories should be documented and retold as long as there is an America.

Acknowledgments

I WOULD LIKE to thank the following individuals and organizations for helping me ferret out interesting, underappreciated characters from the past: Elizabeth Cruce Alvarez, Texas State Historical Association; Ned Blackhawk, University of Wisconsin-Madison; Don Bullis and Mike Stevenson, New Mexico Historical Society; William Convery and Barbara Dey, History Colorado; Nick Cullather, Indiana University; James A. Davis, State Historical Society of North Dakota; Robert K. DeKosky, University of Kansas; Matthew Dennis, University of Oregon; Allison DePrey, Indiana Historical Society; Barbara Dunn, Hawaii Historical Society; Michael Edmonds, Wisconsin Historical Society; Linda Fabian, Wyoming State Historical Society; Andrea Faling, Nebraska State Historical Society; Robert Friedel, University of Maryland; Michael Griske; Steven Hahn, University of Pennsylvania; Michael Hill, Josh Howard, and Ansley Wegner, North Carolina Office of Archives and History; Elbert R. Hilliard and Peggy Jeanes, Mississippi Historical Society; Andrew J. Huebner, University of Alabama; Michael Kazin, Georgetown University; Kevin Mattson, Ohio

Acknowledgments

University; Colleen McKnight, Historical Society of Washington, D.C.; Neil McMillen, University of Southern Mississippi; Mark Miller; Nick Noyes, Maine Historical Society; Jill Padelford, Connecticut Historical Society; William M. S. Rasmussen and Nelson D. Lankford, Virginia Historical Society; Eric Rauchway, UC Davis; Katherine Reeve, Arizona Historical Society; Philip J. Roberts, University of Wyoming; Jason D. Stratman, Missouri History Museum; Marilyn Terrell and Susanne Hackett, National Geographic Society; Jim Turner; and Carroll Van West, Middle Tennessee State University.

I'd also like to thank the helpful staff at the Library of Congress—my second home—as well as the many friends who aided and encouraged me in this project, especially Robert L. Breeden, Keith Bellows, and—for suggesting the secret word—Jonathan Tourtellot. Finally, thanks to my partners in making this book a reality: my agent, Erin Malone, and my editor, Michael Signorelli.

—PM

Sources

VOYAGERS

Carl Akeley

Akeley, Carl E. *In Brightest Africa.* Garden City, NY: Garden City Publishing Co., 1923.

Akeley, Carl E., and Mary L. Jobe Akeley. *Lions, Gorillas and Their Neighbors.* New York: Dodd, Mead & Co., 1932.

"Akeley Hall of African Mammals." American Museum of Natural History. http://www.amnh.org/exhibitions/permanent/mammals/african.html.

Andrews, Roy Chapman. *Beyond Adventure: The Lives of Three Explorers.* New York: Duell, Sloan and Pearce, 1954.

Bodry-Sanders, Penelope. *Carl Akeley: Africa's Collector, Africa's Savior.* New York: Paragon House, 1991.

"Carl Akeley Dead in Belgian Congo." *Boston Globe*, December 1, 1926: 3.

"Carl E. Akeley Dies in Gorilla Land He Loved." *Chicago Tribune*, December 1, 1926: 4.

de Cartier de Marchienne, Baron, and others. "Akeley Memorial Number." *Natural History*, March-April 1927: 114–175.

Sources

Clark, James L. *In the Steps of the Great American Museum Collector Carl Ethan Akeley*. New York: M. Evans & Co., 1968.

Fisher, Clyde. "Carl Akeley and His Work." *Scientific Monthly*, February 1927: 97–118.

"Geology, Botany, and Zoology Collections." Africa, Field Museum. http://www.fieldmuseum.org/exhibits/exhibit_sites/africa/collection5.html.

Pond, Seymour G. *African Explorer: The Adventures of Carl Akeley*. New York: Dodd, Mead & Co., 1957.

"Report: Central African gorillas may go extinct." CNN, March 25, 2010. http://edition.cnn.com/2010/TECH/science/03/25/gorillas.threatened/?hpt=T1.

"Virunga National Park." UNESCO World Heritage Centre, 2010. http://whc.unesco.org/en/list/63.

Wedge, Eleanor F. "Akeley, Carl Ethan." American National Biography Online, February 2000. http://www.anb.org/articles/13/13-00019.html.

Wilson, Susan. "An Elephant's Tale." *Tufts Online Magazine*, Spring 2002. http://www.tufts.edu/alumni/magazine/spring2002/jumbo.html.

Jimmie Angel

"Angel Falls to Be Renamed Kerepakupai Meru So It No Longer Commemorates U.S. Pilot Who 'Discovered' Them." *Mail Online*, December 24, 2009. http://www.dailymail.co.uk/news/article-1237540/Angel-Falls-renamed-Kerepakupai-Meru-longer-commemorates-U-S-pilot-discovered-them.html#.

Angel, Karen. "The Truth About Jimmie Angel and Angel Falls." Jimmie Angel Historical Project, 2001. http://www.jimmieangel.org/lecture1.html.

"Canaima National Park." Lost World, February 26, 1998. http://www.thelostworld.org/canaimanp/canaima2.htm.

"Canaima National Park." Nature Conservancy, 2009. http://www.nature.org/wherewework/southamerica/venezuela/work/art5336.html.

Gilliard, E. Thomas. "Unchallenged Champion." *Natural History*, December 1940: 258–273.

Holl, John R. "Angel on Silver Wings." *Americas*, August 1980: 53–56.

"Jimmy Angel Dies; Was Jungle Pilot." *New York Times*, December 9, 1956: 87.

Onkst, David H. "Hollywood Stunt Pilots." U.S. Centennial of Flight Commission.

Sources

http://www.centennialofflight.gov/essay/Explorers_Record_Setters
_and_Daredevils/movie_stunt_pilots/EX26.htm.

Robertson, Ruth. "Jungle Journey to the World's Highest Waterfall." *National Geographic*, November 1949: 655–690.

Giacomo Beltrami

Beltrami, J. C. A *Pilgrimage in Europe and America Leading to the Discovery of the Sources of the Mississippi and Bloody River; with a Description of the Whole Course of the Former, and of the Ohio*, vol. 2. London: Hunt and Clarke, 1828.

"Biographical Outline: Giacomo Constantino Beltrami." Civica Biblioteca di Bergamo, "Angelo Mai," 2000. http://www.bibliotecamai.org/cataloghi
_inventari/archivi/archivi_collezioni_doc/inventario_beltrami/beltbio
/bioengl.html.

Crompton, Samuel Willard. "Beltrami, Giacomo Constantino." American National Biography Online, February 2000. http://www.anb.org
/articles/20/20-01594.html.

"Historic Fort Snelling." Minnesota Historical Society, 2010. http://www.mnhs
.org/places/sites/hfs/history.html.

Jones, Evan. *Citadel in the Wilderness: The Story of Fort Snelling and the Old Northwest Frontier*. New York: Coward-McCann, 1966.

Kennedy, Roger G. *Rediscovering America*. Boston: Houghton Mifflin Co., 1990.

Martin, Michael. "Improbable Explorer: Giacomo Beltrami's Summer of Discovery." *Timeline*, February–March 1990: 32–43.

Miceli, Augusto P. *The Man with the Red Umbrella: Giacomo Constantino Beltrami in America*. Baton Rouge, La.: Claitor's Publishing Div., 1974.

Severin, Timothy. "The Preposterous Pathfinder." *American Heritage*, December 1967: 56–63.

Kirk Bloodsworth

Casselman, Anne. "Identical Twins' Genes Are Not Identical." *Scientific American*, April 3, 2008. http://www.scientificamerican.com/article.cfm
?id=identical-twins-genes-are-not-identical.

Fridell, Ron. *Solving Crimes: Pioneers of Forensic Science*. New York: Franklin Watts, 2000.

Sources

Junkin, Tim. *Bloodsworth: The True Story of the First Death Row Inmate Exonerated by DNA*. Chapel Hill, N.C.: Algonquin Books of Chapel Hill, 2004.

Marshall, Claire. "I Was First Death Row Inmate Saved by DNA." BBC News, September 9, 2009. http://news.bbc.co.uk/2/hi/programmes/newsnight /8243991.stm.

"What Is DNA?" *Genetics Home Reference*, U.S. National Library of Medicine, February 21, 2010. http://ghr.nlm.nih.gov/handbook/basics/dna.

Yount, Lisa. *Forensic Science: From Fibers to Fingerprints*. New York: Chelsea House, 2007.

Mary Bowser

Anderson, Ella. "Elizabeth Van Lew's American Civil War Activities." *America's Civil War*, July 1991. Reprinted by History Net. http://www.historynet .com/elizabeth-van-lews-american-civil-war-activities.htm.

Crowe, Eyre. "In the Richmond Slave Market." History Matters. Excerpted from *With Thackeray in America*. London: Cassell and Co., 1893. http://history matters.gmu.edu/d/6762/.

Edwards, Ana, and Phil Wilayto. "The Significance of Shockoe Bottom." Defenders for Freedom, Justice & Equality. http://defendersfje.tripod.com /id33.html.

Grosvenor, Vertamae. "The Spy Who Served Me: A Tale of Espionage from the 'White House' of Jefferson Davis." NPR, July 17, 2009. http://www.npr .org/programs/morning/features/2002/apr/served/.

Jackson, Vernice. "Mary Elizabeth Bowser." Women in History, Lakewood Public Library, March 9, 2009. http://www.lkwdpl.org/wihohio/bows-mar .htm.

Kane, Harnett T. *Spies for the Blue and Gray*. Garden City, N.Y.: Hanover House, 1954.

Markle, Donald E. *Spies and Spymasters of the Civil War*. New York: Hippocrene Books, 2004.

"Mary Elizabeth Bowser." *Richmond Times-Dispatch*, February 9, 2009. http:// www.timesdispatch.com/rtd/news/special_report/black_history/article /mary_elizabeth_bowser/201873/.

"Richmond: History & Culture." Richmond National Battlefield Park, National Park Service, October 30, 2006. http://www.nps.gov/rich/historyculture /index.htm.

Sources

Robinson, Susan. "Mary Elizabeth Bowser." A Day in Black History, *Gibbs Magazine*, August 27, 2001. http://www.gibbsmagazine.com/Eliz.htm.

Rose, P. K. *Black Dispatches: Black American Contributions to Union Intelligence During the Civil War*. Washington, D.C.: Center for the Study of Intelligence, 1999.

Sizer, Lyde Cullen. "Bowser, Mary Elizabeth." Harvard Faculty of Arts and Sciences. http://www.fas.harvard.edu/~aanb/shtml/downloads/Sample%20entries%20for%20Web%20site.pdf.

Van Lew, Elizabeth. *A Yankee Spy in Richmond: The Civil War Diary of "Crazy Bet" Van Lew*. Edited by David D. Ryan. Mechanicsburg, Pa.: Stackpole Books, 1996.

"The White House of the Confederacy." Museum of the Confederacy. http://www.moc.org/site/PageServer?pagename=visit_wh_main.

Eugene Bullard

Carisella, P. J., and James W. Ryan. *The Black Swallow of Death: The Incredible Story of Eugene Jacques Bullard, the World's First Black Combat Aviator*. Boston: Marlborough House, 1972.

"Eugene Bullard, Ex-Pilot, Dead; American Flew for French in '18." *New York Times*, October 14, 1961: 23.

"Eugene Jacques Bullard." National Museum of the U.S. Air Force. http://www.nationalmuseum.af.mil/factsheets/factsheet.asp?id=705.

Fannin, Caroline M. "Bullard, Eugène Jacques." American National Biography Online, October 2002. http://www.anb.org/articles/07/07-00775.html.

"The Jazz Age in Paris: 1914–1940." Smithsonian Institution, 1998. http://www.si.edu/ajazzh/jazzage.htm.

Lloyd, Craig. *Eugene Bullard: Black Expatriate in Jazz-Age Paris*. Athens: University of Georgia Press, 2000.

——. "Eugene Bullard (1895–1961)." History & Archaeology, *New Georgia Encyclopedia*, November 19, 2002. http://www.georgiaencyclopedia.org/nge/Article.jsp?id=h-741.

Smith, Mary. "The Incredible Life of Monsieur Bullard." *Ebony*, December 1967: 120–128.

Stovall, Tyler. *Paris Noir: African Americans in the City of Light*. Boston: Houghton Mifflin, 1996.

Sources

Ishi

Collins, David R., and Kristen Bergren. *Ishi: The Last of His People*. Greensboro, N.C.: Morgan Reynolds, Inc., 2000.

Dillon, Richard H. "Ishi." American National Biography Online, February 2000. http://www.anb.org/articles/20/20-01701.html.

Heizer, Robert F., and Theodora Kroeber, eds. *Ishi, The Last Yahi: A Documentary History*. Berkeley: University of California Press, 1979.

Kroeber, Theodora. *Ishi in Two Worlds: A Biography of the Last Wild Indian in North America*. Berkeley: University of California Press, 1976.

Merton, Thomas. *Ishi Means Man*. Greensboro, N.C.: Unicorn Press, Inc., 1976.

Starn, Orin. *Ishi's Brain: In Search of America's Last "Wild" Indian*. New York: W. W. Norton & Co., 2004.

Hercules Mulligan

Bakeless, John. *Turncoats, Traitors, and Heroes*. Philadelphia: Lippincott, 1959.

Ford, Corey. *A Peculiar Service*. Boston: Little, Brown, 1965.

"Hercules Mulligan: 1740–1825." Fenian Graves, December 5, 2007. http://www.irishfreedom.net/Fenian%20graves/Biographies/Second%20entries/H.Mulligan.htm.

"New York Recalls Hercules Mulligan." *St. Petersburg Times*, November 25, 1970: 6-A. http://news.google.com/newspapers?id=ds0NAAAAIBAJ&sjid=rXUDAAAAIBAJ&pg=4952,3706602&dq=hercules+mulligan.

O'Brien, Michael J. *Hercules Mulligan, Confidential Correspondent of General Washington*. New York: P. J. Kennedy, 1937.

"Personalities: George Washington." Central Intelligence Agency, December 9, 2009. https://www.cia.gov/library/center-for-the-study-of-intelligence/csi-publications/books-and-monographs/intelligence/pers.html.

Poteat, S. Eugene. "George Washington: Spymaster Extraordinaire." *Scottish Rite Journal*, February 2000. http://www.srmason-sj.org/council/journal/feb00/poteat.html.

Rose, Alexander. *Washington's Spies: The Story of America's First Spy Ring*. New York: Bantam Books, 2006.

Sources

Cynthia Ann Parker

"Comanche Nation: The Rise and Fall of An 'Empire.'" NPR, June 23, 2010. http://www.npr.org/templates/story/story.php?storyId=127930650.

"Cynthia Ann Parker." Academic Dictionaries and Encyclopedias. http://en .academic.ru/dic.nsf/enwiki/221466.

DeShields, James T. *Cynthia Ann Parker: The Story of Her Capture.* Dallas: Chama Press, 1991.

Gwynne, S. C. *Empire of the Summer Moon: Quanah Parker and the Rise and Fall of the Comanches, the Most Powerful Indian Tribe in American History.* New York: Scribner, 2010.

Hacker, Margaret Schmidt. *Cynthia Ann Parker: The Life and the Legend.* El Paso: Texas Western Press, 1990.

———. "Parker, Cynthia Ann." American National Biography Online, February 2000. http://www.anb.org/articles/20/20-01262.html.

———. "Parker, Cynthia Ann." *The Handbook of Texas Online*, Texas State Historical Association. http://www.tshaonline.org/handbook/online /articles/PP/fpa18.html.

Hagan, William T. "Parker, Quanah." American National Biography Online, February 2000. http://www.anb.org/articles/20/20-00832.html.

Hosmer, Brian C. "Parker, Quanah." *The Handbook of Texas Online*, Texas State Historical Association. http://www.tshaonline.org/handbook/online /articles/PP/fpa28.html.

Jackson, Grace. *Cynthia Ann Parker.* San Antonio: Naylor Co., 1959.

Maschino, Ellen. "Limestone County." *The Handbook of Texas Online*, Texas State Historical Association. http://www.tshaonline.org/handbook/online /articles/LL/hcl9.html.

"The Tale of the Comanches: The Battle for Texas." *The Economist*, June 17, 2010. http://www.economist.com/node/16374526?story_id=16374526& source=hptextfeature.

Wilson, Claire. *Quanah Parker, Comanche Chief.* New York: Chelsea House, 1992.

James Parker

"Big Ben Parker and President McKinley's Assassination." The Circle Association's African American History of Western New York State, 1900–1935.

Sources

http://www.math.buffalo.edu/~sww/0history/parker_and_mckinley
.html.

"James Benjamin Parker at the Pan-Am." History of Buffalo. http://www.buffaloah
.com/h/panam/panwho/parker/parker.html.

Johns, A. Wesley. *The Man Who Shot McKinley*. South Brunswick, N.J.: A. S.
Barnes, 1970.

"The Legal Aftermath of the Assassination of William McKinley." The Libraries, University at Buffalo, 2005. http://ublib.buffalo.edu/libraries/exhibits
/panam/law/assassination.html.

"Pan-American Exposition, Buffalo, 1901." University of Delaware Library,
December 11, 2007. http://www.lib.udel.edu/ud/spec/exhibits/fairs/pan
.htm.

"Pan-American Exposition, 1901, Buffalo, New York." Buffalo Free-Net Library,
June 15, 2001. http://library.bfn.org/local/pan-am.html.

Peterson, Harold F. "Buffalo Builds the 1901 Pan-American Exposition." History of
Buffalo. http://www.buffaloah.com/h/panam/peter.html.

"Presidential Assassin vs. Giant Negro." Undercover Black Man, July 16, 2007.
http://undercoverblackman.blogspot.com/2007/07/presidential-assassin
-vs-giant-negro.html.

Rasuli, Daryl. "James B. Parker Revisited." The Libraries, University at
Buffalo, 2005. http://ublib.buffalo.edu/libraries/exhibits/panam/essays
/rasuli/rasuli.html.

Rauchway, Eric. *Murdering Mckinley: The Making of Theodore Roosevelt's America*. New York: Farrar Straus & Giroux, 2004.

"Reward for 'Jim' Parker." *Washington Post*, December 22, 1901: 1.

Savannah testimonial. *New York Times*, September 10, 1901.

"This Day in 1901 Archives." *Buffalo Evening News*, September 1901. http://
panam1901.bfn.org/thisday/septemberarchives.html.

"What Happened to Hero Big Ben Parker." The Circle Association's African
American History of Western New York State, 1900–1935. http://www
.math.buffalo.edu/~sww/0history/parker_big.ben.html.

William Van Horne

Bryce, George. "The Real Strathcona." *Canadian Magazine*, December 1915:
156–162.

Sources

"Building the Canadian Pacific Railway." *The Canadian Encyclopedia.* http://www.thecanadianencyclopedia.com/customcode/Media.cfm ?Params=A3railway.swf.

"Canadian Pacific: A Brief History." Canadian Pacific, 2010. http://www8.cpr.ca /cms/English/General+Public/Heritage/History/A+Brief+History.htm.

Eagle, John A. "Van Horne, Sir William Cornelius." *The Canadian Encyclopedia.* http://www.thecanadianencyclopedia.com/index.cfm?PgNm=TCE &Params=A1ARTA0008300.

Folster, David, and Tom Slater. "The Great Railway Bazaar." *Macleans*, August 20, 1979: 20.

"The History of the Rogers Pass crossing of the Selkirk Mountains of B.C. Canada by the Canadian Pacific Railway and later by the Trans-Canada Highway." Excerpted from *Snow War.* Environment Canada, 1991. http:// cdnrail.railfan.net/RogersPass/RogersPasstext.htm.

Keys, C. M. "American Builders in Canada." *World's Work*, January 1910: 12476– 12481.

Knowles, Valerie. *From Telegrapher to Titan: The Life of William C. Van Horne.* Toronto: Dundurn Press, 2004.

Lamb, W. Kaye. *History of the Canadian Pacific Railway.* New York: Macmillan, 1977.

Lavallee, Omer. *Van Horne's Road: An Illustrated Account of the Construction and First Years of Operation of the Canadian Pacific Transcontinental Railway.* Montreal: Railfare Enterprises, 1974.

Regehr, Theodore D. "Van Horne, Sir William Cornelius." *Dictionary of Canadian Biography Online*, University of Toronto, 2000. http://www.biographi .ca/009004-119.01-e.php?&id_nbr=7754.

Sibley, C. Lintern. "Van Horne and His Cuban Railway." *Canadian Magazine*, September 1913: 444–451.

"Sir William Cornelius Van Horne (2002)." Canadian Railway Hall of Fame, 2006. http://www.railfame.ca/sec_ind/leaders/en_2002_VanHorneW.asp.

"Sir William C. Van Horne." *Bulletin of the Pan American Union*, September 1915: 367–368.

"Sir William Van Horne." *Outlook Magazine*, September 22, 1915: 163.

Vaughan, Walter. "Building a Railway." *Century Magazine*, October 1920: 814–821.

——. *The Life and Work of Sir William Van Horne.* New York: Century Co., 1920.

Sources

———. "The Recreations of a Busy Man." *Century Magazine*, November 1920: 88–92.

"William Van Horne." North America Railway Hall of Fame 1999 Induction Awards. http://www.narhf.org/nar99/NAR99awards_WVH.html.

INNOVATORS

Wilbur Atwater

Atwater, W. O. "The Chemistry of Foods and Nutrition." *Century Magazine*, May–Oct. 1887: 59–74.

Atwater, W. O., and A. P. Bryant. "The Chemical Composition of American Food Materials." U.S. Department of Agriculture, *Office of Experiment Stations Bulletin* 28 (1899).

Beecher, Gary R. "Legacy of Wilbur O. Atwater: Human Nutrition Research Expansion at the USDA–Interagency Development of Food Composition Research." *Journal of Nutrition* 139 (2009).

Carpenter, Kenneth J. "Atwater, Wilbur Olin." American National Biography Online, February 2002. http://www.anb.org/articles/10/10-00063 .html.

———. "The Life and Times of W. O. Atwater (1844–1907)." *Journal of Nutrition* 124 (1994).

Combs, Gerald F. "Celebration of the Past: Nutrition at USDA." *Journal of Nutrition* 124 (1994).

Darby, William J. "Contributions of Atwater and CISDA to Knowledge of Nutrient Requirements." *Journal of Nutrition* 124 (1994).

"Fight Fatigue with Energy Foods." WebMD. http://www.webmd.com/diet /fight-fatigue-energy-foods-6/power-up?page=3.

Galbraith, Catherine Atwater. "Wilbur Olin Atwater." *Journal of Nutrition* 124 (1994).

"History Highlights of Nutrition." Purdue University. http://www.ansc.purdue .edu/courses/ansc221v/histnote.htm.

"How to Understand and Use the Nutrition Facts Label." U.S. Food and Drug Administration. http://www.fda.gov/Food/LabelingNutrition/Consumer Information/ucm078889.htm.

Landau, Elizabeth. "How Olympic Athletes Get Their Fuel." CNN Health,

August 15, 2008. http://www.cnn.com/2008/HEALTH/diet.fitness/08/14 /olympic.diet/index.html.

Lusk, Graham. "The Atwater-Rosa Respiration Calorimeter." *The Elements of the Science of Nutrition*. Philadelphia: W. B. Saunders Co., 1919. http:// chestofbooks.com/health/nutrition/Science/Chapter-II-The-Atwater -Rosa-Respiration-Calorimeter.html.

Maynard, Leonard A. "Wilbur O. Atwater—A Biographical Sketch." *Journal of Nutrition* 78 (1962).

McBride, Judy. "Wilbur O. Atwater: Father of American Nutrition Science." *Agricultural Research Magazine*, June 1993.

"National School Lunch Program." Food and Nutrition Service, U.S. Department of Agriculture, October 29, 2009. http://www.fns.usda.gov/cnd /Lunch/.

Nichols, Buford L. "Atwater and CISDA Nutrition Research and Service: A Prologue of the Past Century." *Journal of Nutrition* 124 (1994).

"Welcome to the Beltsville Human Nutrition Research Center." Agricultural Research Service, U.S. Department of Agriculture, October 27, 2009. http://www.ars.usda.gov/main/site_main.htm?modecode=12-35-00-00.

Welsh, Susan. "Atwater to the Present: Evolution of Nutrition Education." *Journal of Nutrition* 124 (1994).

Zelman, Kathleen M. "The Olympic Diet of Michael Phelps." WebMD, August 13, 2008. http://www.webmd.com/diet/news/20080813/the-olympic-diet -of-michael-phelps.

John Wallace Crawford

"Capt. Jack Crawford Dead." *New York Times*, February 28, 1917: 10.

"Captain Jack Crawford—Poet Scout of the Black Hills." *Black Hills Visitor Magazine*. http://www.blackhillsvisitor.com/main.asp?id=14&cat_id=30288.

Cody, William F. *The Life and Adventures of "Buffalo Bill."* New Perspectives on the West, PBS, 2001. http://www.pbs.org/weta/thewest/resources /archives/seven/w67bbauto/w67bb21.htm.

Crawford, Captain Jack. *The Poet Scout: A Book of Song and Story*. New York: Burr Printing House, 1889.

Dary, David. "Cowboys." *The Oxford Companion to United States History*. New York: Oxford University Press, 2001. http://www.anb.org/articles/cush /e0370.html.

Sources

"Deadwood and Lead—The Twin Cities of the Black Hills." *Black Hills Visitor Magazine.* http://www.blackhillsvisitor.com/main.asp?id=14&cat_id=30018.

"Featured at the Bar-D Ranch: Classic Cowboy Poetry, John Wallace 'Captain Jack' Crawford." Cowboy Poetry. http://www.cowboypoetry.com/captain jackcrawford.htm.

"George Crook (1828–1890)." New Perspectives on the West, PBS, 2001. http://www.pbs.org/weta/thewest/people/a_c/crook.htm.

Johns, Joshua. "Buffalo Bill's Wild West Show." University of Virginia, November 11, 1995. http://xroads.virginia.edu/~hyper/hns/buffalobill/home.html.

A Literary History of the American West. Fort Worth: Texas Christian University Press, 1987.

Liukkonen, Petri. "Owen Wister (1860–1938)." Books and Writers, 2008. http://www.kirjasto.sci.fi/owister.htm.

Miller, Darlis A. *Captain Jack Crawford: Buckskin Poet, Scout, and Showman.* Albuquerque: University of New Mexico Press, 1993.

Murdoch, David H. *The American West: The Invention of a Myth.* Reno: University of Nevada Press, 2001.

Nolan, Paul T. "Crawford, John Wallace." American National Biography Online, February 2000. http://www.anb.org/articles/20/20-00224.html.

———. *John Wallace Crawford.* Boston: Twayne Publishers, 1981.

———. *Three Plays by J.W. (Capt. Jack) Crawford: An Experiment in Myth-Making.* The Hague: Mouton & Co., 1966.

"The Poet-Scout." *Literary Digest,* March 24, 1917: 837.

Ramos, Mary G. "Cattle Drives." *Texas Almanac,* Texas State Historical Association, 1991. http://www.texasalmanac.com/history/highlights/cattle/.

Schwantes, Carlos Arnaldo. "West, The." *The Oxford Companion to United States History.* New York: Oxford University Press, 2001. http://www.anb.org/articles/cush/e1644.html.

"Sitting Bull—Tatanka-Iyotanka (1831–1890)." New Perspectives on the West, PBS, 2001. http://www.pbs.org/weta/thewest/people/s_z/sittingbull.htm.

"Wild Bill Hickok & the Deadman's Hand." Legends of America, 2010. http://www.legendsofamerica.com/we-billhickok.html.

George Fabyan

Chiles, James R. "Breaking Codes Was This Couple's Lifetime Career." *Smithsonian,* June 1987: 128–144.

Sources

Clark, Alfred E. "E. S. Friedman, 88, Cryptanalyst Who Broke Enemy Codes, Dies." *New York Times*, November 3, 1980: D12.

Clark, Ronald. *The Man Who Broke Purple*. Boston: Little, Brown and Co., 1977.

"Col. George Fabyan, Scientist, Dies at 69." *New York Times*, May 18, 1936: 17.

D'Alessio, F. N. "George Fabyan Celebrated for Fostering First Think Tank." Associated Press, June 13, 2001. http://lists.jammed.com/ISN/2001/06/0075 .html.

Ehresmann, Julia M., ed. *Geneva, Illinois: A History of Its Times and Places*. Geneva, Ill.: Geneva Public Library District, 1977.

Fabyan, George. *Fundamental Principles of the Baconian Ciphers and Application to Books of the Sixteenth and Seventeenth Centuries*. Geneva, Ill.: George Fabyan, 1916.

———. *The Keys for Deciphering The Greatest Work of Sir Francis Bacon, Baron of Verulam, Viscount St. Alban*. Geneva, Ill.: Riverbank Laboratories, 1916.

"Fabyan Villa and Japanese Garden." Preservation Partners of the Fox Valley, 2005. http://www.ppfv.org/fabyan.htm.

The Friedman Legacy: A Tribute to William and Elizebeth Friedman. Washington, D.C.: Center for Cryptologic History, National Security Agency, 1992.

Friedman, William F. *Elements of Cryptanalysis*. Laguna Hills, Calif.: Aegean Park Press, 1976.

Friedman, William F., and Elizebeth S. Friedman. *The Shakespearean Ciphers Examined*. Cambridge, England: The University Press, 1957.

Glenwright, Fredrick M. "Friedman, Elizebeth Smith, and William Frederic Friedman." American National Biography Online, February 2000. http://www.anb.org/articles/20/20-00371.html.

Kahn, David. *The Codebreakers*. London: Weidenfeld and Nicolson, 1974.

Kopec, John W. *The Sabines at Riverbank: Their Role in the Science of Architectural Acoustics*. Woodbury, N.Y.: Acoustical Society of America, 1997.

"Riverbank Laboratories: Geneva Local Landmark." City of Geneva, Illinois, 2000. http://www.geneva.il.us/riverbnk/riverpag.htm.

Uzzle, Ted. "Journey Through Acoustics." Digitalcontentproducer.com, December 1, 1997. http://digitalcontentproducer.com/mag/avinstall_journey _acoustics/.

"William F. Friedman." *Cryptologic Almanac*. National Security Agency, Central Security Service. http://www.nsa.gov/about/cryptologic_heritage /center_crypt_history/almanac/index.shtml.

Sources

"William Friedman Dies; Broke Japanese Code." *New York Times*, November 3, 1969: 47.

Herman Haupt

"Gen. Haupt Dies Suddenly," *New York Times*, December 15, 1905: 9.

"Gettysburg." Battle Summary. National Park Service. http://www.nps.gov /history/hps/abpp//battles/Pa002.htm.

"Graduates of West Point." West Point in the Making of America, Smithsonian National Museum of American History. http://americanhistory.si.edu /westpoint/graduates_print1.html.

Haupt, Herman. *Reminiscences of General Herman Haupt*. New York: Arno Press, 1981.

"Herman Haupt (1817–1905)." Mr. Lincoln's White House, Lincoln Institute, 2010. http://www.mrlincolnswhitehouse.org/inside.asp?ID=653 &subjectID=2.

"Interesting Railroad Record." *Chicago Tribune*, October 9, 1866. Reprinted by Catskill Archive. http://www.catskillarchive.com/rrextra/Page0005 .html.

Lord, Francis A. *Lincoln's Railroad Man: Herman Haupt*. Rutherford, N.J.: Fairleigh Dickinson University Press, 1969.

"Manassas, Second." Battle Summary, National Park Service. http://www.nps .gov/history/hps/abpp//battles/Va026.htm.

Snow, Richard F. "American Characters: Herman Haupt." *American Heritage*, February–March 1985.

Sterling, Keir B. "Haupt, Herman." American National Biography Online, February 2000. http://www.anb.org/articles/13/13-00718.html.

Turner, George Edgar. *Victory Rode the Rails: The Strategic Place of the Railroads in the Civil War*. Lincoln: University of Nebraska Press, 1992.

Ward, James A. *That Man Haupt: A Biography of Herman Haupt*. Baton Rouge: Louisiana State University Press, 1973.

Andrew Jackson Higgins

"A. J. Higgins Dies of Brief Illness." *Times-Picayune*, August 2, 1952: 1.

"A. J. Higgins, Landing Craft Builder, Dies." *Washington Post*, August 2, 1952: 12.

Sources

"Andrew Jackson Higgins (1886–1952)." Higgins Memorial. http://www.higgins memorial.com/.

Brinkley, Douglas. "The Man Who Won the War for Us: The Neglected Epic of Andrew Jackson Higgins." *American Heritage*, May–June 2000: 49–50.

"D-Day and the Battle of Normandy." D-Day Museum, Portsmouth, 2010. http://www.ddaymuseum.co.uk/faq.htm.

"D-Day, June 6, 1944." U.S. Army. http://www.army.mil/d-day/.

Friedman, Norman. *U.S. Amphibious Ships and Craft: An Illustrated Design History*. Annapolis: Naval Institute Press, 2002.

Goldstein, Richard. "Victor H. Krulak, Marine Behind U.S. Landing Craft, Dies at 95." *New York Times*, January 4, 2009.

Hammond, William M. *Normandy*. Washington, D.C.: U.S. Army Center of Military History, 2003.

"Higgins is the Name." *Time*, May 4, 1942.

"The Higgins 78' PT Boat." PT Boats, Inc., October 17, 2003. http://www.ptboats .org/20-01-05-ptboat-006.html.

Hough, Frank O., Verle E. Ludwig, and Henry I. Shaw, Jr. *History of U.S. Marine Corps Operations in World War II*, vol. 1. Washington, D.C.: U.S. Marine Corps, 1968.

"Military: LC—Landing Craft." Global Security, 2010. http://www.globalsecurity .org/military/systems/ship/lc.htm.

"Normandy Invasion, June 1944." Naval History & Heritage Command. http:// www.history.navy.mil/photos/events/wwii-eur/normandy/normandy.htm.

Omaha Beachhead. Washington, D.C.: War Department Historical Division, 1945.

"Permanent Exhibitions." National World War II Museum. http://www.national ww2museum.org/exhibitions/permanent-exhibits.html.

Strahan, Jerry E. *Andrew Jackson Higgins and the Boats That Won World War II*. Baton Rouge: Louisiana State University Press, 1994.

"USS *Rankin* (AKA-103): LCVP—Landing Craft, Vehicle, Personnel." USS *Rankin*. http://www.ussrankin.org/id41.htm.

Hedwig Kiesler

Braun, Hans-Joachim. "Advanced Weaponry of the Stars." AmericanHeritage .com, Spring 1997. http://www.americanheritage.com/articles/magazine /it/1997/4/1997_4_10.shtml.

Chapman, Gary. "Hedy Lamarr's Invention Finally Comes of Age." *Los Angeles*

Times, January 31, 2000. http://articles.latimes.com/2000/jan/31/business /fi-59503.

Couey, Anna. "How 'The Bad Boy of Music' And 'The Most Beautiful Girl in the World' Catalyzed a Wireless Revolution—in 1941." Harvard School of Engineering and Applied Sciences, 1997. http://people.seas.harvard .edu/~jones/cscie129/nu_lectures/lecture7/hedy/lemarr.htm.

"Female Inventors: Hedy Lamarr." Inventions.org, 2005. http://www.inventions .org/culture/female/lamarr.html.

"George Antheil (1900–1959)." Classical Net, 2009. http://www.classical.net /music/comp.lst/acc/antheil.php.

"Hedy Lamarr: Invention of Spread Spectrum Technology." Famous Women Inventors, 2008. http://www.women-inventors.com/Hedy-Lammar.asp.

"Hedy Lamarr: Military Communications System." Massachusetts Institute of Technology. http://web.mit.edu/invent/iow/lamarr.html.

"Hedy Lamarr, 1914–2000." IEEE, 2009. http://www.ieee.org/web/aboutus /history_center/biography/lamarr.html.

Meeks, Fleming. "Hedy Lamarr, Hollywood Sex Goddess, Was Also a Brilliant Inventor. She Got Paid for Her Movies, but not for Her Invention." Hedy -Lamarr.org, April 4, 2009. http://www.hedy-lamarr.org.

"Movie Legend Hedy Lamarr to Be Given Special Award at EFF's Sixth Annual Pioneer Awards." Electronic Frontier Foundation, March 11, 1997. http:// w2.eff.org/awards/pioneer/1997.php.

"1940's Film Goddess Hedy Lamarr Responsible for Pioneering Spread Spec- trum." *America's Inventor*, December 1997. http://inventionconvention .com/americasinventor/dec97issue/section2.html.

Peterson, Barbara Bennett. "Lamarr, Hedy." American National Biography On- line, February 2000. http://www.anb.org/articles/18/18-03569.html.

Prabakaran, Prabakar. "Tutorial on Spread Spectrum Technology." CommsDe- sign, May 6, 2003. http://www.commsdesign.com/article/printableArticle .jhtml?articleID=53200011.

Schmidkunz, Eliza. "Player Pianos, Sex Appeal, and Patent #2,292,387." Inside GNSS, September 2006. http://www.insidegnss.com/node/303.

Schneider, Mike. "30s, 40s film star Hedy Lamarr dies." *Salon*, January 19, 2000. http://www.salon.com/people/obit/2000/01/19/lamarr/print.html.

Soares, Andre. "Hedy Lamarr: Q&A with Author Patrick Agan." *Alternative Film Guide*, February 13, 2007. http://www.altfg.com/blog/actors/hedy -lamarr-patrick-agan.

Sources

"Spread Spectrum Technology." KMJ Communications. http://www.kmj.com
/proxim/pxhist.html.

Solomon Louis

Allen, Phillip. "Choctaw Indian Code Talkers of World War I." Choctaw Nation, 2010. http://www.choctawnation.com/history/people/code-talkers
/code-talkers-of-wwi/.

Archambeault, Marie J. "World War I Choctaw Code Talkers: 36th Division
of the National Guard." *Whispering Wind*, May–June 2008. http://www
.thefreelibrary.com/World+War+I+Choctaw+code+talkers%3A+36th+
division+of+the+National+Guard.-a0181312753.

Bloor, Col. A. W. "Transmitting Messages in Choctaw." Center of Military History,
U.S. Army, January 23, 1919. http://www.history.army.mil/html/topics
/natam/wwi-choctaw.html.

Chastaine, Capt. Ben H. *Story of the 36th: The Experiences of the 36th Division in the
World War.* Oklahoma City: Harlow Publishing Co., 1920.

"Choctaws—The Original Code Talkers." Choctaw Nation, 2010. http://
www.choctawnation.com/history/people/code-talkers/choctaws---the
-original-code-talkers/.

"Choctaw Stopped War Wire Tappers." Choctaw Nation, 2010. http://www.choctaw
nation.com/history/people/code-talkers/choctaw-stopped-war-wire-tappers/.

Davis, Cheryl. "Our Best World War I and II Weapon: Choctaw Code Talkers." Cheryl Davis' Art Blog, August 2008. http://bymyart.wordpress
.com/2008/08/13/world-war-i-and-ii-choctaw-code-talkers/.

Franks, Kenny A. *Citizen Soldiers: Oklahoma's National Guard.* Norman: University of Oklahoma Press, 1984.

"Germans Confused by Choctaw Code Talkers." *Bishinik*, August 1986.
http://www.choctawnation.com/history/people/code-talkers/germans
-confused-by-choctaw-code-talkers/.

Houghton, Jaclyn. "Woman Relates Stories of Choctaw Nation Code Talkers in
World War I." *Enid News*, January 13, 2007. http://www.enidnews.com
/localnews/local_story_013221737.html?keyword=secondarystory.

Jenkins, Ron. "Choctaw Code Talkers Finally Recognized." *Cherokee Phoenix*,
October 20, 2008. http://www.cherokeephoenix.org/19787/Article.aspx.

Kahn, David. *The Codebreakers: The Story of Secret Writing.* New York: Scribner,
1996.

Sources

Meadows, William C. "'They Had a Chance to Talk to One Another . . .': The Role of Incidence in Native American Code Talking." *Ethnohistory*, Spring 2009: 269–284.

Moseley, Susan. "Choctaw Code-Talkers." *Oklahoma Today*, July–August 1988: 13.

Robinson, Gary, and Lucas, Phil. *From Warriors to Soldiers: A History of American Indian Service in the United States Military*. Bloomington, Ind.: iUniverse Star, 2010.

"Solomon Bond Louis underage when he enlisted." *Bishinik*, March 2000. http://www.choctawnation.com/history/people/code-talkers/solomon -bon-louis/.

Telephone Warriors: Choctaw Code Talkers of WWI. Durant, Okla.: Choctaw Nation.

"World War I and II Choctaw Code Talkers." *Bryan County Heritage Quarterly*. http://www.oklachahta.org/code talkers.htm.

"The WWI Unbreakable Code." *Veterans Magazine*, November 2006: 8–10.

Anne Royall

"Anne Royall Rock Gone." *New York Times*, August 21, 1913: 5.

"Anne Royall, 1769–1854." Workshop 3. http://www.workshop3.freeuk.com /anne_royall.htm.

"Anne Was 'Go-Getter' Reporter; Here's Proof." *Washington Post*, August 30, 1933: 9.

Biggers, Jeff. "America's First Blogger: Anne Royall." *Huffington Post*, June 10, 2008. http://www.huffingtonpost.com/jeff-biggers/americas-first-blogger -an_b_106397.html.

Blankenhorn, Heber. "The Grandma of the Muckrakers." *American Mercury*, September 1927: 87-93.

Brown, Rick. "Anne Royall: America's First Professional Female Journalist?" History Buff. http://www.historybuff.com/library/refroyall.html.

Earman, Cynthia. "An Uncommon Scold." Library of Congress, January 2000. http://www.loc.gov/loc/lcib/0001/royall.html.

"Edited Her Own Paper." *Washington Post*, April 12, 1899: 11.

"Escaped the Ducking." *Washington Post*, February 12, 1905: G4.

"Honored 60 Years After." *New York Times*, May 14, 1911: 16.

Jackson, George Stuyvesant. *Uncommon Scold: The Story of Anne Royall*. Boston: Bruce Humphries, 1937.

Sources

James, Bessie Rowland. *Anne Royall's U.S.A.* New Brunswick, N.J.: Rutgers University Press, 1972.

"Life and Times of Anne Royall." *New York Times*, March 27, 1909: BR179.

Mattingly, Marie. "First Woman Editor." *Washington Post*, October 6, 1901: 26.

Maxwell, Alice S., and Marion B. Dunlevy. *Virago! The Story of Anne Newport Royall. (1769–1854).* Jefferson, N.C.: McFarland & Co., 1985.

"Memorial to Mrs. Royall." *Washington Post*, May 13, 1911: 3.

"Monument to Anne Royall, the Mother of 'Yellow Journalism.'" *Washington Post*, May 2, 1909: M8.

Royall, Anne. *Letters from Alabama on Various Subjects.* Washington, D.C.: Self-published, 1830. Reprinted by University of Alabama Press, 1969.

——. *Sketches of History, Life and Manners in the United States, by a Traveller.* New Haven: Self-published, 1826. Reprinted New York: Johnson Reprint Corp., 1970.

"She Was a Holy Terror." *Washington Post*, February 22, 1891: 9.

Sloan, W. David, and Lisa Mullikin Parcell, eds. *American Journalism: History, Principles, Practices.* Jefferson, N.C.: McFarland & Co., 2002.

Steadman, Jennifer Bernhardt. *Traveling Economies: American Women's Travel Writing.* Columbus: Ohio State University Press, 2007.

Wilson, Vylla Poe. "Anne Royall, Pioneer Woman Publicist." *Washington Post*, May 10, 1931: MF4.

Clarence Saunders

"Business & Finance: Piggly Wiggly Man." *Time*, February 25, 1929. http://www.time.com/time/magazine/article/0,9171,880518,00.html.

"Clarence Saunders, Builder of Fortunes, Dies Suddenly Here." *Commercial Appeal*, October 15, 1953: 1, 14, 35.

"Finance: Piggly Wiggly." *Time*, March 31, 1923. http://www.time.com/time/magazine/article/0,9171,846203,00.html.

"The Piggly Wiggly Beauty Contest Brought Out the Most Beautiful of Memphis Womanhood." *Commercial Appeal*, September 7, 1916: 2.

"The Piggly Wiggly Beauty Contest Will Begin at Ten O'Clock Today." *Commercial Appeal*, September 6, 1916: 3.

"The Piggly Wiggly Believes in Woman Suffrage." *Commercial Appeal*, September 4, 1916: 2.

Sources

"The Piggly Wiggly: $50.00 in Gold to Be Given Away." *Commercial Appeal*, September 5, 1916: 4.

"The Piggly Wiggly: Green Hair, Blue Hair, Black Hair, Red Hair, Blonde Hair, Grey Hair, Curley Hair, Straight Hair—No Hair If You Please—Will Be Welcome Monday Morning As Early As 7 O'Clock." *Commercial Appeal*, September 10, 1916: 9.

"The Piggly Wiggly Price List." *Commercial Appeal*, September 14, 1916: 2.

"The Piggly Wiggly Will Establish a New Fashion." *Commercial Appeal*, September 3, 1916: 3.

"The Piggly Wiggly Won't Be Ready in Tip-Top Shape Until Monday Morning at 7 O'Clock." *Commercial Appeal*, September 8, 1916: 7.

"Pink Palace Museum." Pink Palace Family of Museums, 2009. http://www.memphismuseums.org/museum-overview/.

"Where it began." Piggly Wiggly Corp. http://www.pigglywiggly.com/cgi-bin/customize?aboutus.html.

Eliza Scidmore

"Bloom Watch." National Cherry Blossom Festival. http://www.nationalcherryblossomfestival.org/cms/index.php?id=404.

Cameron, Mabel Ward, ed. *The Biographical Cyclopaedia of American Women*, vol. 1. New York: Halvord Publishing Co., 1924.

Cassel, Susie Lan. "Scidmore, Eliza Ruhamah." American National Biography Online, February 2000. http://www.anb.org/articles/16/16-01459.html.

"Cherry Blossom Festival: History of the Cherry Trees." National Park Service, March 27, 2009. http://www.nps.gov/cherry/cherry-blossom-history.htm.

Conroy, Sarah Booth. "She Painted the Town Pink." *Washington Post*, February 1, 1999: A1.

"Her Blooming Great Idea." *National Geographic*, April 1997: 7.

"History of the Trees and Festival." National Cherry Blossom Festival. http://www.nationalcherryblossomfestival.org/cms/index.php?id=574.

Kennon, Donald R., and Richard Striner. *Washington Past and Present: A Guide to the Nation's Capital*. Washington, D.C.: United States Capitol Historical Society. 1983.

Kunitz, Stanley J., and Howard Haycraft, eds. *American Authors 1600–1900*. New York: H. W. Wilson Co., 1938.

Sources

Martin, Oliver. "How the Japanese Cherry Trees Came to Washington." *The Transmitter*, April 1934: 1–3.

McClellan, Ann. *The Cherry Blossom Festival: Sakura Celebration*. Boston: Bunker Hill Publishing, 2005.

McHenry, Robert, ed. *Liberty's Women*. Springfield, Mass.: G. & C. Merriam Co., 1980.

"Miss Eliza Scidmore, Capital Author, Dies." *Washington Evening Star*, November 3, 1928: 9.

"Miss Eliza Scidmore Dies in Geneva at 72." *New York Times*, November 4, 1928: 32.

Scidmore, Eliza Ruhamah. "The Cherry Blossoms of Japan." *Century Magazine*, March 1910: 642–653.

"The Corps' Connection to the Washington, D.C., Tidal Basin and Its Beloved Cherry Trees." U.S. Army Corps of Engineers, April 2002. http://www.usace.army .mil/History/hv/Pages/048-Cherry_Trees.aspx.

Madam C. J. Walker

Blustain, Sarah. "Black Beauty: Millionaire C. J. Walker." Scholastic Search, 2010. http://www2.scholastic.com/browse/article.jsp?id=4779.

Bundles, A'Lelia. *Madam C. J. Walker: Entrepreneur*. New York: Chelsea House, 2008.

———. *On Her Own Ground: The Life and Times of Madam C. J. Walker*. New York: Scribner, 2001.

"Famous Hair Culturist Is Dead." *Philadelphia Tribune*, May 31, 1919: 1.

"The Harlem Renaissance." Celebrate Black History, Biography.com, 2010. http://www.biography.com/blackhistory/harlem-renaissance.jsp.

Ingham, John N. "Walker, Madame C. J." American National Biography Online, February 2002. http://www.anb.org/articles/10/10-01700.html.

Lommel, Cookie. *Madam C. J. Walker*. Los Angeles: Melrose Square Publishing Co., 1993.

"Madam C. J. Walker." Madame Walker Theatre Center. http://walkertheatre .com/index.asp?p=24.

"Madame C. J. Walker." The Black Inventor Online Museum, 2009. http://www .blackinventor.com/pages/madamewalker.html.

"Mme. Walkers $250,000 Villa at Irvington-on-the-Hudson, N.Y." *Baltimore Afro-American*, May 30, 1919: A1.

Sources

Simmonds, Yussuf J. "Annie Turnbo Pope Malone." *Los Angeles Sentinel*, July 23, 2010. http://www.lasentinel.net/Annie-Turnbo-Pope-Malone.html.

Sullivan, Otha Richard. *African American Millionaires*. Hoboken, N.J.: John Wiley & Sons, 2005.

"Villa Lewaro." Places Where Women Made History, National Park Service, March 30, 1998. http://www.nps.gov/history/Nr/travel/pwwmh/ny22.htm.

"Was Richest Colored Woman in America." *Baltimore Afro-American*, May 30, 1919: 1.

"Wealthiest Negress Dead." *New York Times*, May 26, 1919: 15.

HUMANITARIANS

Grace Abbott

Abbott, Edith. "Grace Abbott and Hull House, 1908–21, Parts I & II." *Social Service Review*, September 1950: 374–394, December 1950: 493–518.

——. "Grace Abbott: A Sister's Memories." *Social Service Review*, September 1939: 351–407.

Abbott, Grace. "Children and the Depression: A National Study and Warning." *New York Times*, December 18, 1932: XX5.

——. "Federal Aid for the Protection of Maternity and Infancy." *American Journal of Public Health*, September 1922. Reprinted by the U.S. Department of Labor Children's Bureau, 1923.

——. *From Relief to Social Security: The Development of the New Public Welfare Services and Their Administration*. New York: Russell & Russell, 1966.

——. *The Immigrant and the Community*. New York: The Century Co., 1917.

——. "Ten Years' Work for Children." *North American Review*, August 1923. Reprinted by the U.S. Department of Labor Children's Bureau, 1923.

——. "Victories for Child Welfare Won in the Last Two Decades." *New York Times*, April 10, 1932: XX4.

Adams, Mildred. "Guardian of the Children of America." *New York Times*, November 9, 1930: SM6.

"Child Labor Fight Reaches the Senate." *New York Times*, May 4, 1924: XX10.

"Child Labor in U.S. History." University of Iowa Labor Center and Center for Human Rights, 2000. http://www.continuetolearn.uiowa.edu/laborctr/child_labor/about/us_history.html.

Sources

"Children's Bureau Seeks Crime Cure." *New York Times*, December 16, 1929: 12.

"The Children's Bureau." Social Security Online. http://www.ssa.gov/history /childbl.html.

Costin, Lela B. *Two Sisters for Social Justice: A Biography of Grace and Edith Abbott.* Urbana: University of Illinois Press, 1983.

"Family's Name Famous." *New York Times*, June 20, 1939: 19.

"Jane Addams (1860–1935)." Harvard University Library Open Collections Program, 2011. http://ocp.hul.harvard.edu/immigration/addams.html.

Krugman, Paul. "Leaving Children Behind." *New York Times*, February 27, 2011. http://www.nytimes.com/2011/02/28/opinion/28krugman.html ?_r=1&hp.

Longo, Julie, and VanBurkleo, Sandra F. "Abbott, Grace." American National Biography Online, February 2000. http://www.anb.org/articles/15/15 -00002.html.

"Miss Grace Abbott Resigns U.S. Post." *New York Times*, June 15, 1934: 18.

Nutter, Kathleen Banks. "Abbott, Edith." American National Biography Online, February 2000. http://www.anb.org/articles/15/15-00001.html.

Sorensen, John, and Judith Sealander, eds. *The Grace Abbott Reader.* Lincoln: University of Nebraska Press, 2008.

"12 Women Declared Nation's 'Greatest.'" *New York Times*, February 24, 1931: 18.

"Urge Grace Abbott for Cabinet Post." *New York Times*, June 1, 1930: 6.

Walsh, Winifred A. "Grace Abbott and Social Action, 1934–1939." Doctoral dissertation, University of Chicago, 1965.

Henry Beachell

Barclay, Adam. "How Wild Rice Species Help Their Cultivated Cousins." *Rice Today*, January 2004. Reprinted by Bioversity International, June 26, 2008. http://www.bioversityinternational.org/news_and_events/news/news /article/how-wild-rice-species-help-their-cultivated-cousins.html.

Conway, Gordon. *The Doubly Green Revolution: Food for All in the Twenty-first Century.* New York: Penguin Books, 1997.

"Critchfield, Richard. "China's Miracle Rice: A New Rivalry with the West." *New York Times*, June 17, 1992. http://www.nytimes.com/1992/06/17 /opinion/17iht-edcr.html.

Ganzel, Bill. "The Green Revolution—Agriculture to Prevent War." *Farming in*

Sources

the 1950s & 60s, Wessels Living History Farm, 2007. http://www.living historyfarm.org/farmingin the50s/crops_13.html.

——. "Green Revolution Legacy." Farming in the 1950s & 60s, Wessels Living History Farm, 2007. http://www.livinghistoryfarm.org/farmingin the50s /crops_18.html.

——. "Miracle Rice." Farming in the 1950s & 60s, Wessels Living History Farm, 2007. http://www.livinghistoryfarm.org/farmingin the50s/crops_17.html.

——. "Norman Borlaug & Henry Beachell." Farming in the 1950s & 60s, Wessels Living History Farm, 2007. http://www.livinghistoryfarm.org /farmingin the50s/crops_15.html#beachell.

——. "The Sustainable Ag Movement Begins." Farming in the 1950s & 60s, Wessels Living History Farm, 2007. http://www.livinghistoryfarm.org /farmingin the50s/crops_19.html.

"Henry M. Beachell & Dr. Gurdev Singh Khush—1996 World Food Prize Laureates." World Food Prize Foundation, 2010. http://www.worldfoodprize .org/en/laureates/19871999_laureates/1996_beachell_and_khush/.

"International Rice Genebank: Sharing the Seeds." Genetic Resources Center, International Rice Research Institute, 2001. http://www.irri.org/GRC /irg/biodiv-genebank.htm.

Kral, E. A. "Henry M. Beachell: Leading 20th Century Rice Breeder and Co-Pioneer of Asia's Green Revolution in Rice." NSEA, 2009. http://nsea .org/news/BeachellProf.htm.

Pearce, Jeremy. "Henry M. Beachell Dies at 100; Developed New Rice Plant." *New York Times*, December 28, 2006. http://query.nytimes.com/gst/full page.html?res=9C07EFDF1F31F93BA15751C1A9609C8B63.

Rost, Thomas L. "Where Rice Came From." University of California, Davis, 1997. http://www-plb.ucdavis.edu/labs/rost/Rice/introduction/intro.html.

"Scientist, Rice Breeder Hank Beachell Celebrates 100th Birthday." News Section, *SeedQuest*, September 19, 2006. http://www.seedquest.com/News /releases/2006/september/16953.htm.

"World Wide Rice Production." Rice Trade B2B Marketplace, 2010. http://www .rice-trade.com/world-wide-rice-production.html.

Inez Boissevain

Banner, Lois W. *Women in Modern America: A Brief History.* Belmont, Calif.: Thomson/Wadsworth, 2005.

Sources

Churchill, Allen. *The Improper Bohemians: A Re-creation of Greenwich Village In Its Heyday*. New York: E. P. Dutton, 1959.

Covey, Alan, ed. *A Century of Women*. Atlanta: TBS Books, 1994.

Eastman, Max. *Enjoyment of Living*. New York: Harper & Brothers, 1948.

Harvey, Sheridan. "Marching for the Vote: Remembering the Woman Suffrage Parade of 1913." American Women: A Library of Congress Guide for the Study of Women's History and Culture in the United States, Library of Congress, 2001. http://www.memory.loc.gov/ammem/awhhtml/aw01e/aw01e.html.

"Icon: Inez Milholland (Boissevain) (1886–1916)." Profiles: Selected Leaders of the National Woman's Party, Library of Congress. http://memory.loc.gov/ammem/collections/suffrage/nwp/profiles3.html.

"Inez Boissevain to Be Buried Here." *New York Times*, November 27, 1916: 11.

Lumsden, Linda J. *Inez: The Life and Times of Inez Milholland*. Bloomington: Indiana University Press, 2004.

Marlin, John Tepper. "Inez Milholland Boissevain." Boissevain News USA, 2010. http://www.boissevain.us/inezmilholland.html.

"Mount Renamed 'Inez.'" *New York Times*, December 12, 1916: 7.

"Mrs. Boissevain Is Recovering." *New York Times*, November 23, 1916: 13.

"Mrs. Inez Boissevain Dies in Los Angeles." *New York Times*, November 26, 1916: 1.

Nevins, Allan, and Frank Ernest Hill. "Henry Ford and His Peace Ship." *American Heritage*, 2008. http://www.americanheritage.com/articles/magazine/ah/1958/2/1958_2_65.shtml.

Perry, Marilyn Elizabeth. "Boissevain, Inez Milholland." American National Biography Online, February 2000. http://www.anb.org/articles/11/11-01094.html.

Phemister, Jennifer Beck. "Freedom Hero: Inez Milholland Boissevain." Freedom Heroes. http://www.myhero.com/go/hero.asp?hero=im_boissevain.

Sherr, Lynn, and Jurate Kazickas. *The American Woman's Gazetteer*. New York: Bantam Books, 1976.

Stevens, Doris. *Jailed for Freedom: The Story of the Militant American Suffragist Movement*. Chicago: R. R. Donnelley & Sons, 2008.

"Tribute at Capitol for Mrs. Boissevain." *New York Times*, December 25, 1916: 11.

"Wilson—A Portrait: Women's Suffrage." American Experience, PBS, 2001. http://www.pbs.org/wgbh/amex/wilson/portrait/wp_suffrage.html.

Sources

Joseph Dutton

Dutton, Joseph. *Joseph Dutton: His Memoirs.* Edited by Howard D. Case. Honolulu: *Honolulu Star-Bulletin,* 1931.

"Hansen's Disease (Leprosy)." Kalaupapa National Historic Park. http://www.nps.gov/archive/kala/docs/hansens1.htm.

"Historical Chronology." Remembering Kalaupapa. http://www.whirledwydeweb.com/kalaupapa/chronology.html.

"Joseph Dutton Papers." Notre Dame Archives, University of Notre Dame. http://archives.nd.edu/findaids/ead/index/DUT001.HTM.

"Kalaupapa National Historic Park." National Park Foundation, 2009. http://www.nationalparks.org/discover-parks/index.cfm?fa=viewPark&pid=KLHS.

"Molokai, Kalaupapa." Visit Molokai. http://visitmolokai.com/kala.html.

"National Hansen's Disease (Leprosy) Program." Health Resources and Services Administration, U.S. Department of Health and Human Services. http://www.hrsa.gov/hansens/.

"Settlement History—Why Here?" Kalaupapa National Historic Park. http://www.nps.gov/archive/kala/docs/history1.htm.

Skinsnes, Anwei V., and others. *Brother Joseph Dutton, 1843–1931: A Saint for Vermont.* Edited by Richard Halpern. Stowe, Vt.: Blessed Sacrament Church. 1981.

"St. Damien's Wisconsin Assistant." Odd Wisconsin Archive, Wisconsin Historical Society, October 11, 2009. http://www.wisconsinhistory.org/odd/archives/004010.asp.

Yenkavitch, Joseph. "A Glimpse into the World of Kalawao." Heart of New England. http://www.theheartofnewengland.com/travel-Kalawao.html.

Gertrude Elion

Altman, Lawrence K. "Gertrude Elion, Drug Developer, Dies at 81." *New York Times,* February 23, 1999: A21.

Andrews, Edmund L. "First Woman In Inventors Hall of Fame." *New York Times,* March 2, 1991: 1.32.

Bouton, Katherine. "The Nobel Pair: Mavericks of Medical Research in a Shared Quest." *New York Times Magazine,* January 29, 1989: SM28.

Brokaw, Tom. *The Greatest Generation.* New York: Random House, 1998.

Sources

Camp, Carole Ann. *American Women Inventors.* Berkeley Heights, N.J.: Enslow Publishers, 2004.

Colburn, Don. "Pathway to the Prize: Gertrude Elion, from Unpaid Lab Assistant to Nobel Glory." *Washington Post,* October 25, 1988: Health 10.

Elion, Gertrude B. "Autobiography." Nobel Foundation, 1988. http://nobelprize .org/nobel_prizes/medicine/laureates/1988/elion-autobio.html.

———. "The Purine Path to Chemotherapy." Nobel Lecture, December 8, 1988. http://nobelprize.org/nobel_prizes/medicine/laureates/1988/elion -lecture.html.

Gerber, Judith B. "Elion, Gertrude." American National Biography Online, September 2000. http://www.anb.org/articles/12/12-02091.html.

"Gertrude Elion Biography." Academy of Achievement, February 1, 2005. http:// www.achievement.org/autodoc/page/eli0bio-1.

"Gertrude Elion Interview." Academy of Achievement, March 6, 1991. http:// www.achievement.org/autodoc/page/eli0int-1.

MacBain, Jennifer. *Gertrude Elion: Nobel Prize Winner in Physiology and Medicine.* New York: Rosen Publishing Group, 2004.

Marx, Jean L. "The 1988 Nobel Prize for Physiology or Medicine." *Science,* October 28, 1988: 516–517.

St. Pierre, Stephanie. *Gertrude Elion: Master Chemist.* Vero Beach, Fla.: Rourke Enterprises, 1993.

"What Is DNA?" Genetics Home Reference, 2011. http://ghr.nlm.nih.gov/hand book/basics/dna.

Wickelgren, I. "Two Americans, Briton Share Medical Nobel." *Science News,* October 22, 1988: 261.

Golden Rule Jones

Barclay, Morgan J. "Reform in Toledo: The Political Career of Samuel M. Jones." *Northwest Ohio Quarterly* L, no. 3 (Summer 1978): 79–89.

Bremner, Robert H. "The Civic Revival in Ohio—Samuel M. Jones: The Man Without a Party." *American Journal of Economics and Sociology* 8, no. 2 (Jan. 1949): 151–161.

———. "The Civic Revival in Ohio." *American Journal of Economics and Sociology* 8, no. 1 (Oct. 1948): 61–68.

De Angelo, Laura. "Titusville, Pennsylvania." *Encyclopedia of Earth,* June 14, 2007. http://www.eoearth.org/article/Titusville,_Pennsylvania.

Sources

Jones, Samuel M. *Letters of Love and Labor: A Series of Weekly Letters Addressed and Delivered to the Working-Men of the Acme Sucker Rod Company, Toledo, Ohio, During the Summer and Fall of 1901.* Toledo: Franklin Printing & Engraving Co., 1901.

——. *The New Right: A Plea for Fair Play Through a More Just Social Order.* New York: Eastern Book Concern, 1899.

"Ohio Oil Company." Ohio History Central, Ohio Historical Society, 2010. http://www.ohiohistorycentral.org/entry.php?rec=950.

Pitzer, Donald E. "Revivalism and Politics in Toledo: 1899." *Northwest Ohio Quarterly* 41, no. 1 (Winter 1968–69): 13–24.

"The Progressive Era (1890–1920)." Eleanor Roosevelt National Historic Site, National Park Service, 2003. http://www.nps.gov/archive/elro/glossary/progressive-era.htm.

"Samuel M. Jones." Ohio History Central, Ohio Historical Society, 2010. http://www.ohiohistorycentral.org/entry.php?rec=218.

Teaford, Jon C. "Jones, Samuel Milton." American National Biography Online, February 2000. http://www.anb.org/articles/06/06-00324.html.

"Toledo, Ohio." Ohio History Central, Ohio Historical Society, 2010. http://www.ohiohistorycentral.org/entry.php?rec=808&nm=Toledo-Ohio.

Warner, Hoyt Landon. *Progressivism in Ohio, 1897–1917.* Columbus: Ohio State University Press for the Ohio Historical Society. 1964.

Jonathan Letterman

Adams, George Worthington. *Doctors in Blue: The Medical History of the Union Army in the Civil War.* New York: Henry Schuman, 1952.

"The Battle of Antietam." Antietam National Battlefield, November 28, 2006. http://www.nps.gov/anti/historyculture/index.htm.

"Battle of Second Manassas (Second Bull Run)." Manassas National Battlefield Park, August 1, 2009. http://www.nps.gov/mana/historyculture/second-manassas.htm.

Clements, Bennett A. *Memoir of Jonathan Letterman, M.D., Surgeon United States Army and Medical Director of the Army of the Potomac.* New York: G. P. Putnam's Sons, 1883. Reprinted from the *Journal of the Military Service Institution*, September 1883.

Goellnitz, Jenny. "Civil War Battlefield Surgery." eHistory, Ohio State Univer-

Sources

sity Department of History, 2011. http://ehistory.osu.edu/uscw/features
/medicine/cwsurgeon/amputations.cfm.

——. "Civil War Medicine." eHistory, Ohio State University Department of History, 2011. http://ehistory.osu.edu/uscw/features/medicine/cwsurgeon
/introduction.cfm.

Heiser, John. "Camp Letterman General Hospital." Gettysburg National Military Park Virtual Tour, September 1998. http://www.nps.gov/archive
/gett/getttour/sidebar/letterman.htm.

Keegan, John. "The American Civil War: The Gruesome Suffering of Soldiers Exposed." *The Telegraph*, September 17, 2009. http://www.telegraph
.co.uk/culture/books/6199297/The-American-Civil-War-the-gruesome
-suffering-of-soldiers-exposed.html.

Leland, Anne, and Mari-Jana Oboroceanu. "American War and Military Operations Casualties: Lists and Statistics." Congressional Research Service, February 26, 2010. http://www.fas.org/sgp/crs/natsec/RL32492.pdf.

"Medical Care, Battle Wounds, and Disease." Civil War Home, February 10, 2002. http://www.civilwarhome.com/civilwarmedicine.htm.

Musto, R. J. "The Treatment of the Wounded at Gettysburg: Jonathan Letterman: The Father of Modern Battlefield Medicine." *Gettysburg Magazine* 37: 120–127.

Savage, Douglas J. *Civil War Medicine*. Philadelphia: Chelsea House Publishers, 2000.

Schaadt, Mark J. *Civil War Medicine*. Quincy, Ill.: Cedarwood Publishing, 1998.

Schroeder-Lein, Glenna R. *The Encyclopedia of Civil War Medicine*. Armonk, N.Y.: M. E. Sharpe, 2008.

Tooker, John. "Aspects of Medicine, Nursing and the Civil War." *Transactions of the American Clinical and Climatological Association*, vol. 118, 2007: 215–223. http://www.ncbi.nlm.nih.gov/pmc/articles/PMC1863579/.

Uschan, Michael V. *A Civil War Doctor*. San Diego: Lucent Books, 2005.

"Weapons of the American Civil War." Civil War Home, February 16, 2002.
http://www.civilwarhome.com/weapons.htm.

Hugh Thompson

Angers, Trent. *The Forgotten Hero of My Lai: The Hugh Thompson Story*. Lafayette, La.: Acadian House Publishing, 1999.

Sources

"'Blood and Fire' of My Lai Remembered 30 Years Later." CNN, March 16, 1998. http://www.rpadden.com/docs/HughThompson2.htm.

Bock, Paula. "The Choices Made: Lessons from My Lai on Drawing the Line." *Seattle Times Pacific Northwest Magazine*, 2002. http://seattletimes.nwsource.com/pacificnw/2002/0310/cover.html.

Bujol, Jessica. "My Lai Hero Hugh Thompson Jr. Dies at 62." Associated Press, January 6, 2006. http://www.rpadden.com/docs/HughThompson.htm.

Cummins, Joseph. *The World's Bloodiest History: Massacre, Genocide, and the Scars They Left on Civilization.* Beverly, Mass.: Fair Winds Press, 2010.

Goldstein, Richard. "Hugh Thompson, 62, Who Saved Civilians at My Lai, Dies." *New York Times*, January 7, 2006. http://www.nytimes.com/2006/01/07/national/07thompson.html.

"Hugh Thompson's Crewmember Remembers Helping to Stop the My Lai Massacre." *Democracy Now*, January 18, 2006. http://www.democracynow.org/2006/1/18/hugh_thompsons_crewmember_remembers_helping_to.

Linder, Doug. "An Introduction to the My Lai Courts-Martial." University of Missouri-Kansas City School of Law. http://law2.umkc.edu/faculty/projects/ftrials/mylai/Myl_intro.html.

"My Lai Hero Hugh Thompson Jr. Dies at 62." Associated Press, January 7, 2006. http://www.mishalov.com/hugh-thompson.html.

"My Lai Pilot Hugh Thompson." NPR, January 6, 2006. http://www.npr.org/templates/story/story.php?storyId=5133444.

Olson, James S., ed. *Dictionary of the Vietnam War.* New York: Peter Bedrick Books, 1987.

Spector, Ronald H. "Vietnam War." *Britannica Concise Encyclopedia*, 2011. http://www.britannica.com/EBchecked/topic/628478/Vietnam-War.

Thompson, Hugh. "The Heroes of My Lai." University of Missouri-Kansas City School of Law. http://law2.umkc.edu/faculty/projects/ftrials/mylai/myl_hero.html.

"3 Honored for Saving Lives at My Lai." *New York Times*, March 7, 1998. http://www.nytimes.com/1998/03/07/us/3-honored-for-saving-lives-at-my-lai.html?scp=2&sq=&st=nyt.

"Who Are the War Criminals?" *The Economist*, April 3, 1971. http://www.economist.com/world/united-states/PrinterFriendly.cfm?story_id=15709500.

PAUL MARTIN spent three decades as a book and magazine editor with the National Geographic Society, the final ten years as executive editor of *National Geographic Traveler*. His assignments have taken him around the world. Early in his career, he spent a year in Vietnam as a military journalist and was the assistant editor of *Outdoors* and managing editor of *Continuing Education for the Family Physician* magazines. A graduate of the Missouri School of Journalism, Martin lives near Washington, D.C. When not writing, he builds acoustic guitars.